"HERE'S TO OUR FRATERNITY"

לָךְ עִיר הַצֶּדֶק קִרְיָה נֶאֱמָנָה :
: וְשֶׁבֶר פְּשָׁעִים וְחַטָּאִים יַחְדָּו וְעֹזְבֵי

Zion shall be redeemed with judgment,
and those that return to her with
righteousness.

ישעיה א :בז
Isaiah 1:27

"Here's to Our Fraternity"

ONE HUNDRED YEARS OF
ZETA BETA TAU
1898–1998

Marianne R. Sanua

PUBLISHED BY
ZETA BETA TAU FOUNDATION, INC.
Distributed by Brandeis University Press and
University Press of New England / Hanover and London

Published by Zeta Beta Tau Foundation, Inc.
Distributed by Brandeis University Press and
University Press of New England, Hanover, NH 03755
© 1998 by Zeta Beta Tau
All rights reserved
Printed in the United States of America   5 4 3 2 1
Library of Congress card number: 98–61347
ISBN: 0–87451–879–2

CONTENTS

ILLUSTRATIONS

FOREWORD

Here's to Our Fraternity is published in Zeta Beta Tau's 100th year. As we choose our paths for ZBT's second century, we need to clearly understand where we have been.

The ZBT experience has had a significant impact on the lives of many men over the decades—men who have become leaders in society as well as men who have struggled with daily worries—yet all with a common bond and hoped-for goal.

We wish to thank our author, Dr. Marianne Sanua, whose interest in ZBT will serve to record in historic chronicles the social history of Jewish collegiate life in the late nineteenth and twentieth centuries. The reader will quickly recognize the depth of Dr. Sanua's knowledge, her ability to communicate, and her love of her subject.

Ronald J. Taylor, M.D.
National President
History Publication Editor

Here's to Our Fraternity

(to the tune "Gaudeamus Igitur")

Here's to our Fraternity, may it live forever,
May we always faithful be, and its bonds ne'er sever.
Though the troubles may be nigh, boys,
With our standard raised on high, boys,
We'll be loyal to our Z B T
Ever loyal to our Zeta Beta Tau.

Let us raise our glasses boys, and pledge our friendship ever,
Though life may have its cares and joys, that friendship we'll ne'er sever.
In life's sorrow and in its sadness,
In its joys and in its gladness,
We'll be brethren of the Z B T
Always brethren of Zeta Beta Tau.

Lord of Heaven and of Earth, keep watch o'er us ever,
Fill our hearts with love and mirth; let our bonds ne'er sever,
By the heaven that smiles above us,
By the faith of those that love us,
God protect our Z B T
God protect our Zeta Beta Tau.

—*Written 1899 by Maurice L. Zellermayer,*
a founder of Zeta Beta Tau

"HERE'S TO OUR FRATERNITY"

CHAPTER ONE

"ZION BE-MISHPAT TIPADEH"

The Origins of Zeta Beta Tau

Zion shall be redeemed with judgment, and those that return to her with righteousness. — Isaiah 1:27

It was unlikely that Greek traditions as expressed in the American college fraternity would someday merge with the ancient traditions of the Jewish people, particularly the part of it that sought the rebirth of the Land of Israel. The long-standing conflict between Hellenism and Hebraism, annually celebrated in the holiday of Hanukkah, would have seemed to preclude it. However, it was precisely such a merger and an evolution of these two forces over a number of years that brought about the foundation in 1898 of the oldest of a series of historically Jewish college fraternities in America—the ZBT Society or, as it later became known, the Zeta Beta Tau Fraternity.

At the turn of the twentieth century, student fraternities were enjoying tremendous popularity both in Europe and in the United States, and in many schools they were coming to dominate student life. In the case of Zeta Beta Tau, the strength of the American "Greek system" helped to turn what began in 1898 at Jewish Theological Seminary in New York City as a highly idealistic, religiously and intellectually oriented Zionist debating and discussion society, made up of advanced students from several colleges, into a collegiate social fraternity modeled on its non-Jewish counterparts. ZBT was not unique among American fraternities in its religious origins. Until the mid-nineteenth century a central purpose of American higher education was to prepare educated candidates for the ministry, and many of the older and larger fraternities had been founded by avowedly Christian men studying to enter the clergy. Crosses and other Christian symbolism thus remained an integral part of their badges and rituals.

That soon after its creation ZBT jettisoned much of its original religious emphasis never ceased to be a source of considerable distress to some of its founders. However, evidence of the basic roots of the organization remained throughout the generations. For more than a half-century after its founding the fraternity's membership was limited exclusively to men of Jewish birth, a fact that could not help but have an enormous impact independent of each member's level of commitment to the actual practice of Judaism.

Neither the general goal of service to the Jewish people nor the depth and intellectual traditions of Zeta Beta Tau's rabbinical origins were rejected. Instead, the organization's ideals soon became displaced from the national or political arena, which was in any case better served by the plethora of other American Jewish organizations springing up. ZBT's arena instead became the day-to-day realm of social affairs, business, and personal interactions, where most of life truly was lived and most of life's battles were actually won or lost.

The primary goals of ZBT in its earliest years were, on an individual basis, to provide members with all the joys, companionship, and social opportunities that they saw as their right by virtue of their education, background, and class standing but that were denied them in the non-Jewish world. Collectively, through extremely select standards of membership, followed by intense socialization, the fraternity would prove first on the college campus and later to all the world that young Jewish men could be the equal of their best Gentile counterparts in achievement, breeding, appearance, behavior, and gentlemanly bearing.

Fraternities in America

In forming a college fraternity the young men of 1898 were joining a long-established tradition. Such organizations had existed from the dawn of the American republic; the first, Phi Beta Kappa at the College of William and Mary, was established in 1776. Although it later evolved into a strictly scholarly group, "Phi Bete" began as a literary, social, and recreational outlet for the students. Next came Kappa Alpha, Sigma Phi, and Delta Phi at Union College in New York State in the 1820s. By the beginning of World War I in 1914, *Baird's Manual of American College Fraternities* counted more than seventy national Greek-letter groups for men and women established on over five hundred campuses. Their combined membership exceeded 350,000 and the value of their chapter houses was estimated to be over thirteen million dollars (1920: 779–81).

By choosing Greek letters and mottoes to represent themselves, students could identify with the glories of this ancient civilization—its athleticism, art, literature, philosophy, and democratic values. It was a world not unfamiliar to them, for Classical Greek was a prerequisite for attending college in those days, and the study of Greek and Latin classics remained central to American private higher education from the time colleges and universities were first established into the early years of the twentieth century.

Through the hard work and fervor of the original members, new chapters of each fraternity were gradually established at other campuses, and many stayed together even when the North and South were torn apart during the Civil War (1861–65). In time, these Greek-letter societies developed passwords, secret handshakes, and often elaborate rituals with details and symbols borrowed from the humanistic, Masonic, and Christian traditions. The secret rituals served an almost quasi-religious function, establishing the identity of each group and revealing its values to the initiates. They also served, naturally, to cement the bonds of brotherhood and friendship within each particular group against a sometimes hostile outside world.

College fraternities also began to serve a much-needed function when the tradition of building chapter houses with dining facilities began, early in the 1870s. College administrations, for the most part, did not assume direct responsibility for the room and board of their students, leaving them to fend for themselves. However, college officials, who had originally bitterly opposed the fraternities because of their secrecy and rebelliousness, saw wisdom in allowing the societies to house and feed the students and regulate their behavior and often cooperated with the fraternities by supplying them with land and guaranteeing their mortgages. Officials also observed that there was nothing like a chapter house building campaign to arouse the interest and involvement of their wealthy alumni.

By the turn of the century the "Greek system" was an integral part of American higher education. Unfortunately for those excluded from them, however, their professed values of brotherhood and friendship were sometimes subsumed under the values of snobbishness and exclusiveness: wealth, family, connections, appearance, and religious faith often became the most important considerations for membership. When a flood of largely southern and eastern European immigrants came to the New World in the late nineteenth and early twentieth centuries, the American Greek system reacted by closing its doors and writing into its constitutions clauses that would ban all but white Protestants.

Before the mass migration of Jews from eastern Europe beginning in the 1880s, an occasional exceptional Jew of great talent might be asked to join a Gentile fraternity—particularly if the members were not aware of his Jewish identity when they recruited, or "rushed," him. However, for the most part the Greek system was closed to Jews, as it was to Blacks, Orientals, and sometimes Roman Catholics as well. The trend toward restrictions in fraternities was part of a larger trend in the late nineteenth century that saw Jews systematically excluded from country clubs, town clubs, neighborhoods, firms, private schools, resorts—indeed, from any kind of social institution. Coupled with exclusion, both overt and covert, from student societies already in existence, Jewish students were everywhere subject to insults and social ostracism by their non-Jewish fellows and occasionally even by their professors in their early days on the campus.

In addition to the possible presence of secret sectarian clauses and overt anti-Semitism, Jewish students themselves could not easily feel comfortable with the common use of a cross on the fraternity's insignia, professions of faith in Jesus Christ as part of the ritual, requirements of regular prayer and church attendance for new members, trees and caroling at Christmastime, required fraternity activities that coincided with Jewish High Holy Days, or a Christian grace recited daily before meals. While it was natural and suitable for early Christian brotherhoods to reach for these symbols to cement the members' unity, solemnity, and faith, a Jewish male student could not take part in these rituals with a full heart if he wished to remain true to his people. Nor was it easy for either Jew or Gentile to live comfortably under the same roof, sharing jokes and stories and socializing intimately with those whose religion he did not share, whose presence would likely not be welcomed by his parents during visits at home or at school, and whose sisters he could neither date nor marry.

All of these forces helped propel Jewish students into forming their own sectarian societies. Indeed, across the board, American Jews of both genders and all ages responded and retaliated by forming parallel institutions of their own, a phenomenon that constitutes a major part of American social history.

The Germanic Heritage: Fraternities in Central Europe

In reaching for models to form their organizations, Jewish students could look to Central Europe as well as to the glories of classical civilizations. Even without the parallel of anti-Semitism the model of the Central European student fraternity, which included beer-drinking, good fellowship, heated discussion, and physical recreation as well as political activity, had its appeal to American young men, especially those who had the opportunity to study in the universities of Germany, Austria, or Czechoslovakia. Novels and the popular operetta *The Student Prince*, set in the German university town of Heidelberg, fixed in the public mind the heroism, joys, and glamour of European student fraternity life.

In general, the bonds between ZBT's founders and the best of German language and culture ran deep. In the late nineteenth century, when the United States was still considered a young country and somewhat uncivilized, it was common for young men of higher class or culture to receive all or most of their education abroad at the great German-speaking universities. The majority of university professors and presidents in America in the nineteenth century, including the mentors of ZBT, had in fact received their final degrees from either German or British universities.

Even if they had not studied there, the young American Jews who founded the organization were themselves only one or two generations removed from German-speaking lands, an origin they proudly held in common with millions of American immigrants' descendants. In 1900, Germany was still considered one of the most academically, technologically, and scientifically advanced nations in the world. It was not until World War I, when the United States declared war against the "Dirty Hun," that the American higher educational establishment in general and American Jews in particular would seek to wrench themselves away from any identification with the ancestral German language and culture.

Within the existing framework of popular student groups, a precedent for the establishment of separate Jewish student societies already existed in late-nineteenth-century Central Europe, particularly in the

Universities of Vienna and Berlin. In the German lands, student fraternities, known as *Burschenschaften,* were first formed as part of a patriotic, romantic, and nationalist reaction against invasion by Napoleon's
armies. Many of these groups eventually took the form of "dueling"
fraternities, in which young men would defend the honor of themselves and their group and proudly wear the scars on their cheeks to
prove their bravery and manhood. The *Burschenschaften* rapidly expanded into almost all the German universities.

Jewish students participated fully in the early years of the *Burschenschaften*'s development. Indeed, Theodore Herzl himself, the founder
of modern political Zionism (who, we are told, came from such a completely assimilated Viennese Jewish milieu that he was accustomed to
having a Christmas tree at home), belonged to such a dueling fraternity
at the University of Vienna, as did the well-known political novelist
and journalist Arthur Koestler during his years of study in Berlin.

The waves of anti-Jewish hatred that would explode during the years
of Adolf Hitler's rule in the 1930s and 1940s were, however, many years
in coming, and European Jewish students directly felt their influence
long before the rise of the Nazi Party. Beginning in the 1870s and
through the 1890s, student fraternities in Germany and Austria, which
became increasingly influenced by trends of nativism and nationalism,
associated themselves with the growing anti-Semitic movement and refused to admit or recognize Jews on racial grounds. Furthermore, they
either expelled or forced the departure of those Jewish students, including Herzl, who had managed to become members in the past.

The assimilated middle- and upper-class Jewish men of Vienna, who
did not feel themselves to be so different from their fellow students, felt
especially bewildered by the hatred they were encountering. They
therefore attempted a variety of means both to reassert their pride and
self-respect in the face of rejection and also, from a more practical aspect, to protect themselves from the physical attacks and verbal abuse
that threatened them every day as they went to classes or walked the
streets of their university town. One of the most obvious and most
popular solutions was to attempt to "disappear" as a Jew, to do everything possible to erase signs of an identity that seemed to have become
not only meaningless but physically dangerous. This might be done by
changing one's name; modifying one's clothing, speech, or general appearance; ceasing to admit one's Jewishness; not associating with anyone in the Jewish community in the hope that one would not be linked
with them; and finally, formally converting to Christianity.

To form nationalist student fraternities of their very own was another solution that Jewish university men could reach for. Certainly, they could practice the art of fencing and dueling as easily among themselves as among non-Jews. Furthermore, the radical notion of modern Jewish statehood, just then gaining currency at the turn of the century, matched Teutonic nationalism well and could serve as an antidote both to anti-Semitism and to the students' own sense of demoralization. Modern Zionism glorified a Jewish people reborn, living a natural life on their ancestral soil, displaying all the courage and physical prowess that non-Jews accused them of lacking. With their own state or at least their own ideal of muscular patriotic nationalism behind them, Jewish male students believed, no non-Jews would dare to mistreat them as they had in the past, and it would no longer be necessary for any of their number to betray his ancient people by "disappearing." On the contrary, they, as young, strong, healthy, fit, and educated men, could and should turn themselves to their people's service.

In 1883 the first Jewish nationalist dueling fraternity, *Kadimah* ("forward" in Hebrew) was founded at the University of Vienna, and it inspired a host of followers. The founders—Nathan Birnbaum, Reuben Bierer, and Maurice Schnirer—pledged to use their organization to fight anti-Semitism, raise Jewish national consciousness, resist assimilation, and work for the Jewish colonization of Palestine. They later sought to defend Jewish honor by dueling with the anti-Semites who insulted the Jewish name—until the anti-Semites declared that it was even beneath their dignity to duel with them! When Theodore Herzl published his ground-breaking pamphlet *The Jewish State* in 1896, the first declaration and manifesto of the modern political Zionist movement, the young men of *Kadimah* were among his first followers and co-workers. Eventually, *Kadimah* became known around the world, and it thus served as one of the earliest models for the original ZBT Society even before the members became cognizant of the importance of the conventional American college "Greek" system.

Dr. Richard James Horatio Gottheil (1862–1936)

The story of Zeta Beta Tau would not be complete without acknowledgment of the great role that Dr. Gottheil, an eminent Columbia professor, played in its founding. From the beginning, Dr. Gottheil was the inspiration, guide, and for ten years actual head of the fraternity, and his tall, gentlemanly, and immaculate presence was a constant influence. In the words of one of the early brothers, "Professor Gottheil was every inch an aristocrat, a true Prince in Israel." Although he occasionally betrayed some disappointment when, in his view, the group "strayed" from his original goals for them, he nevertheless remained as mentor and role model to "his" boys until the end of his life. In 1925, the fraternity's highest award, the Gottheil Medal, was named after him; and in a letter of final instructions written only a few months before he died in 1936, he requested that "my ZBT boys" line the aisle of Temple Emanu-El as his casket was carried in and out.

Richard James Horatio Gottheil was born in Manchester, England, October 13, 1862, the son of Rabbi Gustav Gottheil, who later served as the spiritual leader of Temple Emanu-El, a leading Reform Jewish congregation in New York City. The young Gottheil graduated from high school in England and then, after his family moved to New York, received his B.A. degree from Columbia College in 1881. Nicholas Murray Butler, who later became the powerful president of the university, was an undergraduate at the same time, and the two were classmates and friends.

After graduation, Gottheil continued his studies abroad at the universities of Berlin, Tuebingen, and Leipzig, where he received his doctorate in Semitics in 1886. Upon his return to America, Gottheil was appointed an instructor at Columbia University, where his career was to span forty-nine years. He quickly rose to the rank of full professor and chairman of the Department of Semitic Languages, publishing numerous learned works. He also served as chief of the Oriental Department of the New York Public Library from 1896 until his death.

In the academic world, Gottheil became known for helping to bring the most rigorous European standards of critical scholarship to the United States and for training dozens of students who later became leaders in their field. Among his many noted protégés was the American rabbi and Zionist leader Stephen S. Wise (1874–1949), who received his B.A. degree from Gottheil at Columbia in 1892 and his doctorate in 1901.

Gottheil did not limit his activities purely to professorial pursuits in his own field of Semitics. It was taken for granted that the university would call upon him to supervise any thesis in any academic department that had a Jewish theme, whether related to Gottheil's philological specialty or not. As one of the first Jewish professors at Columbia, he quickly became the semiofficial advisor and advocate to Columbia's entire Jewish student body, whether for academic or extracurricular activities. Gottheil's sympathy and championship of Jewish students, which he did not hesitate to carry up to the level of President Butler himself when necessary, was especially effective when cases of anti-Semitic prejudice occurred on the Columbia campus. In addition his home, presided over by his erudite wife Emma Leon—herself a strong Zionist, born in Beirut and educated in France—became an intellectual and social center not only for Columbia's Jewish students but also for young men studying at other institutions of higher education in the New York area, including the Jewish Theological Seminary, New York University, and the City College of New York.

Beyond Columbia, Gottheil's entire career was filled with public service to various groups and organizations, holding offices in the American Jewish Historical Society, the American Oriental Society (which he served as president in 1933–34), and the Jewish Institute of Religion, a rabbinical seminary in New York that was later merged with the Hebrew Union College.

Zionism and the Founding of ZBT

Of all Gottheil's public activities in the early years of the century, however, one took precedence over others. With the encouragement of his father, Gottheil embraced the goal of modern political Zionism, then in its infancy. It seemed an odd embrace, for Zionism at that time was looked upon with contempt or at least skepticism by a vast majority of American Jews. There was a widespread belief that the movement was relevant only to those few traditional, Yiddish-speaking immigrants who were unable to accept that the United States of America was in fact the new "Promised Land." Especially to well-established, upper-middle-class German Jews of the Reform denomination, the precise class to which Gottheil and many of his students belonged, Zionism seemed a dangerous doctrine, a waste of energy that exposed their people to the dreaded charge of "dual loyalty." Equally widespread was the belief that anyone who dreamed, as Theodore Herzl did, that the tiny, barren, backwater Ottoman Turkish province of Palestine could be turned back into some kind of national Jewish homeland, had to be either a crackpot or a fool.

Gottheil, however, was neither. He traveled the country, speaking to fashionable audiences in either fluent English or German, trying to convince them of the integrity and "respectability" of the Zionist movement. In 1898, the same year as the founding of ZBT, he was elected president of the Federation of American Zionists (later the Zionist Organization of America [ZOA], with the very young Rabbi Stephen S. Wise as secretary, a post Wise held until 1904. In this position, Gottheil was in constant touch with Herzl and Zionist leaders all over the world, traveling every year to the World Zionist Congresses held in Switzerland and England, where much of the groundwork for what later became the modern State of Israel was laid.

In recruiting adherents for the new movement, Gottheil could not overlook the splendid raw material presented to him almost every day. His well-educated, American-born or -raised, and fluent-English-speaking Jewish students were precisely the flower of young Jewish manhood that the movement needed desperately. Moreover, both Gottheil and his father, Gustav, along with Jewish leaders all over the world, were noting with regret that, in their rush to embrace higher education and the best of mainstream culture, Jewish youth seemed to be deprecating and drifting away from their own ancient heritage. As had been the case in Europe, the excitement and enrichment of modern Zionist ideals might help revive young men's waning enthusiasm for that heritage and inculcate in them renewed feelings of pride and self-worth.

This pride was badly needed. Gottheil could witness the covert and overt currents of anti-Jewish feeling that ran through Columbia University; he saw weekly the grief experienced by Jewish men when they met with complete rejection in social and extracurricular spheres or even active hostility from other students who were their equals in every respect. Gottheil had probably experienced this grief himself during his undergraduate days. The situation was dangerous, and the incentives for young men to opt out of Judaism and to reject the Jewish people altogether at the first possible opportunity were strong. Without doubt, Gottheil believed, the formation of their own separate and independent fraternity would afford his charges essential protection against both physical and spiritual harm and possibly serve as an antidote to campus anti-Semitism.

The eminent professor did not have to work too hard to convince his followers. The young men in the Gottheil circle, most of them "dual curriculum" students—learning at the seminary in the mornings and at Columbia, City College, or NYU later in the day, were receptive. As the historian of Zeta Beta Tau in the 1920s noted, they were "thrilled" at the prospect of forming a Zionist group. Indeed, there is some evidence that a group known as the Young American Zionists, an intercollegiate Zionist group formed from this circle in 1896, was the actual predecessor to ZBT and that the students' interest in the Zionist movement had arisen independently. In any event, on December 29, 1898, with the encouragement and inspiration of the Gottheils, fifteen young men gathered at Jewish Theological Seminary to form officially a new organization, specifically citing Vienna's *Kadimah* as their model. Their names were

Herman Abramowitz	Aaron W. Levy
Bernhard Bloch	David Liknaitz
Isidore Delson	Louis S. Posner
Aaron P. Drucker	Bernhard D. Saxe
Bernard C. Ehrenreich	Herman B. Sheffield
Menachem M. Eichler	David A. Swick
Aaron Eiseman	Maurice L. Zellermayer
David Levine	

The initials ZBT and the group's chosen Hebrew motto, *Zion be-mishpat tipadeh* (Zion shall be redeemed with justice), a quotation from the book of Isaiah, well known in learned circles, had been the suggestion of the men's Bible instructor, Rabbi Bernard Drachman (1861–1945). The ancient phrase had already been taken up by the budding Zionist movement, and the full quote—*Zion be-mishpat tipadeh ve-shaveha be-tzedakah* (Zion shall be redeemed with justice, and they that return of her, with righteousness)—is emblazoned in Hebrew on the delegate's badge, which Gottheil himself wore to the fourth Zionist Congress in August 1900 in London. It is today preserved among the Gottheil papers at the American Jewish Archives in Cincinnati, Ohio.

Not all of ZBT's founders intended to go on to ordination. In fact, the more theologically minded group who aimed to become rabbis were good-naturedly termed "sky-pilots" by their contemporaries who planned to go into more "practical" fields, such as law or medicine. The latter took courses at the seminary only because they and their families believed that a good religious education to accompany one's secular studies was proper and desirable. Despite any divergence in their ultimate professional paths, however, all were thoroughly dedicated to the Jewish cause and looked to Jewish and Zionist iconography in forming the basic framework of their society.

The "Home Fraternity" in New York City, c. 1899. Founder Maurice L. Zellermayer, author of the song "Here's to Our Fraternity," stands in second row, second from right; founder Louis S. Posner sits first row, second from right.

In addition to a Hebrew motto the students chose the customary Jewish "national" colors of blue and white as their own, and the six-pointed Star of David was their emblem. ZBT's first officers also took on Hebrew titles (some of which, in modern Hebrew, are today used to identify officers in the Israel Defense Forces). These were Nasi (president), Segan Rishon and Segan Sheni (first and second vice presidents), Sopher (corresponding secretary), Ro'eh Cheshbonoth (financial secretary), Gizbar (treasurer), and Shomer Hasaph (sergeant-at-arms). Presiding over the Beth Din (advisory and executive board) was the Av Beth Din, a title going back to the sixth century. Membership was open to all Jewish men at least eighteen years of age who were enrolled at a college, university, or professional school and were of "unimpeachable character." The group's formal objectives, according to its first charter, were "to promote the cause of Zionism and the welfare of Jews in general; and to unite fraternally all collegiate Zionists of the United States and Canada."

The Cafe Logeling on New York's West Fifty-seventh Street was the favored gathering spot of the founders. There members would listen to notable speakers, discuss Zionism and other burning issues of the day, and enjoy beer and pretzels and each other's company—activities as much in keeping with the traditions of a German student society as of an American college fraternity. Writing in the fraternity's twenty-fifth anniversary volume, its historian acknowledged the ZBT Society's similarity to these groups: "Smoking their long pipes, drinking real beer, singing their college songs, and enjoying their sandwiches and cake, these men must have had jolly gatherings, more like those of the students in Berlin or Vienna than like the gatherings of students in America." The organization grew rapidly in its first year and a half. By 1900 it had chapters in New York, Baltimore, and New Haven and had received recognition as a Zionist organization in both *The American Jewish Year Book* and *The American Hebrew*, an influential German-Jewish English-language newspaper. City College's annual for that year listed sixteen men as members of ZBT, including Mordecai Kaplan, later a leading American rabbi and founder of Reconstructionism, and Alfred Frankenthaler, who went on to become a New York State Supreme Court justice.

Rapid turnover, however, is an inevitable feature of any organization composed of students, and ZBT was no exception. Within two years the founders, four of whom went on to distinguished rabbinical careers, had graduated, and the early Zionist enthusiasm of ZBT faded. The philosophy was still too atypical and alien to the vast majority of American Jews, most of whom were far more interested in establishing themselves in America than in Palestine and often regarded those who dreamed of a Jewish homeland with contempt or pity. In addition, the organized American Jewish community was growing in complexity; many more groups now existed that served the goals of Jewish and Zionist education and social welfare. Indeed, ZBT had grown, with over one hundred members studying at eighteen different colleges and professional schools; but the new Zionist philosophy could not unite so many different members, and it seemed time to move in other directions.

In November 1900, therefore, a new administration took over the helm of ZBT, and thus began the gradual evolution into a Greek-letter collegiate fraternity more like the common American model. As one of the founders, Maurice L. Zellermayer, reported, in an early history of ZBT, "Zeta Beta Tau: The First Twenty-Five Years, 1898–1923," "It was found that it would be for the best interests of the Fraternity not to limit ourselves solely to the question of Zionism, that as a Jewish College

Fraternity we ought not to shut out those Jewish college men who were desirous of entering our Fraternity but had not as yet taken any definite stand on the Zionist question." Within a year (November 1901), ZBT's administration had revised its charter to eliminate the goal of promoting Zionism and had resolved that the new object of the fraternity would be simply "the promotion of Judaism."

To those involved in ZBT's early transformation, the movement away from an organization of rabbinical students and toward a conventional college fraternity for Jewish men did not appear in any way to be a frivolity or a luxury or an abandonment of service to their people. A Jewish fraternity appeared to be a necessity for reasons both positive and negative. The need for a traditional American college fraternity, with its chapter house and well-organized social activity, had not been so acute in the big city, for either Jews or Gentiles. But ZBT was rapidly expanding beyond the boundaries of New York City. In rural areas and small towns, where many American institutions of higher education were located, to be deprived of fraternity affiliation because of prejudice or religious restrictions could be a catastrophe for a young college man, and students began to demand an exclusively Jewish Greek-letter college fraternity.

In the decade after its abandonment of the purely Zionist ideal, ZBT became truly national in scope, establishing chapters in upstate New York, Pennsylvania, Massachusetts, Louisiana, Ohio, and Illinois, and even Canada. By 1906, after a year of tension and sometime bitterness among the older and younger members of the fraternity, the reorganization was complete. On October 21 of that year, the Supreme Beth Din issued a new constitution and preamble, and the name of the society, after several years of informal use, was officially changed to "The Zeta Beta Tau Fraternity." The official crest of the new fraternity still featured the traditional Jewish Star of David, but now it was redrawn to include other, more common fraternity symbols—the censers of justice, the lamp of learning, the clasped hands of friendship, and a Greek temple representing nobility of spirit.

In addition to adopting a Greek name and Greek symbolism and eliminating some of the traditional Hebrew names for its institutions and officers, the fraternity adopted a new set of goals. The purpose of Zeta Beta Tau, according to the preamble of their new constitution, was to "promulgate, foster, encourage, strengthen and continue the friendship gained at college"; to "inculcate in the lives of its members a love and respect for all things Jewish, and to help them exemplify in their lives the highest ideals of the Jewish people"; and finally, "to . . . form a more perfect society." Thus came the final merging of Hellenistic and Hebraic influences. From that day on, for another half-century, although it was still a Jewish fraternity serving Jewish young men and included Jewish elements in its ritual and pledge training, Zeta Beta Tau would function in every way as a modern American collegiate Greek-letter fraternity, participating fully in the national Greek system wherever it existed.

Privately, Professor Gottheil deplored what he saw as the dwindling interest of his beloved fraternity in Zionist and Jewish matters. The elements of Judaism that very clearly remained within ZBT were never enough to satisfy him, and he took every public opportunity to encourage the young men to "mend their ways." However, so high was his regard for the membership and so high, in turn, was their regard for him, that he remained at the helm of Zeta Beta Tau for another fourteen years and maintained close contact with it until the day he died.

World War I and the Challenge of Reconstruction

Within less than two decades of its founding, the new Zeta Beta Tau found it necessary to pass through the first of several precarious periods in which its very existence was threatened. The fraternity's first major test was the "Great War," when young men all over the world abandoned their normal activities to take part in the worldwide struggle, sparked by a pistol shot on June 28, 1914 in Sarajevo, the capital city of Bosnia. In short order Russia declared war on Austria, and Germany, Belgium, France, England, and Italy joined the conflict. It was not until April 1917, however, that the United States entered the war, and the strength that ZBT had managed to build up during its years of peace stood it in good stead when the crisis finally came upon them.

Indeed, by the second decade of the century, ZBT, despite its relative youth as an organization, was already functioning as a well-organized fraternity on the Greek-letter model and was spreading throughout the country. The year 1913 brought especially momentous signs of progress. The first issue of the ZBT *Quarterly* appeared that October, edited by Louis William Greenstein and Philip Spira, both of Western Reserve University. The fraternity's first sectional gathering, a Western Conclave held in Cleveland in March, was attended by all the national officers and eighty-three men, including a group of students from McGill University who were installed as the first Canadian chapter. November 29, 1913, was the first time that Zeta Beta Tau was represented at the annual National Interfraternity Conference, a distinction that conferred legitimacy upon it within the American Greek-letter world. In the following four years graduate clubs sprang up in New York, New England, and Cleveland. Chapters were installed in 1914 and 1916 at the aristocratic University of Virginia and the University of Alabama. National administration became more sophisticated as an index card system, membership directory, and traveling adviser system was instituted under Harold Riegelman (Cornell '14), who rose from Supreme Sofar in 1915 to Supreme Vice Nasi in 1916.

Weekly meetings of the Zeta Beta Tau Club of New York took place in the Hotel Ansonia, while the fraternity conducted a quest for proper quarters they could call their own. Finally, enough funds were gathered to rent a handsome "gray stone front" at 127 West Eighty-eighth Street. There open-house teas could be held every Sunday afternoon, entertainment for the undergraduates could take place every Saturday night, and living quarters were available for all New York–area ZBT men who wished them. With great satisfaction the New York Club prepared to act as hosts for the nineteenth anniversary celebration of ZBT's founding.

It was not to be, however, for less than a month after the official housewarming at West Eighty-eighth Street, U.S. president Woodrow Wilson, on April 2, 1917, asked for and soon received a declaration of war from Congress. There was no doubt in anyone's mind what the next step of any good ZBT member should be. Here was a chance for patriotic young men of Jewish ancestry to prove their worth and their gratitude to the country that had given their families shelter and prosperity. In addition, as the national leadership of the fraternity reminded them, to enlist promptly and to serve with as much bravery and distinction as possible, would ultimately bring honor not only to all Jewish men in general but to the fair name of Zeta Beta Tau specifically.

"It is the duty of every man to do his best in the great work in which the democracy now participates—to free the earth from those that wish to tyrannize over it and to lay the foundations for a peace that shall be durable," declared Supreme Nasi Richard Gottheil in a proclamation issued from New York City immediately after the declaration of war:

Men of the Fraternity! We desire ardently that we Jews in America shall acquit ourselves worthily of the opportunity that is afforded us. Together with others, our fathers found here a refuge. But even more than have many of our fellow citizens, we have found release here from the bondage of oppression and from the onus of government overlordship. The occasion now is forward for us to show by immediate action our abiding gratitude. . . . You have with me in addition, the good name of Zeta Beta Tau at heart. Let it be said that to a man we, in our various chapters, have not waited for a summons from our government, but that we have freely and cheerfully offered the best we possess—ourselves—to its service. Long live the United States of America! Long may they stand and may they fight for that which is true and right! ("ZBT . . . 1898–1923")

At the time of the U.S. declaration of war, ZBT had grown to twenty-one chapters and three graduate clubs. Now, however, the ranks of both the chapters and the national administration were decimated as each day more and more left their posts to enter the armed forces. Several lost their lives, including Brother Alwyn Gordon Levy, a pilot who wrote to his fraternity brothers of the risks of training to fly a plane at the very dawn of military aviation. Colleges were taken over by the army for training purposes through the organization of the SATC (for Student Army Training Corps, although its critics derogatorily referred to it as "Saturday Afternoon Tea Club" or "Safe at the College"), and the War Department went so far as to prohibit fraternity meetings or initiations for a time as inimical to the war effort. Soon the entire running of the national fraternity fell upon the shoulders of Samuel Stark, a graduate of City College and Columbia known as the "Grand Old Man of Zeta Beta Tau," who almost single-handedly rescued ZBT from complete disintegration.

Even after the armistice was declared in November 1918 and chapter rolls swelled in the spring of 1919 with returning veterans, ZBT was torn by dissension and the challenges of readjustment to civilian life. Among other things, undergraduates vehemently protested what they saw as the old-fashioned, excessively New York–centered nature of the national leadership; they refused at first to sing the fraternity song, "Here's to Our Fraternity," considering it antiquated and old-fashioned (a resolution to abolish it was introduced at a convention but did not pass); they chafed at Professor Gottheil's constant reminders that they were Jewish members of a Jewish organization first and members of a Greek-letter fraternity second; and they complained that letters written to the *Quarterly* to express their displeasure were being censored by alumni.

By the end of the December 1919 convention, however, the spirit of opposition had faded and the forces of unity had again taken hold. Professor Gottheil was elected for the ninth time as Supreme Nasi, with Harold Riegelman as the new Supreme Vice Nasi. The matter of the *Quarterly* was settled when one alumnus reminded the others, in a 1919

Letter to the Editor, of the "dry as toast" nature of their magazine before it had been opened up to undergraduate editorship and noted that the very arguments they were having were the sign of a vital, red-blooded organization. "Go to it, print what you want," he declared to the editors. "We will criticize; we will roast you; we will tear you to pieces if you print anything improper; but go to it, if it is going to be for the purpose of creating thought in the fraternity." ZBT grew in strength and by 1921 could count twenty-eight chapters, with thirteen owning their own homes.

Richard Gottheil: In Memoriam

It is a reflection on Richard Gottheil's enormous influence in the early years of Zeta Beta Tau that when he passed away after a brief illness at the age of seventy-three on May 22, 1936, the entire fraternity joined together to mourn him. Nicholas Murray Butler, Columbia's president, noted in his memorial that Gottheil had not ceased to teach his classes until two weeks before his death. The entire September 1936 issue of *The Zeta Beta Tau Quarterly* was dedicated to his memory, and brothers and friends contributed their tributes and reminiscences about the gentleman who had served as their guide and mentor for so long.

One founder, Rabbi Herman Abramowitz of Montreal, wrote: "Our Zeta Beta Tau Fraternity is indeed fortunate in having had Richard Gottheil as its founder; and wise in building up a Memorial for him to act as an inspiration for the future. For in his personality we had embodied the ideals our fraternity aims most to foster. He was the sincere Jew; the profound scholar; the polished gentleman. That is the combination of qualities that his memory will continue to preach to our membership as to all Jewish students." Another founder, Aaron Eiseman, wrote of Gottheil's constant attendance at ZBT meetings; his ready offering of advice, counsel, and inspiration; his interest in his students' personal problems, particularly those who were preparing for the rabbinate; and of how they would always remember him as "the pilot who steered the old ship on its earliest travels over many tempestuous seas and brought it, under his splendid leadership, to a place of pre-eminence and importance."

Bernard C. Ehrenreich wrote of how Gottheil joined their founder's group without a moment's hesitation, despite his busy schedule, and of the inspiration he was to them all back in the days when ZBT meetings were attended by a mere handful of people. "When he came," Ehrenreich recalled, "he carried with him a world of enthusiasm and every young fellow was made to feel that the Professor was interested in him. From that day until the last it was my good fortune to enjoy the friendship of the professor and his good wife, and my memories of him will always remain. . . . His interest in ZBT never lagged even to the last when as an old man he was no longer able to take an active part in fraternity matters. Yes, we loved him then, and we love his memory now and always will look with joy for having known him."

Others remembered the joy of visiting him and his wife at home, where fascinating guests from all walks of life and all social classes could be found; his devotion to Columbia University; his ability to enjoy the company of younger people while never giving the impression of being an elder; the honor and respect granted him by both Jew and Gentile, and the dignified service he gave to the cause of breaking down the barriers of anti-Semitism and creating better understanding between Jews and Christians.

Some remembered visits to the professor's cloistered study in Philosophy Hall on the Columbia campus. "There he seemed to be in his natural setting," recalled Simon J. Jason, a former secretary and treasurer of ZBT. "Picture the dignified gentleman in a quiet, secluded study, the walls lined with books, the light fairly dim, and there you have him—the whole world for the time being shut out." Stanley I. Fishel (Columbia '34), president of ZBT's fourth, or "Delta," chapter, had perhaps more contact with Gottheil than most undergraduates had and missed him keenly. He wrote:

For those of us who attended Columbia University, Richard J. H. Gottheil was more than a ZBT legend, more than the venerable patriarch whose enthusiasm and inspiration gave birth to an ideal that he was to live to see become an institution, the largest and finest of its kind.

Brother Gottheil was proudly claimed as Delta's own, and many a newly installed and earnest, but woe-begone chapter president found the courage to face difficult tasks ahead after the privilege of an hour's heart to heart talk with the Professor in his cloistered office. . . .

Succeeding classes of Delta undergraduates must recall with mixed feeling the many luncheon and dinner visits that this soft-spoken, grey-bearded, kindly gentleman paid the House; and how classes were forgotten under the spell of a magnetic personality and the wisdom and unforgettably interesting reminiscences that many decades of travel and research gave to a figure so many years the senior of his listeners but so decidedly their equal in the youthfulness of his outlook.

The fraternity's loss is great, but to those whose honor it was to know him personally, it is irreplaceable.

The Founders: Whither?

Despite the fraternity's change in its original direction, most of the fifteen founders remained active and interested, often helping to establish new chapters near their homes, faithfully attending conventions, advising the younger men, and in many cases serving as officers. All fifteen graduated to distinguished careers, and their achievements were followed with interest by Zeta Beta Tau members in the pages of the *Quarterly.*

Aaron P. Drucker entered the field of secular education, following graduation from Columbia and a period of study at the University of Chicago. He taught at various colleges and universities and was the author of several books. Three of the founders—Aaron W. Levy, Louis S. Posner (both born in England), and Bernhard Bloch—entered the legal profession, at the same time holding a host of positions in legal organizations, Jewish charities, and state government. Isidore Delson, who served as Supreme President of Zeta Beta Tau in 1905 (as did Aaron W. Levy in 1904), became a civil engineer, employed by the city of New York. Mrs. Delson, the *Quarterly*'s editors were pleased to note, was none other than Frances Zellermayer, the sister of Maurice Zellermayer, who unfortunately died at an early age. Zellermayer was remembered as being an enthusiastic and devoted member of the original group and author of the ZBT anthem: "Here's to Our Fraternity." Dr. Herman B. Sheffield, or "Sheff" as he was known, followed a promising medical practice. He had in fact already graduated from the university at the time of Zeta Beta Tau's founding and was thus several years older than the others. Nevertheless, he was a part of the original group, and during the first year and a half of its existence many of the official meetings were held in his office.

Four of the founders completed the full course of rabbinical study at Jewish Theological Seminary and received ordination. Aaron Eiseman became a pulpit rabbi and one of the founders of the Jewish Welfare Board during World War I. Herman Abramowitz became rabbi of Congregation Shaar Hashomayim in Quebec, president of the United Synagogue of America, and honorary vice-president of the Zionist Organization of Canada. Among his many posts, he served during World War I as chaplain to His Majesty's Canadian Jewish Forces. Dr. David Liknaitz studied at the University of Pennsylvania, Columbia

University, and the Jewish Theological Seminary. He helped to organize the first Zionist Society in Philadelphia and was for many years Jewish chaplain of the federal prison at Fort Leavenworth, Kansas.

The name of one of ZBT's most distinguished founding rabbis—Dr. Bernard C. Ehrenreich, or "Doc E" as he was known to his friends and fraternity brothers—cannot be separated from the history of the Jews of the American South, and his life has attracted much scholarly attention. Born in Kis Szeben, Hungary in 1876, Ehrenreich came to America with his family at the age of three. A leading interest in his life was the establishment of resources for the physical, spiritual, and intellectual development of youth. A Progressive in his politics, while still an undergraduate at New York University he helped establish the community playground system of New York City. Later he served as recording secretary of the Federation of American Zionists, the organization of which Richard Gottheil was president.

Ehrenreich began his rabbinical career with pulpits in Atlantic City and Philadelphia, then moved with his wife and family to Congregation Beth Or in Montgomery, Alabama, in 1906. The social causes he supported included Zionism, the establishment of juvenile courts, and higher education for southern Blacks. None of these goals were designed to increase a southern Jew's popularity in the first quarter of the twentieth century, yet he could not help but react to what he saw around him. His biographer notes that at a meeting of the Peanut Association attended by Ehrenreich in 1917 in Montgomery, he witnessed George Washington Carver's having to enter the hall via a freight elevator. This experience made a shocking impression on him and led him to speak up even more forcefully for the cause of equal rights.

Perhaps the height of Ehrenreich's career came during World War I, when he served as a civilian chaplain under the auspices of the Jewish Welfare Board for soldiers stationed at Camp Sheridan in Montgomery. The "Buckeye Division" included many young Jewish soldiers from Ohio, away from home for the first time. One of them, who became an acquaintance and corresponded with Ehrenreich during the war years, was Jacob Rader Marcus of Cincinnati (1896–1995). The young Sergeant Marcus would go on to become the founder of the American Jewish Archives and one of the country's leading scholars in the history of American Jewry.

To all Jewish soldiers, Bernard and Irma Ehrenreich opened their homes, ceaselessly feeding, caring, advising, and ministering to their needs. Sometimes these needs included obtaining translators to write letters to the boy's parents; more than a few came from families of such recent immigrant origin that their parents knew no English, and the young boys were unable to write to them in Yiddish.

Contact was not broken after the young men left the camp. The Ehrenreich papers, preserved at the American Jewish Historical Society, are filled with literally hundreds of letters from soldiers written from all over the world, praising the Ehrenreichs and thanking them for their hospitality. In return, Ehrenreich sent hundreds of letters filled with comfort and encouragement in the face of the terrible dangers his soldiers were confronting. In 1917 a mother of one of these soldiers wrote to the *American Israelite*: "Without Bernard Ehrenreich who would know what would become of the Jewish soldiers. To him they look up as a father, to him they confide their troubles. When they cry, when they are homesick . . . to him they go for money and his hand is always in his pocket, never refusing one. He feeds twenty-five to forty twice a week out of his own pocket." In addition to opening his home, Ehrenreich made regular visits to the army base, where he not only visited the sick but taught hundreds of illiterate soldiers how to read and write English.

At the end of World War I, Ehrenreich began to realize a dream that had begun on the streets of New York City while he was working to develop a public playground system. Long before summer camps, much less Jewish summer camps, existed, Ehrenreich conceived of establishing a rural setting where all the physical and spiritual potentialities of youth could be nurtured. Being away from the city, forced to be self-reliant, and living close to nature were for him the essentials of developing character and physical stamina. In 1915 he purchased the campsite of Camp Kawaga in Minocqua, Wisconsin. The camp opened that year with twelve campers living in tents—with no cabins, no running water, no electricity, and no phone. By 1920 the camp had grown sufficiently to warrant his full-time attention, and Ehrenreich therefore resigned his pulpit to spend the next twenty years of his life as a camp director. "He takes with him," declared the state's governor, Thomas Kilby, "the respect, esteem and all good wishes of the people of Montgomery and thousands of friends throughout Alabama."*

---

*Bryon L. Sherwin, "Portrait of a Romantic Rebel: Bernard C. Ehrenreich (1876–1955), in *Turn to the South: Essays on Southern Jewry*, ed. Nathan M. Kaganoff and Melvin I. Urofsky (Charlottesville: University Press of Virginia, 1979), 10.

The Founders Remember

ZBT's founders for the most part remained in touch with the fraternity, guiding it through its changes and marveling at its growth. It was clear that none of them visualized that the small group they began with fifteen men in 1898 would grow into a national fraternity with thousands of members and scores of chapters. Ehrenreich was especially thrilled when he was invited as a special guest to the fiftieth anniversary banquet, held in New York City at the Waldorf Astoria in December of 1948. Writing to his wife, wishing she could be with him, he declared: "Of course I am having a good time. Not until I came to the convention did I realize the kind of organization we started fifty years ago. Imagine, there are 1,000 ZBT's in the land. What a fine bunch of kids! To hear them argue large subjects is a treat for the mind and heart and soul. As long as the Jewish people grow this kind of youthful crop there is nothing to worry about. I was thrilled when I first came to the meeting and now I am up in the clouds—way above the clouds, since last night's banquet. Such arrangements and such speeches. Marvelous, one after another . . ."

At the fortieth anniversary convention of Zeta Beta Tau, also held in New York—1938, two years after the death of Richard Gottheil—founder Louis S. Posner was asked to give the keynote address. He gave a long and moving account of his memories, of the founders and of their group's earliest days, which was reproduced in full in the *Zeta Beta Tau Quarterly* of March 1939 and which captures perhaps better than anything else the atmosphere at the dawn of the fraternity:

The few minutes assigned me are intended, I realize, as a tribute not to me personally, but to all of us who constitute the founders of Zeta Beta Tau. Allow me at this point, therefore, to present to you two of the founders who are here with us tonight, Bernhard Bloch and Aaron Levy. For them and for myself, also, the confession must be made that even if it be a wise child that knows its own father, it is an even wiser father that in this instance could possibly recognize his own offspring. But I can hear the father speak: It is many years, my children, since you left home and scattered yourselves over the length and breadth of our land; today you have returned, and I look upon you and my heart is warmed by your shining countenances, your bright eyes, your determined bearing—you have done honor to the family name, and with pride I welcome you back into the family circle, to the City where you were born.

Forty years, you say! I deny it. Time, you thief, out with you and your ruffian calendars! We deny that forty years of your reckoning have passed since those fateful days when we young fellows met in one another's homes, my own included, and when in the house next door to mine lived a boy with whom I occasionally rode downtown, he to City College, I to work—there's a lad that will make his mark and be heard of someday—this young Felix Frankfurter. We deny that forty years have passed since we foregathered in the beerstubes of 57th Street, drank beer, enjoyed pretzels and free lunch, and looked forward with confidence to the paths we were yet to tread; since we sat at the knee of Richard Gottheil and drew strengthened faith in the dawn of a better day and of a Zion redeemed.

Look in on us as we meet—there is Bernhard Bloch with his whole life before him, as indeed it is before all of us—he says he will be a lawyer some day and you can see he is ambitious and able, and intelligence radiates from his round face; there's Aaron Levy, he also plans to be a lawyer, and you know he will be a good one too, for he is keen and quiet and understanding and has great charm of manner for so young a chap; as for young Posner over there, he also expects to be a lawyer—he is an eager boy, but I'd rather not say much about him, at least not tonight. Here are Ehrenreich and Drucker and Abramowitz and Liknaitz and Eiseman—they are all going to be sky-pilots and we don't envy them their student days and studies and dreams at the theological institute—they know so little of the outside world, poor fellows, while we know so much—but the trouble is they think they must be Cantors as well as ministers, for they are trying to harmonize in Zellermayer's fraternity song, "Here's to Our Fraternity, May It Live Forever"; there is Sheffield, that young doctor of great promise; and modest Delson, he's going to be an engineer; and Eichler and Levine and Saxe, and Zellermayer too, fingering his new song carefully on the piano.

Mr. Chairman, Dr. Gottheil, gentlemen: I suggest we discuss the causes of anti-Semitism—are the racial or social or religious or economic, or all of these—do you believe, Dr. Gottheil, that anything short of a miracle can bring us the answer to the age-long prayer for the restoration of Zion—you over there, why do you assert that the educational systems of the country are not adequate—shall women have the vote, or is her place in the home—what do we think of Zangwill as compared with other writers—what can be done to bring more people to the synagogue and to enforce a greater attendance of children at Hebrew schools, one of our theological students asks—this strife between labor unions and employers, will it ever reach a sensible point of agreement, or is the battle to go on until in the effort to find a remedy the pendulum swings, as it often does in such a case, too far the other way—and now we're discussing whether the country still needs the protection of a tariff or whether free trade is best.

The hour grows late. A voice is heard—it is quiet, deep with emotion and suppressed excitement. I ask you, Dr. Gottheil, and the others present—can you see in this room, as I do, dimly but unmistakably, a throng of young men, educated, well dressed, all Jews. Their faces are strange, they seem to belong to another era! Notice how determined they appear to be—they are leaders, or the stuff of which leaders are made! Here they sit, silent, grim, as though ready for the summons to gird on their armor and sally forth in the battle for freedom of faith, for equality before the law, for the security of freemen, for a land where democracy shall rule, and where they shall know justice and brotherly love! No, no, I object to this interruption, Dr. Sheffield—don't tell me about this new psychology stuff, and that we are young and imaginative and always dreaming dreams and seeing visions. Look, you can see them for yourself! But—yes—you are right. It is a vision! For slowly the faces fade, and slowly, softly, the strange group melts away into the limitless depths of space.

We are about to adjourn. We fix the time and place for the next meeting. We arrange for sandwiches and refreshments and decide upon the subject then to be discussed. And so we part, full of vigor and ideals and faith in the future of the world, the betterment of man and the improvement of the lot of Jews everywhere. To these purposes we have dedicated ourselves, and made our pact with God!

> "What happy pictures then we drew
> Of coming joys; of sorrows few
> We thought, as in those days so fair,
> We built great castles in the air."

(pp. 7–9)

CHAPTER TWO

"LOVE AND MIRTH"

Zeta Beta Tau in the "Roaring Twenties"

The decade of the 1920s was the veritable "Golden Age" of the American college fraternity, for at hardly any time before or since did the Greek system enjoy such a spectacular rise in size, wealth, power, and influence. The fads and fashions of college life itself became enshrined in American popular culture, and movies, musicals, novels, and songs attempting to depict this new aspect of American youth were devoured by the non-college-attending population. Much of this material was sheer fantasy, but the new importance and accessibility of a college education and its concomitant fraternity experiences were not.

In a trend accelerated by the postwar prosperity, the number of students in the United States who were attending some kind of institute of higher education shot up from 150,000 in 1910 to well over one million men and women by the end of 1929. The majority of these were enrolled in coeducational residential colleges, one of the most fertile grounds for the growth of the Greek-letter movement. College administrations were, for the most part, unprepared to handle the sudden influx and welcomed the fraternities' ability to sort, house, feed, and regulate the behavior of their students. Strong opposition thus gave way to grudging cooperation or even active recruitment of new fraternity chapters by the colleges themselves. During the decade the number of fraternity chapters in the country more than doubled, and the reported value of their property increased more than fivefold.

Zeta Beta Tau enjoyed its share of the new prosperity, as did more than a dozen of its fraternal competitors. The historically Jewish fraternity system blossomed during the 1920s, with new chapters being established virtually overnight. Zeta Beta Tau could no longer see itself as reigning in solitary splendor, and only an expanding system could accommodate the tens of thousands of young American Jews seeking a college education for the first time. On the other hand, as its officers pointed out to each other, ZBT was still the largest Jewish fraternity and would always be the oldest, and moreover, it was blessed with outstanding leaders who were respected throughout the entire fraternity world. ZBT might be despised by some of its competitors, but such was the price of prestige, and in any event their organization could never be ignored.

Indeed, it can be said that Zeta Beta Tau reached its full maturity in the years between the signing of the peace treaty in Versailles in 1919 and the crash of the New York Stock Exchange in October of 1929. The fraternity expanded until its chapters were to be found in every section of the country, and the most important foundation for its financial solvency—a national permanent endowment fund (the NPEF)—was established. Its new leaders played an important role in the defense and advancement of the Greek system as a whole and in the defense and advancement of Jewish college students in particular. In addition, its members were able to partake of all the joys that the fabled "Jazz Age" was able to offer to affluent young people.

The Departure of Richard Gottheil

An era in ZBT ended when, in the spring of 1920, Richard Gottheil announced his resignation as Supreme Nasi, citing his need to make an extensive tour of postwar Europe. Never again was he to have daily contact with the national officers of the fraternity. But he was still consulted frequently by the members of the Columbia chapter, and his commanding presence and spirit dominated the fraternity until the day of his death in 1936 and long afterward. At the January 1921 convention in New York City, members elected to that office the colorful and popular Congressman Julius Kahn of California (1861–1924) who had been a member of Zeta Beta Tau since 1908 and had been instrumental in establishing its West Coast chapters. The end of the Great War found him eager to take an active part in the fraternity's national affairs.

Born in Kuppenheim, Germany, in 1861, Kahn had been taken to the

United States at the age of five, where his family chose to settle in San Francisco. At the height of the German army's advances in Europe during World War I, when it seemed that the kaiser's forces might well be victorious, Kahn was the ranking Republican member of the House Military Affairs Committee and a fervent proponent of national defense. (Upon his death his wife, Florence Prag Kahn, was appointed to take his congressional seat, which she held until 1937.) In a long and distinguished career, Julius Kahn became best known for leading the fight to secure the passage of President Woodrow Wilson's Selective Service Act, opposing those who believed that an all-volunteer army would be sufficient to repel the military threat. "If for nothing else," noted the writers of the *Zeta Beta Tau Quarterly* in 1922, "Julius Kahn will go down in history as the man who insured American victory at a time when Flanders Fields were staggering under the onslaught of an approaching German success." Above all, they noted, his career served as "a staggering answer to the bigoted theory that the Jew is selfish, unpatriotic, and a detriment to his community."

The Architects of Zeta Beta Tau:
George Macy, Harold Riegelman, and Lee Dover

The 1920s were also the most important years for three remarkable leaders who were to leave their mark on Zeta Beta Tau for generations. George Macy (1900–1956), Columbia '20, a native of New York City who was honorably discharged from the U.S. Army in December 1918 and who began a promising and innovative publishing career as undergraduate editor of *The Columbia Jester* and the *Columbian* yearbook, assumed the editorship of the *Zeta Beta Tau Quarterly* immediately upon his graduation. In 1923, he became the fraternity's first general secretary, a position he held for more than five years. During the time of the fraternity's most dramatic growth he toured the country, visiting, counseling, strengthening old chapters, helping to establish new ones, and achieving fame for giving football-type "fight talks" at Graduate Club meetings, urging payment of alumni dues.

Macy's official role within the fraternity was of relatively short duration. Still, in ZBT's critical formative years he was remembered for setting a high cultural and intellectual standard for the fraternity and for using his talent for editing, typography, and layout to produce a quarterly that was the envy—and at times the despair—of the Greek-letter world. It was with the backing and support of his fraternity brothers that he was eventually able to serve as founder and director of the Limited Editions Club, a company that monthly distributed fine illustrated editions of literary classics to discriminating bibliophiles; that was followed by the Heritage Club, which made books of similarly high quality available at regular trade book prices to eager readers who otherwise would never have been able to obtain them.

In time, George Macy was to establish a publishing empire and to receive international recognition for his contribution to the art of fine bookmaking, but to the end of his life he remained in close touch with his fraternity and the friends he had made there. As would be the case of many other men of high achievement, contacts originally made within the fraternal training ground would always enrich him both personally and professionally. "He made our society a first class power in the fraternity world," recalled Harold Riegelman, a contemporary and distinguished alumnus of the fraternity "I count it no mere coincidence that at the end of his term a ZBT man was elected Chairman of the NIC" (the National Interfraternity Conference).

Harold Riegelman (Cornell '14), another Zeta Beta Tau leader who rose to prominence in the 1920s, was that first ZBT president (his title at the time was Executive Nasi) elected as NIC chairman, for the academic year 1927–1928. This was an honor remarkable for the leader of any fraternity and at the time almost unthinkable for one whose members were all Jewish. A tall, imposing man and an eloquent speaker, Riegelman held meetings at his law offices, served continually on the Supreme Council, presented ZBT's most important awards at its annual conventions, and in general served as ZBT's "elder statesman" until the very end of his life in April 1982, when he passed away at the age of eighty-nine.

Born August 19, 1892, in Des Moines, Iowa, Riegelman moved with his family at the age of five to New York City, where he attended De-Witt Clinton High School. At Cornell, which he entered in 1910, he rowed Varsity Crew, was a champion debater, and served as president of his Zeta Beta Tau chapter. He graduated from Columbia Law School in 1916, having written a master's thesis on the Leo Frank lynching case, and soon entered practice; but the entrance of the United States into World War I saw him receiving his officer's commission and serving with distinction in France. As the gas operations officer of the

Fifth Army Corps at the Argonne-Meuse offensive, he planned the largest gas offensives of the campaign and wrote the army's manual on the subject. Significantly, when, twenty-three years later, the by-then Colonel Riegelman, many times decorated for heroism, filled a similar position in the Pacific Islands during the last and most desperate stages of World War II, he recommended that the army *not* use its chemical gas reserves against the Japanese.

After the war, Riegelman enjoyed a distinguished career as a lawyer, writer, Jewish communal leader, and public official, and in 1953 he ran as the Republican mayoral candidate for New York City. Within the Greek-letter system, he served as a leading defender of and apologist for the fraternity world in general and Jewish fraternities in particular. There his skill and reputation as a legal and political leader was established early. In their reports of the December 1928 meeting, at which he took up the NIC gavel for the first time, attendees from other fraternities and from universities throughout the land commented on his unusual "charm," "spontaneity," and "wit." They also praised him for his courage in inaugurating a successful debate leading to passage of a resolution against hazing and roughhouse initiation.

Hazing of some kind had always existed on American campuses, and in its worst forms led to several deaths each year. But in the 1920s it was perceived that the specific issue of fraternity hazing was getting worse. In previous years, when college enrollments had been much smaller, interclass rivalry, an institution passed on by the English public schools, had been an established part of American campus culture. Sophomores routinely fought the freshman in bloody hand-to-hand conflicts, forced them to wear demeaning hats (hence the proverbial "freshman beanie"), forced freshman to perform personal services, and placed severe restrictions on their movement and speech. Interclass hazing was difficult to root out if only because of the successive sophomorism of each class. Sophomorism could be roughly translated as "We suffered through it, they did it to us, and now we can't wait to do it to them." The chain had to be broken at some point, and step by step the universities began to forbid or tightly curtail interclass hazing. However, an urge so primal was not so easily controlled, and it appeared that as campus-wide hazing was abolished, the institution found its outlet within the fraternity system. Of all the NIC officials, Riegelman took the issue with utmost seriousness, insisting that each reported instance of death or injury through roughhouse initiation and hazing was a nail in the coffin of the entire Greek system.

Perhaps the only other Zeta Beta Tau officer whose years of influence equaled or exceeded Riegelman's was Leon David Dover (USC '25). Universally known as "Lee" or "Mr. ZBT," he served as the fraternity's general secretary and editor of its magazine for almost thirty-five years after succeeding George Macy in 1928. Born in Montreal on May 17, 1900, the eldest of five children, Dover's earliest years were spent in the colorful gold rush days of western Canada, where his father served for a term as mayor of the town of Nelson in British Columbia. In 1907 the family settled in Seattle, Washington, where he helped to found the local group that eventually became a chapter of Zeta Beta Tau at the University of Washington in 1924. Upon moving to Los Angeles, Dover was instrumental in founding the fraternity's UCLA chapter in 1927 and served with such distinction as president of the Southern California Alumni Club and chairman of ZBT's 1928 Los Angeles convention that the Supreme Council unanimously invited him to travel to New York and serve as their general secretary.

For many years thereafter, Lee Dover's furrowed brow, shiny pate, jug ears, bow tie, and perpetually dour, worried expression were frequently and affectionately parodied in ZBT's publications. Through years of successive administrations, he ran the Central office and undertook all its mountains of paperwork and record keeping with the help of a faithful staff (including Mrs. Margaret Rossiter, the fraternity's "Lady Friday"). A stickler for proper accounting and administrative procedures—for example, insisting that all communications be limited to one subject per letter—Lee Dover skillfully prodded guilty members' consciences with the impression that it was beneath the dignity of any ZBT gentleman not to pay his bills or otherwise fail to fulfill his fraternal obligations. Moreover, he pursued an exhaustive visitation schedule throughout the country, speaking to alumni, college officials, and active members for much of the year. Many an undergraduate trembled at the announcement that Lee Dover was coming to visit, and there had to be much cleaning and sprucing up of the chapter house before he could step in the door.

On his many college visits, officials of the other fraternities were annoyed no end at Lee Dover's habit of introducing himself as "I'm Lee Dover, secretary of *the* Jewish fraternity in the United States," and among them he was not an especially beloved figure. Even so, all acknowledged his reputation as a man of integrity and self-respect. Perhaps more than any other individual, Lee Dover was throughout the century a guiding spirit and the glue that held the fraternity together.

An Era of Growth

The strong leadership of these men stood Zeta Beta Tau Fraternity in good stead at the beginning of the second decade of the twentieth century, for vast changes in college life in the wake of World War I led to a rapid expansion of the Greek-letter system and resulted in numerous new challenges to be met. "Today entrance into the university is a matter merely of age and dollars," noted one ZBT graduate of the University of Wisconsin in 1928. "Everyone goes; it's hardly the thing for a parent even in moderate circumstances not to insist on a college education for his sometimes utterly unfit progeny." At a 1925 meeting of the American Association of Universities and Colleges, officers lamented that burgeoning enrollments, for which schools were entirely unprepared, were reaching "crisis" proportions. The democratization and greater heterogeneity of college populations in the 1920s—as "college man" rapidly began to lose its aristocratic connotations—plus the expansion of formerly tiny schools west of the Alleghenies, had advantages for the nation but also significant drawbacks.

First and most important, the universities could not keep track of so many new students, and the pool of qualified professors was too small to accommodate them, leading to charges by columnists such as H. L. Mencken that "unqualified idiots" were manning the classrooms. At the same time, the Jewish college student population, which had numbered between eight and twelve thousand before World War I, had reached at least twenty-five thousand by 1927—and possibly more; of these, more than three-quarters were male. Zeta Beta Tau alone had well over one thousand undergraduate members by that time, along with four thousand alumni organized into twenty-six alumni clubs across the country.

Not only were more students than ever before flocking to college and university campuses; they were flocking to college with different expectations. College was now seen as a desirable and even essential forum to make contacts, polish social skills, enlarge one's horizons, enrich one's life, learn new uses of leisure time, participate in extracurricular activities (especially athletics), and find one's mate. In pursuit of these goals, what happened outside the classroom soon became as important as what went on inside if not more so.

The View of College in Popular Culture

Partly responsible for the freshmen's preoccupation with extracurricular activities was the unprecedented romanticization of college life that marked the 1920s. Ever since the publication of *Stover at Yale* in 1912, a stream of popular "college novels" entertained thousands of readers who were unlikely ever to see a real lecture hall, and fraternities and sororities were portrayed as an important part of that life. College humor, songs, fads, slang, and fashion were glorified in advertisements, newspapers, magazines, radio shows, and above all, films. At the moving picture shows, short-skirted flappers, including a very young Joan Crawford, routinely danced the Charleston on fraternity tabletops. ZBT members complained that scenes of extravagant clothes, cheek-to-cheek dancing, smoking, petting, and drinking omitted any visual references to study. High school students and their parents were apt to be unduly influenced by these films, complained Earl L. Wiener (Michigan '18) in the December 1927 *Quarterly*, and too many male students arrived on campus "of the impression that his college life will be one grand and glorious series of fraternity rushings, of dances and of athletics." Reality soon set in for freshmen expecting that and nothing else, and they did not last long on the campus.

Among the silent collegiate films of the 1920s the two most influential and notorious were *The Freshman*, starring Harold Lloyd (1927), and *The Wild Party*, starring the "It" Girl, Clara Bow (1928). As in the case of the movie *National Lampoon's Animal House* fifty years later, sixteen- and seventeen-year-old high school students were attracted to the films and flocked to college and fraternity rushes hoping that they too could participate in such bacchanalia. Zeta Beta Tau's initiated members already knew the importance of the social side of college life and were accomplished at taking advantage of it, but they also knew that attendance required at least a minimum of hard work. Furthermore, they knew very well that the strict in loco parentis campus regulations and curfews restricting contact with the opposite sex, which were characteristic at U.S. colleges until the late 1960s, could in reality seldom be violated as effortlessly as Harold Lloyd and Clara Bow apparently did in the movies. "My main objection to the depictions of college amusements as they are," wrote Alfred B. Engelhard (Wisconsin '24), in 1929, "is that the authors invariably make the mistake of presenting what the student would like to do rather than what he, or even she, actually does. It would be a horrible thing for the world at large if the stories were true; but by the beard of Satan, it would be glorious for the collegian."

The Importance of Fraternities

One essentially truthful impression that could be gleaned from the movies, however, was that fraternities and sororities had indeed become central to American college life. They did not flourish on all campuses, whether because of adverse conditions or the explicit opposition of local campus administrators. Where they did exist, certainly not all wanted or could afford to join them. In the 1920s and 1930s a typical proportion of fraternity and sorority students in a large state school might be only one-third to less than one-half of the entire student body. However, in such schools campus Greeks became the elite who set the tone for others. They dominated student life and politics and embodied the accepted standards of clothing, speech, and behavior. An ambitious college student now felt lost if he or she did not "pledge a good house."

Many university administrators and deans, themselves often fraternity and sorority alumni, came to accept a well-functioning "Greek system" as a valuable partner in the expanding educational process, conferring significant advantages. In times of rapid growth they alleviated critical housing and dining facility shortages, caring for students' physical needs at no cost to the taxpayers. They eased the task of orienting and keeping track of otherwise unwieldy incoming classes. They brought social order out of the chaos of a more diverse student population. Time, energy, and funds could be spared by communicating directly with fraternity chapter representatives, campus interfraternity councils, or adult national officers, rather than trying to contact each student individually.

As an agent in enforcing campus discipline, the corporate system of collective responsibility inherent in fraternity life could be invaluable. Universities could, and did, hold national fraternities and their adult officers collectively responsible for infringements of campus order such as violations of rules concerning sex and alcohol, bad grades, and nonpayment of bills. Among individual students, the threat of seeing the entire chapter put on probation or its charter revoked could be a powerful deterrent against deviant behavior. Even when rules were violated, as they inevitably were, officials could count on the violations being accompanied by a healthy degree of guilt and furtiveness, and deviants might factor into their activities the cost of bad publicity or a possible need to appeal to campus courts. Among Jewish fraternities especially, "good behavior" was of even greater concern because of the constant undercurrent of fear that Gentile administrators would hold Jewish students to higher standards and punish infringements more harshly than they would for a non-Jewish fraternity.

On the more positive side, all fraternities appeared to impart values and teach life skills considered essential for truly educated persons, skills that the deans and presidents themselves might once have chosen to teach their charges in days when student populations were smaller. They gave members a crucial focus of identification after schools had grown so large that no president could ever hope to know or even to meet personally all of the students on the campus. Furthermore, with emphasis on leadership and alumni loyalty actually written into their rituals, it did not take college officials long to realize that fraternities encouraged success in business and a correspondingly high level of financial contributions, and that their largest private contributors were disproportionately fraternity men—a phenomenon that remained constant at the end of the twentieth century. The chapter house itself furthered the process by serving as a priceless center where loyal alumni could always return for visits and through which they could express their love and interest in alma mater and their own college days until the end of their lives.

Given these considerations, it became necessary for the undergraduates to be made aware of the responsibilities of the educational partnership that was being offered them. As Harold Riegelman noted in his chairman's speech before the NIC in December 1928, fraternities had now become "part and parcel of the American system of higher education. . . . They are woven not only into the social warp but the administrative woof of the college life. Deans and presidents have learned to use them. They have learned to be used."

Student Migrancy and the Growth of Jewish Fraternities

The decade of the 1920s was not only the apotheosis of the American college Greek-letter system but the apotheosis of the Jewish college fraternity movement as well. At no point in the twentieth century were

Jewish fraternities and sororities so numerous—more than twenty-five undergraduate groups could be counted in this period—and at no other time did so high a proportion of Jewish students belong to such groups. National Jewish communal leaders lamented that the eagerness of Jewish students to form more Greek-letter chapters was not matched by their eagerness to form student congregations or Zionist or cultural societies, but it was clear even to them that the prevailing winds were blowing from the direction of Athens rather than Jerusalem.

The especially rapid expansion of the Jewish fraternity system in the second decade of the twentieth century was the result of several related factors. Prejudice was first, if not always the most important. If any student who did not pledge a good house was lost then the new Jewish students flocking to the nation's colleges were doubly lost and their houses doubly important. In a survey of sixty-seven college campuses conducted in 1927, fraternity officials found that fifty-two did not admit Jews to their fraternities and sororities at all, while fifteen admitted occasional Jews in only token numbers. On the other hand, Jewish fraternities offered protection, room, board (away from potentially anti-Semitic boardinghouse landlords and landladies), lifelong friendships, a pleasant social life, connections with appropriate females, good contacts, and an extensive program of business and social training. These goals were useful for anyone, but they were crucial for a relatively small, scattered group of upwardly mobile young men who were in large part the children and grandchildren of immigrants and who were trying to make their way in a hostile world.

In addition, young Jewish male students were more likely to be attending school far from home and thus were more dependent upon their fraternities for room, board, and general emotional support. In a trend that began in the 1920s and accelerated during the Great Depression, many thousands of primarily male applicants from the New York tri-state area (where half the entire Jewish population of the United States lived) fled stiff intra-Jewish competition, anti-Jewish quotas, and steep tuition by fanning out to the publicly supported universities of the South and West and to smaller, less expensive, and more welcoming private colleges. Such schools were legally barred from setting up religious restrictions against legitimate taxpaying citizens, and they allowed out-of-state students the time necessary to establish their state residency as a prerequisite for attending a state-supported professional school.

Paradoxically, for the Jewish fraternities the spread of New York City Jewish students across the country was a great boon, for they filled empty house beds and provided a larger reservoir from which to draw; however, at the same time these New Yorkers, or "easterners," were also a source of anxiety because their manners and mannerisms frequently jarred the local populations of small college towns and because too many of them appeared not to be "good fraternity material." The conflict between "New York Jews" and students from other parts of the country was to remain a motif of Jewish college and fraternity life for the next four decades.

Nevertheless, some of the New Yorkers were indeed good material, and in any event there had been an equal rise in the number of Jews going to college from more genteel locations. After years of having the field almost to itself, Zeta Beta Tau Fraternity for the first time found itself in the mid-1920s confronting real competition and a definite need to define itself. At the Supreme Council meeting of May 6, 1924, held at Riegelman's law offices at 67 Wall Street, General Secretary George Macy made the issue a central part of his report. The question of activity in Jewish affairs, he suggested, should be made more explicit; students in the field should be advised as to exactly what the national fraternity desired in terms of raising Jewish consciousness, assisting the Hillel Foundations, pursuing philanthropic programs, or building up student congregations.

To Macy, even more important than defining ZBT's Jewish identity was shoring up its general prestige, which, he warned, was "in great danger." Other Jewish fraternities, he reported, were rapidly coming up and presenting a real challenge. Only that year Sigma Alpha Mu, founded in 1909 at City College, had surpassed ZBT in number of chapters, and Phi Epsilon Pi (founded 1904) and Phi Sigma Delta (founded in 1910) were fast approaching it. Quality, not quantity, would have to become the measure of ZBT's success, and Macy exhorted the fraternity to become even more selective of its members than it had been in the past. A "definite standard of social excellence" had to be maintained so that all would know that within ZBT could be found "the finest group of college Jews." Three months later, at the September 9, 1924, Supreme Council meeting, a new Committee on Standards of Membership set the specific criteria. In evaluating their candidates, members of Zeta Beta Tau were adjured always to ask the following question: "Does his appearance show that he has the manners, culture, and necessary breeding which would compel us to feel that in him we find a truly representative specimen of young Jewish manhood?"

The Specter of Leopold and Loeb

Ironically, at the very same meeting the members of the council were forced to consider the case of two members who, though they were scions of the wealthiest Chicago Jewish families, had conducted themselves in a manner far beneath these impeccable standards. In fact, they had managed to get themselves indicted for kidnapping and murder. These were eighteen-year-old Richard Loeb, a member of their University of Michigan chapter, and nineteen-year-old Nathan Freudenthal Leopold, a graduate of the University of Chicago, whose desire to perpetrate "the perfect crime" had led to the demise of Bobby Franks, their fourteen-year-old neighbor. In what soon became one of the most sensational murder trials yet seen in the United States, Leopold and Loeb, despite a defense led by Clarence Darrow, were both sentenced to life imprisonment plus ninety-nine years. Not content to remain idle, the two men developed a successful correspondence school for penitentiary inmates until Loeb was murdered by a fellow prisoner in 1936.

In time the memory of the horrific crime faded, and Leopold lived long enough to be paroled to Puerto Rico in 1958 and to write a book about his experiences. Shortly after their indictment in 1924, however, Zeta Beta Tau's national officers had no idea to what extent this unwanted publicity would affect the law-abiding majority of their membership, and the tone of anxiety apparent in their minutes of the period indicates that some feared nothing less than a pogrom directed against their houses. It was Harold Riegelman who, not for the first nor the last time, provided leadership in the crisis. He advised the Supreme Council simply to expel the two men and to disassociate themselves from the matter. Thereafter, they were to say and do nothing.

From the point of view of the fraternity, Riegelman's advice proved sound. Though the national leadership through much of 1924 suffered paroxysms of fear and shame, in the long run the Leopold-Loeb affair did not noticeably affect the progress of Zeta Beta Tau.

Legacies and Expansion

In many ways, Zeta Beta Tau appeared to enjoy both the problems and the advantages of the oldest and most prestigious non-Jewish fraternities. This could be measured in the second decade of the twentieth century through the development of a strange challenge: the "legacy problem," legacies being the sons, sibling brothers, and sometimes nephews and cousins of older initiated members. The desire for continuity of the generations and high prestige coupled with a small number of available places frequently caused fathers to place inordinate pressure on the fraternity, including the threat of financial penalties and complete withdrawal of support, if their kin were not accepted into ZBT. In this sense, a ZBT pedigree or the pedigree of any high-ranking fraternity carried as much weight as admission to an Ivy League school. If the boy measured up to ZBT's standards of appearance, personality, and academic strength, then chances were that he would be accepted. If he did not and alumni forced the undergraduates to initiate him anyway, this could lead to a group of what apocryphally were called "closet cases" or the "cellar squad." This was campus slang for members who were so discreditable to their fraternity that they would presumably have to be carefully hidden when important personages came to visit.

"Let us look at the situation in a practical light," implored Robert E. Lederer (Syracuse '30), an undergraduate ZBT officer, in a plea, published in the May 1930 *Quarterly*, against being forced to take unwanted legacies. "When the freshman is rushed he undergoes nothing short of an academic examination in character, background, manners, personality. His examination may last three days or three weeks. His proctors may be ten brothers or there may be twenty. He may rate an A, B or C. Any of these three and he passes. An F is a failure. If he 'flunks' should his brother or father or cousin be allowed to take another examination for him? The answer is obvious" (p. 34). Until national officers began to learn to appreciate the unjustness of the legacy institution and take a courageous stand against it, he wrote, the problem would continue to make its yearly appearance at chapter houses across the country. What Lederer did not say, or perhaps did not realize, was that there were many worse problems his fraternity could have had than prestige and alumni loyalty so intense that graduates would do all but physically break down the door to make sure that their sons got into ZBT.

As in the case of fraternities many generations older, the name of Zeta Beta Tau was now known throughout the land, for its efforts to expand and grow had met with success. Members were thrilled at the expansion of their fraternity from coast to coast. It was a matter for great pride that New York City and its environs was no longer ZBT's only center and that regular regional conventions had become a necessity. A Canadian chapter had existed at Montreal's McGill University since

1913. In 1920 the fraternity established its first West Coast chapter at the University of California at Berkeley. In rapid succession came the University of Nebraska and the University of Wisconsin in 1922, Washington University in St. Louis in 1923, the University of Washington in Seattle in 1924, the University of Arizona in 1926, and both the University of North Carolina at Chapel Hill and, with the help of Lee Dover, the University of California at Los Angeles in 1927. In 1928 the fraternity held its first national convention west of Cleveland—in Los Angeles—and the impressions that members gained of Southern California were undoubtedly positive because ZBTs from elsewhere in the country began to flock there. Soon the Southern California Graduate Club took its place among the largest and most active clubs of the entire fraternity.

Scholarship and Honors

Good scholarship and worldly achievement also brought joy to the fraternity's leaders. Scholarship especially was an area where historically Jewish fraternities were proud of their differences. ZBT was the oldest and largest of a group that for generations had taken for granted that its constituents would rank in the top fifteen out of sixty in the NIC national scholarship rankings each year. In the face of attacks on Jewish fraternities, this was taken as a cause for pride, self-respect, and self-justification. In their correspondence on the subject the national officers of this group seldom even mentioned the need to compete with historically Gentile fraternities for top spots in the scholarship rankings. In that category, their competitive eyes lay only on one another. In the 1928–29 academic year, for example, historian Alfred Breslauer (Berkeley '20) was proud to report that thirteen brothers nationally, out of fewer than two hundred graduating seniors, had been elected to Phi Beta Kappa, including three in their Columbia chapter alone. Not only the Columbia chapter but those at Western Reserve, Michigan, University of Chicago, Vanderbilt, Nebraska, and UCLA had attained the highest scholastic standing of any fraternity groups on their respective campuses.

For the 1929–30 academic year the historian could announce in his annual statistical report that the fraternity had grown to 32 chapters, 32 graduate clubs, and over 5,000 members, although Lee Dover was working on increasing the number (800) who were actually dues-paying members of their local graduate clubs. The Syracuse Club and the El Paso Club had recently been founded, and a group of alumni in Memphis had just applied for a charter. In the area of Jewish student life, ZBT could claim two presidents and one vice president of Hillel Foundations, four Menorah Society presidents, and one president of the Jewish Students' Association. In the crucial area of sports, varsity letters had been won by 69; there were 8 ZBT team captains and 30 team managers. In other extracurricular activities, campus publications led the way, with 136 actively engaged in them; dramatics came in second with 52.

The fifth annual Old Timers' Day, the fraternity's "homecoming" holiday founded in 1924, was reported to have been an unusual success. Affairs, whether small get-togethers, "stag" banquets, dinners, or actual balls, had been held in forty principal cities of the United States and Canada, and at the key affair in New York City the Gottheil Medal had been presented to Felix Warburg as "a philanthropist and lover of his people, Israel." The Central Office in New York, as it was called, inaugurated a National Rushing Program, wherein all members were requested to list names of recent high school graduates who were to enter college in the fall. Over three hundred prospects were recommended to the office through that procedure alone. In the fall of 1929, perhaps prescient of the economic disasters that might befall the country later, the fraternity also inaugurated its National Permanent Endowment Fund (NPEF) toward which every new ZBT was required to contribute upon his initiation. With the support of the NPEF and the enthusiastic fund-raising efforts of University of Pennsylvania (Theta chapter) alumni, the chapter was able to tear down the old house and rebuild a new one at the cost of $250,000. The house opened on schedule in the spring of 1930, several months after the crash.

The Pursuit of Happiness

Stereotypes of the "roaring twenties" and the glamorous college life of the Jazz Age have proved, upon closer historical examination, to be highly exaggerated. Not all Americans enjoyed the ostensible prosperity of the decade, and many a college student, if he could afford to attend at all, was forced to pursue an unrelenting grind of hard study, spare living, and outside jobs, which did not allow time for the relative frivolities of extracurricular activities and athletics.

Such students, however, for the most part did not apply and were

Formal stag dinner at the 22nd Anniversary Convention of Zeta Beta Tau, held at the Hotel Astor on December 26, 1920. Man in uniform at the Harvard table is Abraham Robert Ginsburgh '17, who later rose to the rank of Brigadier General and served both in World War II and the Korean War.

not pledged by Zeta Beta Tau. In the 1920s its explicit criteria for membership included an established family background in the United States, a high degree of social adeptness, and sufficient means to enjoy some of the finer things in life. This was understood when Henry C. Segal (OSU '18), editor of the *Quarterly's* feature "Who's Who among the Alumni," made mocking reference in his geographic sweep of the country to "the First Families of Virginia," "the Loyal Legion of Connecticut," "the Sun Kissed Southern Californians," and "the Stalwart Sons of Cincinnati." Seldom again was the acronym "Zillions, Billions, and Trillions" (or worse, "Zion Bank and Trust") as applicable to Zeta Beta Tau's membership as it had been in the years before the stock market crash. Members' journals and writings from the period are filled with details that indicate a high social status (at the time usually correlated with membership in the Reform denomination of Judaism) coupled with a lively social life and the ability to partake of all the joys that the decade offered to affluent, intellectual, and adventurous college fraternity men.

In terms of physical realities, it was seldom the fraternity house itself that offered residents great luxuries, as Alfred B. Engelhard (Wisconsin '24) described in a December 1927 feature entitled "Ulysses Universitatis, or Four and Twenty Hours from the Life of a College Youth." Students awoke for eight o'clock classes, and members slept in dormitories equipped with bunkbeds, never fewer than four to a room (frequently an entire chapter would sleep in one long room). The "Great Trek bathroomward" dispensed with, members attempted to dress from a single pile of clothing on one of their dressers and then proceeded downstairs, where they fought vehemently over which of twelve men would get to read the four morning newspapers. Breakfast, according to Engelhard, was deplorable, the day's luncheon was composed of leftovers from "Sunday dinners for three months back," albeit accompanied by excellent conversation, and the evening meal sent all on a pilgrimage to the nearest restaurant.

Evening activities, however, offered compensations. Among the men themselves, many pleasant hours in those pre-video days were whiled away playing bridge or poker, despite house rules against gambling. The most popular diversions were the perennial "bull sessions," where undergraduates would expound upon and discuss sex, sports, and all the great philosophical questions of Life until the wee hours of the morning. (Of all their memories of college, it would appear, the alumni remembered and enjoyed those bull sessions most). Another favorite college social activity was making fudge in the "kitchen fudge foundry," in mixed or unmixed company, and consuming it.

Spending time with women was another obvious and favorite evening activity for the ZBT man. One of the first duties that upperclassmen had to their wet-behind-the ears freshmen pledges, after guiding them properly in their fraternity responsibilities, was teaching them how to date and mate. Formal or informal dancing lessons were provided in case new members had arrived at college still ignorant of the finer points of the waltz, fox-trot, cha-cha-cha, or the lindy hop. If a sympathetic female partner was necessary, a cooperative sister, girlfriend, or sorority member could sometimes be enlisted for the purpose. Once the proper chemistry had been established by holding a young woman in one's arms on a chaperoned dance floor, settings of greater intimacy might be sought. "Ulysses Universitatis" reportedly spent much time scouting for the best outdoor trysting places, toward which he would carry a blanket and romance his girl with the quintessential instrument of the 1920s, a ukulele. Fraternity membership was seen as a valuable asset in these activities, for a jeweled pin hooked center vest was supposedly just the thing "to break down the sales resistance of some alluring yearling damsel."

"Canoe dates" were another option peculiar to the 1920s and were recalled with nostalgia by alumni. Since they obviously took place without the presence of a lifeguard or the wearing of flotation devices, it can be assumed that in the interest of water safety the universities must have discontinued them at some point. In the 1920s, however, they were common at any coeducational university near a sizable body of water. Late at night, preferably under a full moon, the man would paddle at least a half mile into the middle of the lake while his date lay facing him upon a pile of pillows. When distance had reduced the houses by the shore to a string of twinkling lights, the man would lay down his paddle and the two would enjoy a solitary romantic interlude before he would paddle back, take her for coffee, and then see her to her front door.

The Importance of College Football

During the day, ZBT men were known for their participation in a wide range of extracurricular activities, an area of college life that reached new heights of importance in the 1920s. Pledges were required to make a start in at least two of them. Development of the individual and obtaining glory for the fraternity were not the only goals; the pride of the entire Jewish people was also at stake. A ZBT man who "made good" brought honor both to his fraternity and to his people; that the converse was also true was a powerful incentive to take one's collective responsibilities seriously.

Anti-Jewish feelings on any campus frequently manifested themselves in the denial of honorary or elective offices to Jewish students. ZBT officers were therefore specific in their directives that ZBT men should seek to smash whatever anti-Semitic stereotypes or barriers might exist on their campus by asserting their leadership in both expected and unexpected places. In the fall of 1929, for example, the *Quarterly* noted with pride that ZBT's undergraduate membership included 2 Menorah Society presidents, 4 Hillel Foundation presidents,

21 debating team members and captains, 9 golf team members, 13 Phi Beta Kappas, 25 team managers, and 22 football players.

It was the last achievement that aroused the greatest pride, for never before had college football reached such heights of popularity as it did in the 1920s. College football was king; football was the mania of the age, and it is perhaps not surprising that charges of corruption followed not far behind. Universities vied with each other in building huge stadiums and recruiting coaches whose salaries far outstripped those of the academic faculty. ZBT and other fraternity houses became overrun by hordes of guests on football Saturdays, and football results became a national obsession, covered by every newspaper in the land. For the most popular event, the annual Harvard-Yale game, ticket scalping was rampant, with prices running into the hundreds of dollars; this was perhaps inevitable, for late in the decade more than eighty thousand people were applying for the fifty thousand available seats.

The reasons for football's unprecedented popularity at that point were many. It was a thrilling form of entertainment and a safe emotional release, handily replacing nationalist contests, medieval jousts, or the outright warfare that had recently destroyed a generation of young men in Europe. In football, symbolic blood could be shed and a gentleman's honor won on the gridiron rather than on the battlefield. The impulse to admire military strategy could be channeled toward admiration of the coach's plays and formations instead. The tensions of student nationalism and patriotism that were soon to become so ominous overseas, not to mention the boredom of long hours of study, could easily be discharged through the rooting and sacrificing for the victory of one's team, especially if cheering crowds were properly whipped into a frenzy by exuberant cheerleaders. The enormous revenues football generated fueled all other sports programs and provided necessary funds for collegiate expansion. Moreover, football served as a superb social event around which dances, teas, cocktail parties, rallies, homecomings, dates, and alumni reunions could be organized. For at least one weekend, visitors could reexperience the best joys of college life without the bothersome necessity of attending any classes.

Finally, college football was the ultimate leveler. The sport permitted everyone, male or female, college student or not, to become part of the romanticized collegiate culture, and it permitted men of even the humblest backgrounds to integrate into the nation's mainstream by becoming players. "They are a testimony to the melting pot, and to that super melting pot, college athletics," editorialized the *Chicago Tribune,* in a commentary on how many immigrant names had recently been in the football headlines. "Who thinks or who cares whether their fathers or grandfathers came from Holland or Germany, Poland or Czechoslovakia. They battle across the white lines of the gridiron the way they fought over the shell holes of the Argonne, and that's American enough for us. . . . What the automobile is doing geographically public schools and colleges are doing socially, stirring the races into one race. School and college athletics are the great mixing machines. The ability to make a touchdown does not belong to the Slav, or an Italian, or an Irishman. It belongs to an American."

Neither did the ability to make a touchdown belong specifically to a Jew, and ZBT's record was more than creditable in that area. However, it was never enough to satisfy Executive Nasi Harold Riegelman, who had rowed Varsity Crew in college and always spurred his undergraduate brothers to disprove whenever possible the stereotype that Jewish men were poor at sports. He constantly criticized ZBT men for being overrepresented in debating, publications, drama, and above all, team managerships. The last was supposedly the haven of Jewish boys who dearly loved sports and had the brains to understand and appreciate athletics in all its complexity but lacked the brawn to participate in them directly. The popularity of being a team manager would later express itself in a disproportionate number of ZBT men, as well as men from the other historically Jewish fraternities becoming the owners of professional football, baseball, and basketball teams; but at that time, it was being a college football player that really counted. In a Jewish fraternity, one good football player carried more weight than ten debate team captains and twenty Hillel presidents.

And indeed, good Jewish football players were not lacking. In a feature entitled "The All ZBT Football Team" published in March 1929, the writers took delight in writing up the exploits of the "eleven greatest ZBT players of all time," plus twenty-eight honorable mentions. These included "Irish" Levy at Tulane (class of '25), who was a tackler and captain of his team; Joseph Alexander '21, better known as Juddy, who was the first Jewish captain at Syracuse; Joe Silverstein, the only Jewish captain ever at Washington and Lee; Jonah Goldman (Syracuse '27), a fullback, "that tough little ZBT [who] could do everything with a football except eat it and he is tough enough to do even that if it was boiled a trifle before taking." By 1929, Goldman was playing professional baseball with the Cleveland Indians.

Fads, Fashions, and Prohibition

All ZBT men, regardless of their athletic or football ability, took with great seriousness the other collegiate fads and fashions of the day. Proper clothing at all times was a topic of special importance, discussed extensively in chapter house conversations and *Quarterly* articles. "There are numerous infallible methods for distinguishing a college man from the outside," read one in 1928. "He disdains hats and garters; he plays the saxophone or banjo, or, at least, shows tolerance toward those who do; he smokes a pipe or has a blind-fold cigarette technique; he knows at least one version of 'Frankie and Johnnie'; wears one or more jeweled badges on vest or watch-chain, and can turn conversation into football from almost any channel." From his fraternity house he had acquired a fashionable "manner of talking to a girl by phone, a facile slang, and a way of turning up his nose at food." (Long lines for a single phone were a fact of fraternity life, and freshmen were warned *never* to get fresh with any girl on the line, for she might easily be somebody's sister.) If inclined to wear a hat at all, a crushed-in felt that looked as if it had come from the bottom of the trunk was a favorite style. Of utmost importance was owning a bearskin or raccoon coat and a yellow oilskin slicker painted by one's friends with various mottoes and designs. It helped, too, to always carry a hip flask and to have one's own personal bootlegger.

Prohibition, or the Volstead Act, which under the Eighteenth Amendment to the U.S. Constitution made the manufacture, sale, or transportation of intoxicating beverages in the United States a federal crime, was in fact on the books from January 16, 1920, until December 5, 1933. However, the evidence suggests that, honorable as the act's intentions were, its effects on ZBT men, as on the population as a whole, were not entirely positive. Drinking appeared to increase rather than decrease, and public drunkenness became more tolerated. In a March 1930 *Quarterly* article, John B. Quigley, a 1924 graduate of the University of Missouri, recalled with nostalgia hearing older alumni's stories about springtime "Beer Busts" where brothers reveled out in the country all night, sitting around iced beer kegs, singing together, and filled with brotherly love. Then as later, actual consumption within the confines of the fraternity house was forbidden. However, "in those days," as he recalled, men drank with men for pleasure in male company exclusively. At social events, a woman might refuse to dance with a man if, through a camouflaging clove, she detected liquor on his breath. For a gentleman to "show his liquor" at a public event in full sight of the male and female college community or to act in any way that might cause harm or bring embarrassment to the fraternity was, for generations in Zeta Beta Tau and other fraternities, grounds for severe censure, fines, or suspension. "Alas," he wrote of the present day, "Bacchus has been dethroned and Ceres has been enshrined in his stead" (p. 14).

Of those who commented on Prohibition, the advent of routine coeducational drinking seems to have caused more discomfort than almost anything else, for it appeared to signal the moral collapse of society. However, the negative effects of Prohibition, including the hypocrisy and organized crime it encouraged, not to mention the death or injury students risked by drinking bootleg substances, directly affected both genders. In the same article, Quigley recalled his own college days, which coincided with Prohibition's onset. In the 1920–21 academic year, he wrote, students in desperation would seek out lemon extract, orange peel concoctions, patent medicine, or whatever was available at the local pharmacy. Soon, "back-alley, shady bootleggers" began selling a poor grade of gin or white corn whiskey. It was filled with pieces of charcoal and it stank, "but it got results." Students would drink it at parties, killing the taste with gum, oranges, or grapefruit. Then in 1923, the writer recalled, bolder female students began drinking as well and going out on late-night dates with men in order to partake; their excursions became so common that the universities stopped expelling them for it. In 1924 "we entered a period more cosmically wet than ever before." The old white corn whiskey improved as bootleggers strained the charcoal out and poured it into fancy bottles with labels and stamps. Bootleggers were so ubiquitous that one could simply pick up the phone and have liquor delivered. At private parties all guests were welcomed to drink, even numerous female students "from the shyest families who wouldn't let their daughter drink coffee. . . . There she stands doing 'bottoms up' with the best of them. The lips that touch liquor belong to both sexes" (p. 15).

Prohibition presented the relatively cultured and well-traveled members of Zeta Beta Tau fraternity with an additional problem. If the only liquor available to them at home was bathtub gin and corn whiskey and they then passed beyond the bounds of Prohibition, how would they know what to order when given the opportunity? The problem was partially solved when Lawrence G. Blockman, a 1921 graduate of the University of California at Berkeley, "viewing with alarm the bootleg tastes being forced upon the younger drinking set by the ginger-ale manufacturers," proceeded, in the October 1929 *Quarterly*, to write for ZBT undergraduates a detailed treatise on the indispensable, gentlemanly art of drinking wine. He explained the mysteries of matching the right wine with the right food, correct years and bouquets, proper serving procedures, and the merits of various kinds of Burgundies, Bordeaux, Champagnes, Sauternes, sherries, and liqueurs. The author, an obvious gourmet, concluded that he could have gone on for much longer, "[b]ut I've said enough to last until Prohibition is modified. Or if you can't wait that long, clip this out and carry it with you the next time there's a ZBT meeting of some kind in Montreal. Or take it along when you win that European scholarship" (p. 15).

Travel and Culture

Zeta Beta Tau men indeed had numerous opportunities to enjoy legal drinking, as well as other pleasures, in places beyond U.S. borders. Many appear to have had at least a working knowledge of French and other languages, either through formal education or through their families. Junior years spent abroad, world travel by ship, or best of all, the traditional gentleman's Grand Tour of Europe were such entrenched customs that in 1924 the Cunard Steamship Lines offered ZBT brothers staterooms at reduced rates so that they could more easily travel together. By the late 1920s the fraternity maintained registries for its members in both London (at the office of the *Times*) and Paris (at the American Express office on 11 rue Scribe). Members scattered throughout the Continent left their itineraries with ZBT's Central Office in New York; they could then pick up mail and messages, and check on the whereabouts of their friends at the registry. Late in the summer each year, a ZBT reunion would be held in both cities. Favorite articles in the *Quarterly* concerned members' travels to England, to Germany, to France, and even to the Soviet Union.

The expectation that a ZBT man would be well traveled was matched by the expectation that he would be cultured as well. A regular and popular feature in the *Quarterly* during the 1920s was "A College Man among the Arts," written anonymously (very possibly by George Macy himself), in which the author reviewed the latest books, plays, operas, art exhibits, symphonic festivals, and musicals, including, upon occasion, the finest offerings of the Yiddish theater. Members were urged to forgo the raccoon coat or another party in favor of buying tickets for the entire chapter to see a good performance together. They were also informed precisely what books and what records of classical music (not just jazz or boogie-woogie) were best to have in a chapter house library and were advised that a specific amount from the chapter's budget should be regularly set aside for that purpose.

The emphasis on classical music did not mean that ZBT members were not appreciative of popular dance music and jazz; at their annual conventions in particular, after business sessions were concluded, they had the opportunity to hear some of the finest live bands in the country playing music "so hot," according to one description, that the brass in the instruments melted. Interest in attending was generated by an annual slogan contest for the chosen city. Those for New Orleans, the jazz capital of the world, were especially picturesque, including "Say YES to N.O." and "Ze Best Time of Your Life"; and for the thirty-first annual convention in 1929, "Four Days to Live." "The story of the 'Four Days to Live,' which slogan proved to be more than an idle publicity gesture, does not appear herein," announced Lee Dover in the exoteric *Quarterly* the following month. "A full and informed account is in the January *Confidential News.*" In the wake of the stock market crash, before the full impact of the Great Depression had been felt, the fraternity blithely named their 1930 convention "Lose the Blues with the St. Louis Blues" (the slogan "When Better Times Are Had, ZBTs Will Have Them" was soon to become a general all-purpose cry for improved morale).

Social Life

On the whole, ZBT annual conventions were lavish affairs, held at the finest hotels and the available Jewish town and country clubs. The 1924 convention, held in late December in Norfolk, Virginia, took the form of a cruise (a diversion that became more popular in the 1920s not only because of its pleasantness but because traveling by ship presumably made Prohibition rules easier to evade—hence the advent of the "booze cruise" tradition). A special ZBT boat left New York at 3 P.M. and Baltimore at 6 P.M. Upon arrival in Norfolk, guests registered at the Hotel Monticello and were treated to an Oyster Roast at Cape Henry that evening, and the weekend's activities included one informal and two formal dances at the Ghent Club. The old Waldorf-Astoria in

Flappers and bathing beauties, all dates of ZBT delegates, pose at the fraternity's 1928 convention in Los Angeles. The availability of 100–200 Jewish women ages 17–30 who could be matched with unattached fraters was a key requirement of any ZBT convention city through the 1950s.

New York City was also a favorite convention spot, and members of the fraternity mourned when the old building was demolished and a new one put up in its place in 1929.

Matchmaking was always a key concern at all ZBT social gatherings held between, during, and after conventions. The natural urge to mate was augmented by strong religious, social, and even professional pressure for a man to be married. The number of women on the social chairman's "date list," passed on to him by men and women in the community, were an important draw for unattached ZBT men seeking a pleasant evening—after all, one could not waltz or fox-trot alone—or a good wife. Convention applicants who wished dates were asked to fill in forms that included such information as age and height and were also allowed to specify the age, height, and hair color ("blonde, brunette, or redhead") of the lady they were to be matched with. Strangers though they might be at the beginning of the festivities, a ZBT man could always be sure that any female from his fraternity's dating pool had already been carefully preselected to meet certain minimum standards of youth, charm, good appearance and dress, family background, intelligence, and membership in a congenial branch of Judaism.

Since a ZBT man was considered to be the ultimate "catch" and the social chairman could always promise that ZBT female guests would be properly chaperoned, Jewish mothers in far-flung communities were inclined to be pleased that their daughters had made the grade, and were cooperative with and indulgent of those who had to travel long distances to reach a ZBT dance or party. "And then there was Alpha Pi's [North Carolina] house party," bragged the columnist in the "What's What among the Chapters" feature of May 1929. "They merely said the word, these boys at North Carolina, and the gals flocked to the weekend from Chicago, Cleveland, and the entire South." Throughout the year, ZBT bachelors permitted their names and addresses to be published in chapter newsletters and the *Quarterly* in the hope that the entire fraternity and their extended relatives would conspire to send eligible women their way.

Success in the matchmaking area was measured in the scores of wedding announcements that appeared in each issue, such as the marriage of Gene Kruger to Miss Helen Labenberg of Richmond, Virginia on May 8, 1930 ("the ceremony took place at the Plaza Hotel, New York City"). Significantly, the evidence suggests that ZBT brides in those days were primarily Jewish women of the upper classes, although it was frequently possible for the men to date members of the Gentile sororities while at college. A sure tip-off of a mixed marriage or any other kind of mésalliance was when the announcement did not, as was the custom, include the bride's name. Usually, ZBT bridegrooms were proud to publish the characteristically Jewish names of their brides, who were commonly siblings of other members and who often came from families of no less wealth or distinction than their own. But vague references to having married "a Holyoke girl"—one member, when asked, simply growled, "Her name is Koch now"—were perhaps an indication that in the 1920s and 1930s, traditional restrictions of religious and class endogamy were not yet so easily violated.

Professions

ZBT members, in their youthful optimism, hoped that their lives after college graduation would be no less exuberant and exciting than their lives before. The numerous articles on professional and vocational choices that ran in their journal each quarter, ranging from the outrageous to the most traditional, were a testimony to the belief that all the gates of the world were open to them.

The entertainment industry, especially Hollywood, was perhaps the ultimate choice for those seeking glamour, excitement, creative fulfillment, great wealth, and possible stardom. No known ZBT ever became a Hollywood superstar, although many made the attempt. In a 1928 essay entitled "We Eat Every Thursday" by the pseudonymous "Don Juan Dardanella," a recent ZBT graduate described the desperate poverty that was the common lot of would-be actors and extras, who, though "dressed to kill" as they walked up and down the boulevard, had not the price of a square meal in their pockets nor the price of a railroad ticket home when they finally despaired of ever reaching their goal. Furthermore, in front of the camera Jewish studio heads adhered more strictly than anyone to the idea that a stereotypically American and "Nordic" look, even in performers of non-Anglo-Saxon ethnic heritage, offered the most appeal and safety—a fact that put some Jewish performers at a disadvantage. For example, it was a common belief accepted by both Jews and non-Jews that the natural Jewish nose was too large to be attractive, and the art of correcting it through plastic surgery was still in its infancy in the 1920s.

The call of actual screen stardom, however, was not the only siren song that attracted young, educated Jewish men and women into various aspects of the industry. Show business also had the advantage of offering them, without overt discrimination, good starting jobs as technicians, painters, designers, costumers, musicians, makeup artists, scriptwriters, editors, researchers, secretaries, typists, clerks, mailroom workers, messengers, or any one of a hundred jobs necessary to keep such huge enterprises running smoothly. At a time when young Jews encountered serious difficulties finding employment, Hollywood studios headed by Jews were a vocational haven. For example, the initials MGM, for the great Metro-Goldwyn-Mayer headed by Louis B. Mayer, were humorously said to stand for "Mayer's Ganze Michpocha" (Yiddish for "Mayer's whole family"). Services to the actual stars was another professional option, as in the case of ZBT graduate Dr. Emanuel Woolfan (Chicago '18), "Doctor to the Stars of Hollywood," who in 1928 was reported to be building a Spanish castle in Beverly Hills. "Think I'll be a doctor," remarked journalist and editor Henry C. Segal of Cincinnati, as he wrote up the news in his regular alumni column.

For those perhaps less photogenic but equally attracted to risks, Wall Street was a popular alternative for ZBT graduates, as it was for many thousands of young men in the most prosperous days of the 1920s. Advertising and journalism also had strong appeal, although a ZBT practitioner of the latter (Stanley S. Friedman, Western Reserve '29) complained of the social stigma some attached to his trade. Nevertheless, for him the work was exciting and satisfying, and his newspaper office was one of the few places where "democracy is practiced, not talked about." "In all," he concluded, "there is a unity, I have found, which ties together the men in the profession; a sort of fraternity without a written ritual and with no badges save a black pencil, and a well-worn trouser seat."

Father's Business

In all of the discussions concerning possible career choices for the young ZBT man a common theme emerged: an almost desperate desire to enter some kind of exciting career or profession and not their fathers' businesses, which were usually centered on the manufacture and sale of clothing.

The garment industry, from the lowliest tailor to the mightiest factory owner, had for generations been a traditional area of economic concentration for Jews. Indeed, it can be said that American Jewish manufacturers revolutionized the field of mass clothing production and helped to make Americans among the best-dressed people in the world. Clothing, after all, had the advantage of being a universal and eternal need. Sewing was a relatively portable skill (in early days little more than a needle tucked in a collar and a good pair of scissors had been necessary). In America, professional education had been neither practical nor obtainable for immigrant grandfathers. English was not a first language, and as for nonbusiness fields, a Jew had little hope of anyone but another Jew hiring him for any kind of job. Garment work was also flexible enough for a Jewish-owned establishment to allow some time off for religious observance and for work in the businesses' early stages to be done at home.

For all these reasons, Jews concentrated in the manufacture and sale of clothing, and many eventually prospered enough to be able to send their sons to college. Numerous ZBTs had been offered the choice of either attending college or entering their fathers' businesses directly.

Even after choosing college and becoming "educated," alumni columns were filled with announcements of young men who had followed that route and become partners. Nevertheless, despite garment work's advantages, for college-educated second-, third-, and fourth-generation American Jewish men, the free professions and hope for an independent practice of some sort offered a far more interesting way to acquire a livelihood and community standing.

Professionalization and specialization were the bywords of the 1920s, and higher education and training were altogether achieving a new popularity. For Jews, acquiring a private practice and standing purely on one's merit circumvented possible job-related anti-Jewish discrimination. It made less critical the need to rely on upper-class Protestant social skills in the event that a Jew was unwilling or unable to become expert in them. Professions also had the advantage of allowing one's capital to be stored all in one's head should disaster strike and sudden movement be necessary. There were great risks in hanging out a shingle and then sitting for weeks or months in an empty office with nary a patient or a client to cross the threshold, as many Jewish fraternity graduates complained was their lot at the beginning of their practices. However, both they and their families were willing to take that chance.

Foremost was the perception that professions were infinitely more fulfilling intellectually and offered Jewish college men the kind of social standing that they could never have achieved as merchants or as members of what was pejoratively called "the rag trade." "Ladies-skirts-wholesale is O.K. for the Old Gent, if that's the sort of thing he likes, but not for you," wrote Herbert Lippman (Columbia '09), in 1929, in an article focusing on the glories of architecture as a career. "During the few years at college you think over the offerings." On a career in law, S. L. Lowenstein Jr. (Penn '17) wrote, "It will take a long time, and you won't make as much money as if you had expended the same amount of talents and energy in the field of business; but you will become a lawyer, and you will be honored and revered in your community as one of its outstanding citizens." Not money alone but honor became the most sought-after attribute. In an article on the rewards of a medical career, one of ZBT's best-known doctors warned that love of the profession's responsibilities, not making a fortune, had to be the primary motive. "If making [a fortune] is your main object . . . you had better give up the idea at once and start in business with your father selling cloaks and suits or whatever it is that he does for a living."

Medicine was the most coveted profession, after law, though it could take as much as a decade to build a career in it. If a businessman father had accrued enough funds to support his son's education for a period of many years, then an excellent medical education could be obtained, particularly since in the 1920s and 1930s this still meant traveling abroad. Dr. Clarence Weil himself suggested replacing college Latin with French or German so that a student would be able to read excellent medical articles in those languages, as yet untranslated to English, and spend six months to a year after medical school graduation in Berlin, Amsterdam, Paris, or Vienna (others suggested visiting clinics in London and Budapest as well) to get tutoring in one's subjects of interest. For anatomy or pathology, he informed his readers, "Vienna or one of the German cities is not to be beat." For urinary disease, "Paris is the place par excellence, and this is true in two ways"; for diseases of children, Germany was best. In Vienna especially, each year the medical schools would hold special postgraduate short courses, and physicians would flock there from around the world, sometimes alone and sometimes with their families. It was not until World War II destroyed the great European centers and the resulting human carnage forced U.S. Army physicians and researchers to cram the equivalent of fifty years' medical progress into five, that the United States would become the medical center of the globe and the direction of physician's visits would be reversed.

Jewish Identity

Perhaps the only profession conspicuously absent from the ambition of the average ZBT was that of the rabbinate—the only profession, as Rabbi Stephen S. Wise had once quipped, that did not discriminate in some way against Jewish boys. For Rabbi Jehudah Cohen (UCLA '27), a ZBT graduate of Hebrew Union College, the absence was due partially to the absence of the rabbi as an equal partner in the religious life of the college campus. With chapel services a daily requirement for non-Jews in many places, it did not seem fair to him that colleges did not provide within easy reach the same opportunities of worship for Jewish students. For Rabbi Henry J. Berkowitz, writing for that audience in 1927, the exclusion made no sense at all. In England, he pointed out, "at least one rising young hopeful of almost every old 'county family' took it as a matter of course that he was to enter the Church and find a good 'living' in some ivy-covered chapel." Among their Jewish ancestors, becoming a rabbi had ranked as the most honorable profession of all. A father's chief pride was a son who entered the rabbinate, and a rabbi was also considered the greatest "catch" "among the Jewish maidens of not so many generations ago." But now, he lamented, modern Jewish young men seemed completely indifferent to it. At such a critical point in Jewish history, he charged, the communities of the United States could no longer afford the loss of the potential religious leadership of their finest young men:

We are confronted with the overwhelming fact that college-bred young Jews of culture . . . are simply not entering the Seminaries. . . . In America today we have only one spiritual leader for about every 12,000 Jews. Most other faiths have about one minister per 600 of the population. We are in dire need, and especially for men from American homes with a background of more than one generation of American environment. Our communities turn to the rabbinical Seminaries and ask that they send them men of this type, and yet they are themselves unwilling to supply such individuals. The profession is going begging. It is high time that a cry of protest arose that is loud enough to be hear within the sequestered Jewish homes of wealth and influence, of culture and refinement. It is a challenge to the Zeta Beta Tau Fraternity. ("On Becoming a Rabbi," *Zeta Beta Tau Quarterly* [Dec 1927]: 10.)

In time a number of ZBT men did enter the rabbinate, and several rabbis were initiated as honorary or associate members. In the case of laymen, it was taken as a matter of course that ZBTs would rank among the upstanding members of their Jewish communities and sit as presidents and board members among all its institutions. A high degree of Jewish communal involvement and contribution was even more the rule among the antecedents of Phi Epsilon Pi, Phi Sigma Delta, Phi Alpha, and Kappa Nu.

However, Zeta Beta Tau was first and foremost an American fraternity. It rose according to the same criteria that governed its American non-Jewish counterparts: expansion, maintenance of standards, the achievements of its members, respect from the administration, good financing, volunteerism, and alumni dedication. It fell according to the same common criteria: poor finances, discreditable behavior of members, alcoholism, hazing, charges of snobbery, bad relations with alumni, and bad relations with the university administrations upon whom their very existence depended.

For Zeta Beta Tau, serving and harnessing the Jewish communal network was crucial in securing an adequate supply of rushees, female dates for social events, and alumni support. On a day-to-day basis, however, it made sense that most of the organizational time and energy of this particular fraternity would be concentrated on issues of concern and joy to *any* fraternity. There is little doubt that the members and national officers of ZBT would have preferred that this be the case all the time. There is also little doubt, however, that to be considered solely a fraternity like all other fraternities was a luxury that Zeta Beta Tau would not be allowed to have.

CHAPTER THREE

"CARES AND JOYS"

The Dilemma of Anti-Semitism, 1920–29

The individual members of Zeta Beta Tau were obviously able to enjoy the prosperity that the 1920s offered to most educated American youth, and as a fraternity it satisfied all the criteria necessary to stand at the forefront of the Greek world. In its early days, however, ZBT was not a fraternity just like any other. It was a fraternity that had been founded by and for Jewish men, and it took its membership only from the small pool of Jewish men available on any one campus. In innumerable ways, these ties of common religion and heritage strengthened the bonds of brotherhood and contributed to the cohesiveness of the group.

At the same time, however, their known Jewish identity made ZBT a target. No matter how strong their desire to be "normal," anti-Jewish discrimination could not help but be an issue of vital concern to all of them. For there was a darker side to the proverbial Roaring Twenties, which came after a major world upheaval and what many believed to have been a disastrous and disillusioning foreign war. Bigotry and intolerance were rampant in the United States of that era, which was characterized by an anti-Communist "Red Scare" (a result of the successful revolution in Tsarist Russia in 1917): hostility to the American labor movement, attempts at federal and state censorship, a rise in religious fundamentalism, a revival of the Ku Klux Klan, and the widespread belief that immigration to America had reached the point of saturation. It was a sign of the times that a serialization of the notorious anti-Semitic forgery, *The Protocols of the Elders of Zion*, appeared regularly in the national newspaper of Henry Ford, perhaps the nation's most popular industrialist. A heightened xenophobia and fear of a refugee flood in the aftermath of World War I led to a cut-off of mass European immigration to the shores of the United States in new laws promulgated in 1921 and 1924.

Dr. Clarence K. Weil of Alabama, a well-known physician and surgeon and the national historian of Zeta Beta Tau, in the pages of the September 1927 *Quarterly* called for the fraternity's members to cry out against the abuses he saw committed in his own state and throughout the nation in the name of "the supremacy of the Nordic and for 100% Americanism":

Intolerance, you see, is not a entirely a thing of the past. It lurks in schools, in churches, in homes, in Senate rooms. It is constantly raising its horrible head in some part of this freedom-loving land. It is conceived by ignorance and sired by greed. You are supposed to be its mortal enemies. For you are the college men of America; you are pictured as carrying on your shoulders the mantle of those who have died for liberty. Knowledge is your weapon. Education is meant to sharpen your intellect, to rectify your viewpoint and send you forth to battle well-armed. Has it? Ask yourself! (p. 27)

To fight the battle against intolerance was difficult, however, when Jewish college students and graduates themselves stood among its targets. Unfortunately for them, the inhospitable era corresponded with the coming-of-age of the second generation of Jewish immigrants' children. Fueled by parental ambition, attraction to opportunities unavailable in the Old World, and the drive toward upward mobility, for the first time Jews applied in large numbers for entrance into the nation's colleges and universities. Also for the first time, soaring Jewish enrollments were checked by quotas and new techniques of selective admissions. Ironically, a significant factor in the rise of the Jewish fraternity system in the 1920s was the flight of Jewish students to state schools where, as one ZBT wrote, "nose-measuring psychology tests" were not yet in fashion and the open-door policy guaranteed those colleges' inability to "resort to the stratagems of the school with selective examinations in halting the Semitic invasions." The fraternity had begun its existence in the Northeast, but as of 1929, nineteen of Zeta Beta Tau's thirty-three chapters were located at semi-rural state schools, and it was precisely these large state schools where the Greek system held its greatest importance.

Since the 1870s and 1880s, Jews had been the victims of exclusion from certain hotels, apartment houses, clubs, resorts, summer camps, and many white-collar or entry-level jobs in non-Jewish firms; in the post–World War I era, however, the pressure intensified, both because it was truly getting worse and because numerically more Jews were seeking to surmount those pressures. Jews seeking entrance to the professions and job opportunities found doors increasingly closed to them, and newspaper advertisements and company hirers did not hesitate to let the world know that they were interested in "Christians only." Assuming that they could be admitted, young Jews on campuses similarly experienced exclusion from societies, clubs, dormitories, and leadership positions in extracurricular activities. Even in the classroom, Jewish students could do nothing but squirm as professors extolled the value of the new pseudoscience of eugenics, which, through the medium of the new IQ tests, purported to divide the world into superior and inferior races. The Anglo-Saxon "Nordic" race was naturally considered superior, while Jewish and other foreign stock was viewed as nothing less than a contaminant.

To their parents, grandparents, and great-grandparents, who might have been happy to be allowed to make a livelihood at all, America still seemed a paradise compared to Europe. But for American-born college men, who felt that they had a right to expect more from their country, the exclusion was a constant source of shame and pain—and of a suspicion that perhaps they, as Jews, might be doing their share to bring this opprobrium upon themselves. As a result, every public incident and instance of anti-Semitism was matched in Jewish fraternity journals by analyses suggesting that changes in behavior might end their suffering, along with disassociation from those other Jews who did not stand at the same level of acculturation as college fraternity men did.

To a certain extent, ZBT members enjoyed some protection from the prevailing winds. Inherited eye, skin, or hair color could not easily be changed, but three or more generations in the country were usually sufficient to eliminate traces of a foreign accent and to advance the acceptable "Americanism" of an immigrant grandchild. ZBT men had been preselected as "representative" Jews, those whose appearance, manners, wealth, family standing, and religious practices should have placed them in the upper brackets of American society. "ZBT men are different" was both a rallying cry and a sought-after compliment from the outside world.

And yet, over and over again, members found themselves facing their disillusionment that all the money and blue blood in the world could never offer complete protection. Gentile acquaintances, when pressed, would frequently justify blanket Jewish exclusion on the grounds that if they let in the "good" Jews, they would eventually have to let in the "kike type" as well; therefore, it was better to make no exceptions rather than to take such a risk. ZBTs as well as other ambitious young Jewish men and women cursed with a stereotypical "Semitic" appearance and a characteristically Jewish name were known to change their names, dye their hair, get their noses fixed at the new "beauty surgeons," or have their required admissions pictures taken by a photographer who specialized in disguising their true features. As to their behavior, there was constant anxiety that the slightest departure from the accepted upper-class Protestant norms would betray them to the world.

The Harvard Affair

The anxiety was exposed most acutely in the spring of 1922, when what one observer called "the bomb that shook American colleges" created a storm of press coverage and controversy. President A. Lawrence Lowell of Harvard, noting with concern that the Jewish enrollment at his school had more than doubled in the first two years of the decade (to almost 22 percent), allowed news to leak out that he was considering establishing a flat 10 percent Jewish quota there. Lowell, who had achieved some notoriety among American Jewry by his strong opposition to the appointment of Louis D. Brandeis to the U.S. Supreme Court in 1916 and by his vice presidency of the Immigration Restriction League, publicly justified his proposal by asserting that a quota would actually help prevent anti-Semitism at Harvard from growing. Furthermore, he insisted, Jews really ought to consider a quota of 10 percent as generous because it was more than three times their actual percentage of the population.

   Harvard's president was not alone in these attitudes, for other universities in the Northeast (where the vast majority of American Jews still lived in the 1920s) had already adapted similar measures to solve their "Jewish problem." Harvard, however, differed because of its ultimate prestige and because of the shamelessness with which its president openly spoke about a quota. The controversy heated up further when the attitudes of the Gentile student body also became public. A professor in the Department of Social Ethics decided to ask his students to discuss the issue of "race limitations" as part of their final exam. More than half the students agreed that a Jewish quota at Harvard was justified and described their reasoning in extended essays. Excerpts were eventually published in the *Nation* and reprinted in the *Zeta Beta Tau Quarterly*, where they became the subject of prolonged discussion and debate by the fraternity's members.

Interestingly enough, in ages past, religious and theological differences would probably have been emphasized more than anything else in negative evaluations of Jews. However, in 1922, college students—themselves hardly religious crusaders—concentrated on the alleged racial and social obnoxiousness of the Jewish parvenu. That Harvard had been founded by and for Anglo-Saxons was the gist of the students' exam essays. The invasion of rude and uncouth Jews, in their view, was spoiling the entire campus atmosphere and would ultimately prevent alumni from sending their sons to their alma mater. The same litany of faults would have been listed at many other campuses besides Harvard: Jews had no interest whatsoever in making contacts, Jews had no interest or capability in athletics, and their tendency to study endlessly was making it too difficult for less maniacally intellectual students to get decent grades. "They memorize their books!" exclaimed one disgruntled student. As a final insult, Jewish alumni allegedly failed to show any loyalty to their alma maters; they were content to come, get their education, and leave, without even paying back the loans that had made their education possible.

Student opinion notwithstanding, the outcry against an overt Jewish quota by faculty, alumni, prominent individuals, and the general public was so great that President Lowell was forced to withdraw his proposal. Eventually, Harvard adopted a complex "geographical distribution" formula for admissions which was as effective as a *numerus clausus*. Other schools, which had not yet taken steps to limit Jewish enrollment and wished to do so, including Yale, took the lesson to heart and adopted similarly indirect, euphemistic methods to obtain the desired goal. Throughout the century young Jews from the New York area seeking to circumvent "geographical distribution" rules at Harvard or any other undergraduate or professional school might try to borrow an alleged home address from a sympathetic aunt or uncle living in Texas or Washington state, but few enjoyed access to that option or were willing to exercise it if they did. By 1928, Harvard's Jewish enrollment had quietly dropped to 10 percent, and it did not rise from that figure until the retirement of President Lowell in 1939 and the new presidency of James B. Conant, under whom the percentage of Jewish students at Harvard promptly rose to 25 percent.

Zeta Beta Tau Responds

The fraternity was severely shaken by the Harvard affair, which caused even the normally unflappable Harold Riegelman to express his exasperation at the barrage of analyses in the press and the negative publicity. "To be subjected to an exclusion which challenges effort and a determination to hurdle the obstacles of prejudice and ignorance is at once a stimulant to ambition, a broadener of capacity, and a developer of a valuable taste for hard-won success," he wrote in his annual report for 1922–23, perhaps recalling the struggles of his own life. "But to be regarded as a 'problem' is bewildering, irritating, and bothersome. We begin to understand how an amoeba feels as he ambles across the field of a Zoology I Lab. microscope."

In the hope that community solidarity and the scientific approach might help, Riegelman spearheaded an attempt to organize the heads of the Jewish fraternities into the short-lived Council on American Jewish Student Affairs, based in New York City. The group operated sporadically as an informal Jewish interfraternity council until it sputtered into inactivity in the late 1920s. A major reason officers gave for not participating was fear that by doing so they would be jeopardizing their hard-won membership in the mainstream National Interfraternity Conference (NIC). The council was revived for a short period after Adolf Hitler's rise to power in Germany in January 1933, but once more it lapsed quickly.

The organization's most significant and lasting contribution in the 1920s was a study, published in 1926, on campus anti-Jewish prejudice, based on questionnaires sent to fifteen hundred fraternity members at sixty-seven colleges and universities. Among other findings, the study revealed that Jews made up approximately 10 percent of the total student body (11 percent of the male students and 8 percent of the female students), that slight to moderate student prejudice against Jews could be found on 41 percent of the campuses, and that severe anti-Jewish prejudice on the part of the faculty was being experienced at 18 percent. The study also permitted the Nasis (presidents) of the respective ZBT chapters to suggest, in essay form, how they thought the problem of anti-Jewish prejudice on the campus could be solved; in so doing they left behind valuable historical documentation of the Jewish role in American college campus life.

Among all the responses a young Jewish man could make to anti-

Semitism, sheer denial was a tempting alternative. Sidney Kaplan (City College '09) in a March 1923 article titled "A Gospel for Zeta Beta Tau Men," counseled that the only way for a gentleman to deal with anti-Semites was to ignore them. He urged his fellow members to work hard, to go out for activities anyway, to remain cheerful, and above all to maintain loyalty to their school, no matter how cruel their foes might be:

> So race prejudice exists in your college! Perish the thought! What if it does exist! To hell with it! Are you feeling good? Then work and play and keep busy. Study hard, present good papers to your instructors and recite well in the class room. Your college mates will have a deal of respect for you. Learn to love your alma mater for the traditions you have imbibed and the education you've received. . . . So you stand high in scholarship, and go big in athletics! What's that you say? Some one on the campus maligned your race? Give him the go-by as you would a dirty crook. Pick out the worthy ones, the upright ones, the lovers of alma mater. That's your company. You're studying at Penn? You've no time to think of Catholic, Jew, or Protestant. It's Penn you must be thinking of. You must be ever loyal to the place. And now you're out of college . . . What's that you say, prejudice again? Still feeling good? Then work harder, for there's more to be done; and play a little too. Think only of the fine things of old college days. (p. 21)

The majority of Zeta Beta Tau undergraduates, however, could not think only of the fine things at college. They did not need special councils or scientific studies to tell them that anti-Jewish attitudes at their schools were a source of continuing disturbance and personal discomfort to all Jewish students. An additional discomfort for Zeta Beta Tau men was the guilt that the Harvard affair aroused in them regarding the exclusiveness and snobbery inherent in any selective Jewish fraternity. If Gentiles were so ready to condemn all Jews to the margins of society, then what sense did it make for Zeta Beta Tau undergraduates to possibly destroy the life of a would-be pledge on the grounds that he did not measure up to their standards? Why make an already painful campus situation worse if it apparently made no difference to the non-Jews?

From the day they were founded, Zeta Beta Tau and the other fraternities had endured criticism from Jewish leaders who charged that there was nothing at all Jewish about a Greek-letter fraternity that had little or no Jewish content in its programming and that regularly discriminated against other Jews. The charges had fallen lightly upon them in earlier years, but after the Harvard debacle the issue of intra-Jewish snobbery, as well as the question of anti-Semitism as a whole, could no longer be ignored so easily. As a result, a noteworthy reaction to the Harvard affair was a flood of articles, impassioned debates, memoirs, and exposés on the subject that poured into the *Quarterly's* offices for months and years, as they did into almost every other Jewish fraternity publication in the United States.

Among the most noteworthy and controversial of those articles was a collection of anti-Jewish feelings and stereotypes virtually identical to those of the Gentile Harvard students, ostensibly written by a Gentile college student under the pseudonym "Cyrus McGinn Mulqueen, A Christian Collegian." It was published in the December 1922 *Zeta Beta Tau Quarterly* at the height of the Harvard controversy under the blatant title "Why I Hate Jews." The next issue contained a companion piece on women, entitled "Why I Hate Jewesses." Other titles in the same issue included "Well, ZBT Men *Are* Different," and "Is Zeta Beta Tau Anti-Semitic?" It is possible that in a fit of sardonic humor the article "Why I Hate Jews" was actually written by a Jewish ZBT member. It is also possible that the editorial board printed the anti-Jewish tract deliberately, as a way of illustrating the attitudes that had helped to bring about the quotas as well as to instruct their readers in precisely what behaviors they should go out of their way to avoid. Whatever the source of the article, it faithfully reflected the tone of anti-Jewish prejudice that was common at the time and was being openly debated in the nation's press.

Mulqueen's article began by noting that prejudice was a fundamental and universal trait and that anti-Jewish reactions, in particular as they centered about "the recent events at Harvard," were a natural response to the overcrowding of Jews in eastern universities to the point that many had become "Semitic institutions, in fact if not in name." Gentiles at these institutions were thus unduly exposed to the objectionable character traits of Jews, which the author proceeded to enumerate. First, Jews cared nothing for their institutions; they came to receive their educations and departed, in the process ignoring such things as athletics, class rushes, social events, and other campus customs. Jews were ceaseless grinds, winning scholastic success only by working at their books day and night and never taking time for such things as friendships or extracurricular activities. Jews lacked college spirit and did not go out for or back college teams because they were "physically lazy" and "not interested." Moreover, the Jewish student was unsociable, unattractive, unfriendly, and hard to get along with—"he is morose, sullen, and too serious about himself"—he was they were also too clannish to permit any friendship with outsiders.

These objectionable characteristics also extended to the areas of civil life, business, and general society, Mulqueen charged. Jews, suddenly released from centuries of restriction, turned drunk with their freedom and showed signs of "exaggerated self-assertion" or not being content to let things rest as they were. The Jew was a destroyer of governments and inevitably "the leader in many of our radical political movements and labor upheavals." In business he was "sneaky, underhanded" and "untrustworthy," using any means short of illegal ones to better his rivals and gain financial success. He was adept at bargaining, hence the popular expression "Jewing one down." In short, Mulqueen wrote, "[a] fair-minded man admires his perseverance, but he must also be disgusted with the business methods of the Jew."

Worst of all, in Mulqueen's opinion, was the Jew's physical appearance and total lack of fitness for life in proper society:

The appearance of the Jew is decidedly against him. The large curved nose; the coarse, curly, black hair; the sallow greasy skin; the stout, phlegmatic body—these make him a very unpleasant sight to look upon. Besides, he is indifferent as to his bodily cleanliness and his clothes are ill-kept, often dirty, frequently wrinkled, and always lacking in dignity. With those who have recently acquired sufficient wealth to be able to buy good things, we find the clothes rich and gaudy—absolutely lacking in taste and refinement. We find their selection dominated by a desire to show off their wealth, rather than to appear as attractive as possible. Jewels in abundance bedeck the women's earrings; ropes of pearls; diamonds of huge dimensions; rings of large size and generally in large numbers. Diamond-studded combs adorn milady's hair, and we almost feel disappointed when we look in vain for anklets and nose-rings. It is almost ridiculous, but it is most annoying to note the social aspirations of these newly-rich. (p. 4)

In addition to a bad appearance and appalling taste in clothing, Jews further allegedly demonstrated abominable manners, gluttony, physical inadequacy, a complete lack of culture, and a determination to push and buy their way into the better parts of society, for which, since most of them were so recently released from near-serfdom, they were not yet ready:

In conversation, the Jew is loud and his guttural voice is quite unpleasant. His loud conversation—coarse and critical—and his even louder laugh are jarring to those of us accustomed to an environment of quiet and refinement.

Their manners are very bad. They eat crudely with special emphasis on the mere act of eating. Their tables are set with rich foods in vast abundance—a marked contrast to the more simple diet of Christians. They fill up on these rich, highly seasoned foods and exercise so little that they grow fat and lazy. . . .

The Jew is a tragic race and has not yet learned to play. His interest in the sports is very slight, golf and poker being his chief acquirements. His dancing is crude, coarse, and "sloppy." . . .

The Jew is decidedly lacking in a true appreciation of the arts. Although a generous patron of painting and prints, he buys more for the sake of showing off than for the love of beautiful things. The emotions of the Jews are too stilted to allow him to appreciate any but the tragic type of music—music resembling his own mournful melodies. True, the Jews compose a large percentage of the patrons of concerts. These are refined Jews, the exception that proves the rule. In drama . . . most of their plays display a great deal of wealth but little taste or else are of the girl and music type. The real dramatic gems are beyond the understanding of the Jew. . . . (p. 5)

The Jews' biggest mistake, in the author's opinion, was that they did not allow sufficient time to unlearn their objectionable traits before trying to climb the social and economic ladder. "He tries to *push* his way into the best society—to *buy* his way in," wrote Mulqueen. "In a few years, he hopes to acquire what other families have taken years to attain. . . . Perhaps the grandchildren of the newly-rich immigrant Jew may attain the desired social prestige, but for the present generation it is impossible, and to try to push or buy oneself into society can only bring a storm of criticism upon one's shoulders." In admitting that such a change was possible, it should be noted, Mulqueen was at least more magnanimous to Jews than those anti-Semites who believed that the whole Jewish race was by nature incorrigible, and hence no amount of time, energy, or Gentile receptivity could bring about their reform.

Mulqueen hastened to conclude his evaluation with the assurance that it did not include "all" Jews and certainly not the "best" ones, but it did fairly represent the "average" Jews, consisting "in actual numbers, of at least 80 per cent of the whole number, and representing in New York perhaps 95 per cent. A group is judged, not by a few outstanding men, but by the rank and file of the great majority."

Justifying the Jewish Fraternity

When they examined their own attitudes, ZBT men frequently could not help but believe that what such personages as Cyrus McGinn Mulqueen said, was essentially correct. After all, the undergraduate leaders of the fraternity were themselves well aware of the current anti-Jewish stereotypes and took care to avoid anyone displaying those characteristics during rush week. According to that school of thought, the prevalence of anti-Jewish attitudes made it all the more important for ZBT members to wield the blackball without mercy when undesirable coreligionists came up for membership. To choose one's company and one's fraternity brothers was a fundamental right that no outside authority, Jewish or non-Jewish, had the right to take from them. "Zeta Beta Tau today, at the highest point she has ever reached, both in number and in quality, is snobbish," Jay Sternberg proclaimed in May 1923, defending their membership policy. "It is snobbishness which requires that man shall be a gentleman to become identified with Zeta Beta Tau. And what are the attributes that gentlemen possess? . . . They are elegance of taste, finesse, savoir faire, sobriety and a number of other traits which mark the person of culture and wholesome refinement. . . . Is this not snobbish? Yes. Is it not just?"

For many members, however, the exclusion of their fellow Jews remained the source of a troubled conscience. One way these consciences could be eased was by rationalizing that the formation of an elite, representative cadre of Jews was paradoxically the best solution to the problem that less fortunately endowed college youth could hope for. Paul Arthur Yawitz of the University of Missouri, in his December 1922 essay entitled "Well, ZBT Men *Are* Different," went so far as to claim that ZBT's exclusiveness was "the death knell to anti-Semitism in American colleges" and the salvation of the Jewish population as a whole.

Remarking on their success in the classrooms and on playing fields, as well as their welcome "within the portals of social acceptance," Yawitz recalled the memory of ZBT's founders at the turn of the century and asked with a rhetorical flourish: "How did a comparatively insignificant band of idealists reach a position which has been sought by a hard-driven, persecuted and libeled race during the past centuries? How and by what miraculous action did Zeta Beta Tau ingratiate itself into the favor and cordiality of the hostile Gentile?" In other words, why did ZBT members constantly hear anti-Jewish remarks with the qualification "but *you're* different," and why should this be considered a compliment rather than an insult? Yawitz's answer was that Zeta Beta Tau men had succeeded by accepting the negative views of Gentiles and deliberately altering their comportment, although not their religious identity. A ruthless selectivity and a shunning of all fellow Jews (especially, by implication, those with origins in Russia) who might bring discredit upon the race were crucial elements in the process.

Yawitz continued:

With all this in mind, Zeta Beta Tau men set out to make themselves as much like their Gentile neighbors as was possible. First they elected new men to their ranks, men who came nearest to the criterion they had established. These men possessed the full appreciation of things American, harbored the ideals of their associates, and offered an appearance that was immaculately that of their best neighbors. . . . Their habits and manners, their polish and breeding, were beyond reproach. In the home their conduct was pleasing; on the campus their courtesy was patent. Only such were chosen! Where such qualities were lacking in its men, Zeta Beta Tau undertook to instill them. That it has been successful is obvious. (p. 7)

Gradually, as Yawitz developed his scenario, Christians realized that some Jews were really better than others: "These men of Zeta Beta Tau were of the flesh and blood he never imagined them to be. They spoke in well-modulated tones, no longer the 'loudmouth Jew' of Gentile tradition; they ate their food with the table manners of royalty, no longer the ill-bred, earth-born; they were generous and considerate, no longer the common, grasping pinchfist; they were clean, kempt, and natty, no longer the careless, slattern immigrant with the grime of generations" (p. 7).

As a result, he concluded, Zeta Beta Tau had produced the "acceptable" Jew, one who was "so like the Gentile" that he was indeed a new entity. "Zeta Beta Tau men need never feel the poisons of prejudice that imperil Judaism," Yawitz insisted. "Zeta Beta Tau men *are* different."

Harold Riegelman and the Philosophy of "Pro-Semitism"

Harold Riegelman, as the de facto spokesman for all the Jewish fraternities, was an eloquent and prolific apologist on the benefits of Jewish fraternities in general and on the importance of ZBT in particular, exclusion and all. He never questioned that personal development, fulfillment, and satisfaction were primary benefits of his or of anyone's involvement. However, he also never doubted that ZBT had a mission in the world aside from the personal fulfillment of its members.

For Riegelman, the cause of eliminating anti-Semitism, the advancement of American Jewry, and the well-being of Jewish fraternities were all intimately connected. He did not believe, as Rabbi Stephen S. Wise charged, that "not one in one hundred of the Jewish students in American colleges is frankly a Jew" and that within their fraternities "not five percent of these students go to the synagogue or link themselves in any way to Jewish religious life." Jewish fraternities, Riegelman argued, were as legitimate an expression of Jewish consciousness as anything else and performed important services to the community. They all taught responsibility, group cooperation, good citizenship, and essential social skills; the good ones helped their members to become active

Jewish community workers as well. They were, moreover, among the most potent instruments with which to fight prejudice in the United States, thus benefiting all Jews whether they were members or not.

College campuses, Riegelman would frequently claim, were like social laboratories, where men from diverse backgrounds gathered and then dispersed across the land. It was from the college campus that the nation and the world drew much of its leadership. During those four formative years, Gentile students could come into continuous contact with Zeta Beta Tau men, a large group publicly identified as being Jewish. Through observation of their achievements and the exchanges of hospitality that the Greek system fostered, non-Jews could learn that Jewish stereotypes had no basis. Upon graduation, they could then carry and spread the message throughout the world. Providing just this education was a sacred mission and the strongest justification for ZBT's existence. Riegelman used this philosophy, which he termed "pro-Semitism" and "race appreciation," to chart a new course for the fraternity, using the same strength of will—and sometimes arousing the same degree of opposition—as Richard Gottheil had when, in 1898, he had helped to found ZBT as a way of bringing American college youth to Zionism.

From the beginning of the Harvard quota controversy until the end of the decade, Riegelman published a series of polemics on the subject in both the Anglo-Jewish press and his own fraternity's quarterly. He also spoke on the theme repeatedly before Jewish audiences. "The battle is not of words," he explained, "not of argument or protest, but of excellent conduct and manly deportment in the advancement of community interests." This was his answer to the charges of critics that Jewish fraternities by their very nature were ridiculous and cruel. The head of Zeta Beta Tau also took the lead in defending Jewish fraternities against the charge, made by a professor at Harvard and published in a national magazine, that Jews were by nature "clannish" and that it was unfair of them to be asked to be treated as individuals as long as they always insisted on forming separate groups. In doing so, the professor was unwittingly echoing charges made on the floor of the French National Assembly more than a century earlier by critics who did not believe that the revolution required granting the Jews of France full emancipation. Riegelman's response, in the May 1923 *Quarterly*, was that, once again, the banding together of individual Jews in groups was necessary if they were ever to surmount the prejudice against them:

Denials and protests avail nothing against predispositions. They but aggravate. If I am predisposed to believe that all residents of New Jersey are commuters and also bowlegged, there is only one cure. I must meet a dozen or two or three dozen straight-limbed Jerseyites who live and have their businesses wholly within Trenton, Bayonne or Hoboken, as the case may be. One won't do. He would be merely the exception which would prove the rule—my rule. I've got to meet gobs of them. I must know them to be Jerseyites before I learn that they are not commuters or observe the straightness of their limbs. (p.23)

Only hundreds of physically fit and socially successful Jewish men, clearly identified as such through their fraternities, could disprove similar prejudices, and only then would every single one of them receive the recognition he deserved:

It is entirely proper, it is more than proper—it is necessary, so long as certain predispositions with respect to Jews exist—that Jewish men should associate themselves as Jews, and as Jews steadily, continuously and persistently, by their sportsmanship on the athletic field, their reserve and decency of deportment, their generous support of movements looking toward relief and communal betterment and solidarity, demonstrate day in and day out on the campus and off the campus the inherent fineness of their character as men among men and the inherent, blatant, stupid falsity of predispositions to the contrary. This is the field of the Jewish fraternity. And this is the watchword of Jewish fraternity men.

"They ask to be treated as individuals, but they form a group." They form a group, if you please, for one purpose only—to demonstrate their right to be treated as individuals. (p. 23)

Although he remained at the helm of ZBT for many years more, Riegelman ceased his public advocating of pro-Semitism in the early 1930s. At that point, the Great Depression deepened, jobs for college graduates evaporated, the Nazis rose to power in Germany, and anti-Semitism worsened both in Europe and at home. In the face of such direct threats to Jewish survival in Europe, much of it helped along by decidedly ill-mannered street brawlers, it no longer seemed appropriate to suggest that education or "excellent conduct and manly deportment" would be enough to stop the threat of guns, tanks, and marching soldiers. Through the decade of the 1920s, however, Riegelman's philosophy reigned within the fraternity.

Pro-Semitism or Anti-Semitism?

Not all agreed with Riegelman's philosophy of pro-Semitism, however, and a number of Zeta Beta Tau spokesmen took public issue with it. Clarence K. Weil, in reply to an article by Riegelman, voiced his suspicion that Zeta Beta Tau was fostering more prejudice than it eliminated.

In his view, Zeta Beta Tau's supposed "mission" was in truth little more than a rationalization designed to relieve their discomfort at abandoning the Zionist ideals of their founders for more purely social ones. The philosopher and educator Horace M. Kallen, one of ZBT's earliest and most prominent honorary members, similarly believed that the proper response to campus anti-Semitism was not redoubled efforts to be like non-Jews, but a return to the Hebraic ideals of Richard Gottheil; he gently chided the membership for what he saw as their departure from the ways of their fathers.

Bernard A. Bergman (Ohio State '16) of Philadelphia, managing editor of the *Jewish Tribune*, took the opportunity to castigate the general membership for using the essay section of their leaders' campus anti-Semitism survey to express views almost identical to the main anti-Semitic writings of the day." "Loud Jews, vulgar Jews, Jews who haven't gotten on to American ways, Jews whose mannerisms are offensive, who don't know how to act, even 'typical Jews,' these and nothing else are the cause of anti-Semitism in our higher seats of learning, according to the answers made by practically all the respective Nasis," he informed them in a March 1923 *Quarterly* column. In voicing these opinions, Bergman warned, the undergraduates were "merely falling into the attitude of the anti-Semite":

The vital thing at hand is our attitude toward our Jewish brothers, who through no fault of their own, merely by the accident of birth, are not in the same fortunate position in which we find ourselves. Most of us, I suppose all of us, were born in America. Many of our fathers are also native-born. But when we indict the newly-arrived immigrant, or the boy who hasn't grown up in the social environment in which we were lucky enough to land, are we playing fair? How did our fathers or our grandfathers disport themselves when they came to America? I doubt if they were any more polished than the loud and vulgar college students we now condemn. . . . Our Executive Nasi hopes, through Zeta Beta Tau, to show the non-Jewish world just what the Jew is, and thus gradually eliminate anti-Semitism. And now the Jew turns out to be an anti-Semite!

Bergman warned that by giving such excuses for anti-Semitism, Jewish students were merely playing into the hands of their foes. In reality, all Jews were open to the same hatred. "They point to our 'black sheep' and to our 'loud and vulgar' as a pretext, when in reality they cherish an inherited, instinctive, and cultivated dislike for all Jews, condescending at times to except from ostracism a few Jews who are 'different,'" he charged.

Can't we be big enough and broad enough to break away from this narrowness of vision, which is so common among those of our people who have lost their vision and their soul, who will stop at no humiliation in order to gain a Gentile smile or a

Gentile pat on the back, when in reality their servility wins them in time only a Gentile kick in the pants? Can't we stand forth at all times as Jews, conscious of our Jewishness, unashamed of our black sheep, for we are entitled to them just as any other race? And as Jews, can't we always be ready to extend the helping hand of brotherhood to those less fortunate than ourselves, rather than spit upon them?

The Jews they condemned, who spoke with heavy accents and had no comprehension of college life, might nevertheless have "fought and faced death" for their religion and race, and a few, Bergman noted, were among "those rare souls who are building up Palestine with their raw, bleeding hands, the most glorious adventure in idealism the world has ever witnessed." Perhaps, he mused, "their culture may be far greater than ours."

Similar objections to internal Jewish anti-Semitism were voiced by Benjamin D. Salinger (Columbia '21) in the May 1923 *Quarterly*. The theme of his article was objection to the use of the term "too Jewish," apparently an epithet of scorn and resentment often used against one's fellow Jews. Also, as Salinger noted, "Jewish jokes" and the expression "kike" were far more widely used in Jewish circles than in Gentile ones. The term was too much of a compromise, he believed, because "whether he wills it or not, every Jew is held accountable for the actions of every other Jew." What, indeed, was it about Jews that Gentiles found so obnoxious?

Salinger enumerated the objections one by one, attempting to strike them down. "The Jew has a Semitic type of features. He is dark complexioned, he has curly hair, he has a prominent nose. Like all generalizations, this is partly true." However, did not the Jews have the same features three thousand years ago when they were a "proud and independent people"? Would any Jew have scorned his own features then? And what of Jews who spoke with accents? So indeed did anyone speak with an accent or use foreign phraseology when emigrating to a country late in life or not using their mother tongue. Certainly no one would accuse a French diplomat, when using a French phrase to help out his English, of being "too French." And what of charges that the Jew was "unsociable, unmannerly, ill-bred, miserly, clannish, ostentatious, cowardly"? These and every vice known to man could justly be ascribed to some Jews—and, in Salinger's opinion, to many Gentiles. The Jew simply served as the Gentile's convenient personification of human faults. As to sneering at Orthodox Jewish practices, the author denounced such attitudes that would deny to any group of people the cherished American freedom to worship in any way they chose.

Of those Jews who were what Salinger termed the "Ghetto type," readers were reminded that the ghetto had been forced upon the Jews by Gentiles, and hence the undesirable traits developed there were not truly Jewish at all. Salinger further showed an admiration and sympathy for East European Jews that was sometimes found among members of the German Jewish upper classes, when he described the "Ghetto Jew" as being inherently superior because he was proud of his Jewishness, whereas other Jews sought unsuccessfully to escape from their identity. The American Jew who denied consciousness of his Jewishness was in fact "far more conscious of it in trying to hide it than the Polish immigrant with his beard and earlocks, whose Jewishness is inherent and is the center of his life."

Salinger concluded by praising what he termed "the true Jewish characteristics," which had and always would outlive the ghetto— namely, superior intellect, intuition, earnestness, a sense of real values that caused him to be "the perfect critic," and personal intensity. After listing some of the major Jewish prophets, intellectuals, and philanthropists throughout the centuries, he concluded by warning that Jews who sought to assimilate would still be labeled as Jews and would also forfeit the characteristics that made them a superior people:

If the Jew cannot be inspired by these examples, if the term "Jew" is repulsive to him, then let him cease to be a Jew. Let him straighten out his curly locks and his curved nose, let him become a Christian Scientist, or an Ethical Culturist, or a Unitarian, or a Protestant, or a Catholic, or a Mohammedan, or a Parsee—let him so completely assimilate himself that he will not wince when his friends tell him the story of an ugly, miserly Jew—and then, above all, let him guard his actions and his words so that he may not commit an indiscretion and be labeled as a "damned Jew."

And he *will* be a "damned Jew"—self-damned, for he has lost the truly Jewish traits as well as those Gentile-given Ghetto characteristics. . . . Had he kept his sense of moral values he would have seen that he was, ostrich-like, hiding his nose, selling his tradition, his heritage, for the outward acceptance of himself socially by the Gentile world. . . .

Damned Jew!

The Jew is damned only in so far as he damns himself—he will be blessed when "too Jewish" is an inspiration to him rather than a slur. (p. 15)

The consciences of those who could not agree with the pro-Semitism model became most troubled during rushing season, when group evaluations of every prospective pledge's faults resulted in many of them being cut from consideration. For one ZBT member, Kalman R. Plessner, the Sacco and Vanzetti trial in 1927 uncovered what he saw as the disturbing intolerance of his fraternity brothers. Why, he wondered in the December 1927 *Quarterly*, in a college where one might expect "straight thinking on their guilt or innocence," did most of his fellow members seem to think that the pair were automatically guilty because they were "dirty reds"? His reflections on what he saw as the inherent unfairness of this attitude led to further reflections on what he saw as fraternity "snobbery and conformism"—the tendency of members to copy and judge each other and to dismiss men "of the poorer dorms" because they were not "our type, " an attitude with which Plessner was obviously becoming disaffected. Of typical rushing procedures and evaluations, Plessner wrote with irony:

The individualist is probably disturbing at times, and we don't want to be disturbed. . . . He is probably careless of some of the social conventions; and, above all else, our men must be social successes. His bridge game is likely to be poor, his dancing inadequate, his after dinner conversation forced. He didn't go to the right prep school, or summer camp, or dancing class; and, most objectionable of all, his parents didn't come from the right part of Europe. He's hardly the sort of fellow we'd like to take home for the holidays. No, the individualist is a poor prospect. (p. 16)

A seventeen-year-old member of Zeta Beta Tau, writing pseudonymously in the fall of 1929, expressed his agony and disillusionment at the recent rushing season, upon realizing that he had virtually ruined a fellow sixteen-year-old Jew's life when he had refused him entrance into the fraternity. "What have I done, with my wildly wielded weapon of the blackball, swung in my 17-year-old wisdom with the vehemence of a Cossack's thong?" he lamented. "And for what? I did not like the cut of his coat or the part of his hair or his handclasp or his manner of speech. . . . I have blackballed a man who is of flesh and blood and bone and human sinew as much as I am, whose family is as decent and worthy as mine if not as refined and educated, for after all the step back to steerage is hardly more than two generations."

Relief in Humor

To many observers in the outside world, the irony of an entire Jewish fraternity seeking to behave as much like non-Jews as possible was a source not for pain but for jokes and ridicule, sometimes coupled with fear. Jewish parents desperately wanted their sons to get an education, but they did not want them to assimilate completely in the process and turn their backs on their people. It was sometime in the 1920s that the ditty "Oy Yoy Yoy, Zeta Beta Toy," ostensibly sung by a

Yiddish-speaking mother lamenting the true effects of a college education on her son, first became a widespread American Jewish folk song, sung even in families where no one had any idea exactly what "Zeta Beta Toy" was.

> Oi yoy yoy, Zeta Beta Toy
> What have you done to my little Jewish boy?
> I sent him off to college to learn to read and write,
> Now he dates a *shiksa* every Friday night
> I sent him off to college, to learn to read and spell,
> Now he thinks *boruch atoh* is a college yell
> I sent him off to college, to learn the Jewish way,
> Now he thinks a *hora* is a girl who's gone astray . . .

Another source of ZBT humor, Columbia graduate Arthur Donald ("Aidee") Swartz, whose parodies and satires of fraternity life entertained the readers of the *Quarterly* throughout the 1920s and 1930s, took careful aim at ZBT's confused Jewish identity in a 1929 piece covering the convention of a mythic "Tau Beta Zeta Fraternity," or TBZ. TBZ was supposedly an outgrowth of an earlier nonsectarian group called the "Young Men's Club for the Restoration of Palestine and Football Managerships to Jews." Upon arriving at the convention and hearing the introductions, the writer commented, he was reminded that "this propaganda of replacing the Aarons with the Arthurs, the Samuels with the Sanfords, and the Jakes with the Johns, has begun to show results. In the first hour of 'getting acquainted,' we met seven Bradys, three Owen's, two Kanes, and any number of 'Bucks.' It suddenly occurred to us that perhaps there had been a merger while we were away, with the Dekes maybe or the Psi Us, one for three perhaps."

At the business meetings of the mythical TBZ, topics for discussion included "How to Finance the National Fraternity without Dues," "How Long May an Alumnus Delay Paying His Undergraduate Senior Dues to His Chapter," "What Is TBZ Material," "How Can a TBZ Man Be Really Jewish and Show It," "How Can a TBZ Man Be Jewish and Not Show It," "The Alumni Problem and Should They Be Shot at 30," "How Can We Make Friends with the Alumni without Asking for Cash," "Blackballing the Nephew of One of the Brothers from the Class of 1900 without Alienating the Brother," and "Keeping the Chapter House Clean." When it came time to distribute the cups, one of the awards included the "*Anti-Semitic Party of Germany Cup—* Awarded to the Chapter whose members are quite willing to admit in public, on the Campus, and elsewhere that they are Jewish in more ways than on their parents' sides; who are old-fashioned enough not to want to adopt every fad that the non-Jewish chapters have; who are perfectly content to tolerate among them a fellow who has come to College to find out what the courses are all about and who once in a while asks the great privilege of being excused from pep rallies."

Assertions of Jewish Identity

The pain and doubt that members expressed over ZBT's supposed snobbery, as well as their willingness to poke critical fun at themselves, was reflective of a deeper attitude and seriousness among ZBT men regarding religious matters and Jewish peoplehood than some outsiders may have been led to believe. The very intensity of their resistance to it belied its alleged lack of importance. ZBT men were not rabbis, but there is evidence that many were deeply religious, in both a universal and a specifically Jewish sense. Judaism was part of the fabric of the fraternity, not always acknowledged and frequently taken for granted, but it was always there nonetheless.

Judaism emerged most strongly in ZBT men during their alumni years, when it was assumed that they would be among the leaders and supporters of their community. As a matter of course they entered such organizations as the B'nai B'rith lodges, temple brotherhoods, and the boards and chairmanships of community synagogues and fund drives; and also as a matter of course, many of their names could be found in succeeding volumes of *Who's Who in American Jewry*.

Among the undergraduates a strong sense of religious identity was usually not expressed openly, but it peeked out from time to time. In one example, pride in the twentieth-century accomplishments of the Jewish people emerged in the continual coverage of the Hebrew University in Jerusalem, opened in 1925 and for decades the recipient of a Zeta Beta Tau scholarship. ZBT men, for the most part, did not burn for the sake of Zion, but the idea of a Jewish collegiate institution taking shape in the Promised Land captured their imaginations; they were devoured with curiosity about student life there and eager to know how it compared with their own. A Jewish identity and childhood memories emerged in snatches of Hebrew, Yiddish, and German, as mentioned in the pages of the *Quarterly* along with references indicating that the average member had some acquaintance with what was called "our racial patois." Baruch Spinoza, whom writers termed "A God for the College

Jew," was held up to them as a man of Jewish background and education struggling to reconcile the teachings of his childhood with the modern enlightened world's demands of science and reason. Identity emerged in the frequent printing of columns by rabbis and Jewish thinkers, discussions on the alienation of Jewish youth, and frequent reviews of Jewish books. That ZBT's editors chose to print such pieces was an indication that the subject was of some concern to them.

Jewish identity emerged most of all from the deepest repository of ZBT's ideals, its rituals. The ritual adopted by the Supreme Council in 1920 might not have satisfied Richard Gottheil or rabbinic figures, but the heritage of the fraternity permeated it. For the "pledgee trial," prospective members were officially required to read one or two books on Jewish history and to take an oral examination on the contents. At the initiation ritual, after the "Levite" administered the oaths, the "seneschal" was to ask: "Who art Thou that seeketh admittance within our gates?" The answer was: "A believer in God and the Brotherhood of Man; I am a Jew." The seneschal would then ask: "What are the watchwords of our fraternity?" Answer: "Justice and Brotherly Love." The seneschal, before explaining the symbolism of the fraternity to the new initiate, would bless him in ancient Hebrew fashion, declaring, "Blessed art thou who cometh in the name of the Lord, for unto thee is afforded the opportunity of being of service to thy brethren."

By all evidence the ZBT ritual was not performed once or twice a year and then forgotten. The record of Jewish activity and leadership of ZBT men on dozens of American college campuses testifies that more than a few took its ideals to heart. For example, ZBT chapters' relationship with the Hillel Foundations on their respective campuses were never as consistently bad as outsiders accused them of being. It was true that, for most of the century, "Greeks" and "Hillel" would be viewed as diametrically opposed groups in collegiate culture, for the other historically Jewish fraternities no less than for Zeta Beta Tau. In individual cases ZBT-Hillel relations ranged from indifference to actual chapter opposition. But in others the relationship was a strong and positive one. Chapter reports regularly and proudly listed the names of ZBTs who had attained high office in their Hillels or other Jewish organizations. In May 1929, for example, on the thirty-three campuses where active Zeta Beta Tau chapters operated, six ZBTs were presidents of their local Hillel chapters or the Menorah Society, and Morris Blank '29 of the University of Illinois and Richard A. Meyer '29 of the University of Michigan served simultaneously as presidents of their ZBT chapters as well. Another leader in the Missouri chapter, Graenum

Berger '30, was president of the Jewish Student Congregation there; he later studied social work and went on to a distinguished career in Jewish communal service, stretching from the spread of the YM-YWHA movement through efforts to aid the Jews of Ethiopia. Indeed, in the mid-1920s, General Secretary George Macy held Missouri up as an example of the type of Jewish involvement the fraternity wished to see in its undergraduate members.

The value placed on Jewish activity could also be seen in the annual awards that ZBT gave for the best chapter. In the late 1920s and early 1930s the consistent winner, indeed the jewel in ZBT's crown, was their "Psi" chapter at the University of Alabama. A 1928 collection of chapter photos published in the *Quarterly* showed twenty-six men immaculately dressed in stiff collars and ties, a large chapter house with a sun-porch, carved mahogany furniture, a chandelier, and a fireplace; in the dining room a ZBT banner hung over the mantel, and the tables were set with white tablecloths, china, and crystal. ZBT's national officers prized Psi chapter for its breeding and gentlemanly behavior, its athletic prowess, its involvement in campus activities, and the fact that it combined all these with an excellent record in Jewish affairs.

Alabama was also the home of Fred Sington '31, ZBT's best all-around athlete, who played both varsity football and baseball while maintaining a 93 average. In the spring of 1930 he was elected vice president of the entire student body, the first time in the history of the university that a Jew had been elected to a major office; he was called by the president of the university "the finest example of an athlete, scholar, and gentleman that the University of Alabama has had." In addition to all this, Sington and the entire chapter remained in close contact with local rabbis and regularly attended services together as a group. Individual members did not hesitate to contribute their talents to this Jewish community, as in the case of Mayer Newfield. During the 1929–1930 academic year he held the lead in the school's operetta, was a lead singer in the Glee Club, and also officiated as cantor at all temple services and congregational groups. In the same year, undergraduate Andre Katz took the initiative in securing a Hillel Foundation for Alabama and served as its first president.

Whether they headed the Hillel Foundation or not, the evidence suggests that many Zeta Beta Tau chapters in those early days took their religious responsibilities seriously and stood up for the entire campus Jewish community whenever they were threatened by outside forces. Rollin G. Osterweis '30, a graduate of the Yale chapter who later returned to teach as a professor and served for a term as ZBT's national vice president, recalled the dances, beautiful women, and prominent alumni who graced their house parties. But also remembered were the friendship and support of men willing to help one another through difficult times. Most of all, Osterweis never forgot the stands his chapter had taken during several outbreaks of anti-Semitism, and the words of one of his brothers: "We've got big problems around here — but when you've got a good bunch together who are willing to tackle them, there's nothing to it. I'm not particularly sentimental, but there's something in it all that gets me — makes me feel as though I were storming the Bastille, or off on some kind of allegorical crusade against Prejudice. . . . There's something magnificent in ZBT" (January 1930 *Quarterly*, p. 30).

Roger Williams

The identity of ZBT was also discernible in its choice of heroes, past and present. It was in the 1920s, under the leadership of Harold Riegelman, that, at the suggestion of Supreme Nasi Julius Kahn, Roger Williams Day became a ZBT holiday and was celebrated intermittently for the next four decades. Roger Williams (1603–1683), born in London, had been banished from the Puritan stronghold of Massachusetts Bay Colony for daring to preach on the need for separation of church and state and freedom of conscience in religion. He eventually became the founder and first governor of Rhode Island colony, the first of thirteen colonies whose constitution separated church from state and granted complete freedom of worship to all its inhabitants. On the date of Williams's birthday, special programs commemorating his life were held in the chapters, and a ZBT delegation laid a wreath at his statue in the Capitol in Washington, D.C. The ceremony fell out of favor for a time but was revived during the rise of Hitlerism in Germany. In the 1940s and 1950s the date of commemoration was switched to National Brotherhood Week. ZBT celebrated Roger Williams Day in tandem with the National Conference of Christians and Jews, and the event drew national press attention.

Louis Marshall

The identity and strong Jewish concern of Zeta Beta Tau members was also discernible in their high regard for Louis Marshall, the premier leader of American Jewry and president of the American Jewish

Committee, who had been initiated as an honorary member of their Syracuse chapter in 1917; the following year he gave a moving speech at ceremonies in New York to honor the fraternity's war dead. Privately, Marshall admitted to loathing the frivolous aspects of fraternities, and ZBT was a minor concern among his many duties. Nevertheless, he never failed to extend a helping hand and counsel when he was called upon. It was he who donated the "Louis Marshall Trophy," the distinctive six-branched candelabrum that was to be awarded annually to the chapter most active in Jewish affairs. When Marshall died suddenly in 1929, the entire fraternity mourned "our dearly beloved Brother" and acknowledged that one of the greatest American Jewish leaders of all time had passed away.

The 1920s: A Sudden End

The passing of Louis Marshall left the American Jewish community bereft of leadership on the eve of one of the greatest crises it had yet faced. The prosperity of the 1920s collapsed in the stock market crash of October 1929, plunging the United States into the worst economic depression of its history. The crash itself was only a symptom of adverse economic forces that had been developing for many years, a reality that was to make economic recovery prolonged and painful. Not long after, the ominous signs of fascism and life-threatening anti-Semitism appeared in Europe, and American Jews became justifiably frightened that aspects of the movement might spread to the United States. In a time of economic disaster, foreign instability, and general fear, the strength of anti-Semitism manifested in the United States grew stronger instead of weaker.

During all the years of the Harvard affair and similar events, Zeta Beta Tau men had clung to the illusion that improved behavior, education, and time would eliminate the prejudice against them and bring about the age of the universal Brotherhood of Man. However, it was difficult to maintain this belief as they watched the land of their ancestors, a light of science and literature and home of one of the most acculturated and successful Jewish communities in the world, descend into barbarism more in keeping with the Dark Ages. At the same time, the economic crisis had severe impact on the Jewish fraternities, as it did on all fraternities, and many groups either disintegrated or went into a decline from which they never truly recovered.

Once again, the affluence of Zeta Beta Tau guaranteed that, with significant exceptions—mainly recent college graduates hitting the job market for the first time—much of the fraternity could continue to survive and even flourish. However, the optimism and hope of the previous age, the ideals that had comforted them and encouraged them to believe that they held their destiny in their own hands, were fast fading as the Roaring Twenties drew to a close.

CHAPTER FOUR

"SORROW AND SADNESS"

Zeta Beta Tau and the Great Depression

The 1920s Golden Age of the American College Fraternity was but one of many phenomena that were rudely interrupted by the crash of the New York Stock Exchange in October 1929. The crash itself was but a symptom of long-standing weaknesses in the U.S. economy, and its effects were not immediately felt outside the circles of stock and bondholders. Gradually, however, like ripples in a pond, the disturbance spread until the American economy was virtually paralyzed and more than a quarter of the population left unemployed.

As a result of the economic paralysis and the evaporation of wealth, thousands of potential students found themselves unable to begin or to continue their education. Those still in school were embittered by the bleak existence and utter lack of job prospects that awaited them, and their frustration and disillusionment at what they saw as the weaknesses of the capitalist system frequently turned to political radicalism. Many looked to the example of the Soviet Union, a nation whose economy seemed to be immune to the catastrophe; indeed, Americans had reason to fear that some kind of revolution might take place on their own shores. At the same time, the American fraternity system found itself facing new challenges, as the trend in higher education moved away from them and toward building in their stead the "house" system, modeled on the British universities of Oxford and Cambridge.

Zeta Beta Tau did not go under during those years, as many other relatively small and young Greek-letter groups did. Its officers managed to pull their fraternity through and even to prosper at times during the lean years. This did not occur, however, without considerable effort, particularly by Lee Dover, who remained at the helm of ZBT throughout.

"These Be Parlous Times"

With budgets slashed and initiates down by 15 percent from the previous year, all the member fraternities of the National Interfraternity Conference (NIC) recognized that by fall 1931 the full impact of the economic crisis was at hand. How should they respond? Ordering local orchestras instead of big name bands, reducing dance ticket prices, skipping party favors, and asking women to agree not to ride in taxicabs on dates so as to save their escorts money—as was done at the Universities of Texas and Wisconsin—were useful but hardly enough in the face of the crisis. The NIC therefore formed a Special Committee on Industrial Depression and the Fraternities, chaired by Harold Riegelman, which performed a survey and presented to the membership techniques that might be used to stave off utter extinction.

In the resulting report, chapters were advised to juggle their finances in whatever way they could and to practice economy at all times. They were also advised to punish waste of electricity and water with fines, to install pay phones, and to have members perform repairs and chores whenever possible even if it meant extending meal credits. Other suggested options were eliminating breakfast, boarding in common with other congenial fraternities, and forming cooperative buying schemes. Collection techniques should be perfected to make sure that all debts owed the chapter were paid. Income from nonmembers might be gained by letting them stay in the house, especially during the summer. During the year the maximum number of members should be encouraged to live in the house, even if it meant lowering the rent. Entertainment should be simplified and competitive entertainment eliminated altogether. Budgets for jewelry, printing, and traveling should all be cut, and the cost of conventions "should be cut to the bone."

In addition, the NIC found itself, at the beginning of the 1930 academic year, forced to issue bulletins with detailed instructions designed to prevent thefts and cons from down-and-out men who showed up at fraternity chapter house doors claiming to be members and who appealed to fraternal promises to always help a brother in need. Secret handshakes and the correct badges were regarded as insufficient proof; handshakes could be seen and copied, while numerous jeweled fraternity badges were now available to enterprising con artists in the nation's pawnshops.

Devoted though individual members might have been to their fraternities, the fear that their organization might go under was not foremost in their minds; too preoccupied were they with anxieties that sudden poverty might force them to leave school, that their education was being bought at too great a sacrifice to their families, or if they managed to graduate, that no jobs would be awaiting them. For the first time, a liberal college education appeared to be nothing more than a "four year loaf"—a waste of four years that did not suit the candidate for any useful occupation. Years spent in schooling, it was feared, would mean only that a graduate would eventually find himself competing with those who had already been in the workforce during that time and would therefore have more experience and seniority than he.

Young alumni castigated undergraduates for taking their education lightly and for not realizing the seriousness of the situation. "All you lucky college students, all you have to worry about is getting a C on a test," wrote Jasper D. Rapoport (Harvard '31) in the October 1932 *Quarterly*. "Get down to 42nd street and join the bread line before they run out of hot water! I'll see you there and we can talk over the good times we had in college." How could millions of people be starving, he demanded bitterly, if they were willing to work? In "They Came for the Ride," Kalman B. Druck (Syracuse '36) warned ZBT undergraduates that if they did not work harder in college, their diplomas would be worthless. As of March 1936, he reminded them in the *Quarterly* of that month, eight million young people in the United States were unemployed, including 35 percent of all college graduates between ages twenty-five and twenty-nine.

The bitterness and disillusionment of a ZBT growing up in the Depression years was perhaps best expressed in an impressionistic autobiography appearing in the December 1938 *Quarterly* entitled "We Grow Up, 1915–1938," written by twenty-two-year-old Jerome L. Schwartz, a 1937 Ohio State graduate. The impact of the crash on his generation was all the worse for their having been born into an era of such hope. For this ZBT, sentience began during the "war to end all wars" in 1917, as he was told that "Papa and big brother are going away across the sea to make the world safe for democracy so that when you grow up there won't be any more wars for you to face." In 1918 there was playing at being a soldier, being carried on adults' shoulders to see the Armistice Day parades, and thinking that "everything was going to be fine now. The war was over. The reign of evil was past." In 1919 the little boy played with mud pies while others talked about progressivism; in 1920, while white-hooded men burned crosses in the South, he and his friends munched popcorn and watched the "magical movies." Next came memories of the Roaring Twenties, accompanied by dreams of success and the awkwardness of entering adolescence. With the stock market crash, however, came an awareness at the tender age of fourteen that none of the dreams would come true and there would no longer be any rewards for hard work and academic success:

1929—The great American balloon burst. Suicides, bankruptcies. But this is still the land of milk and honey! Punch harder! . . . 1931—No, the high school officials said, your class can't have dances, you can't have an annual. People are starving they said. . . . You can't dance when people need bread. . . . 1932—Was this never going to stop? We heard all about the glories of the last generation. But you and your generation must bury your heads in your pillows . . . you must drink in the darkness. 1933—a pounding in our veins, a longing in our hearts, but the world was cold. . . . 1934—The bank failed. No big Eastern University for you, son. Go the State University. You're lucky. Many boys are starving. 1935—Crawling into a warm, academic cloister, feeling the soft touch of books, a desire to lull yourself into forgetfulness of the world outside. . . . 1936—Moonlit nights and a girl. . . . 1937—the firm clasp of friendly hands, and the desire never to let go . . . (p. 14)

Upon graduation, Schwartz found himself facing a life for which he had been neither prepared in college nor brought up for by his family. "1938—You had been a success in college. . . . They patted you on the back, gave you honors, handed you a Phi Beta Kappa key that was excellent to clean your fingernails. They poured more success down your throat. They fashioned you in the image of a lost generation. Then they shoved you into a world which had changed. So pound the pavements, fellow! Slave away! You and your generation have been kicked in the face."

In such an atmosphere, bigotry and anti-Semitism flourished, as well as an exaggerated conservatism and patriotism from those who correctly perceived that the American system was in great danger. It was therefore not surprising that young people, who were aware of the utterly useless slaughter that had resulted from World War I, and who despaired of the capitalist economic chaos that they had inherited, developed an attitude of rebelliousness against their elders that frequently became channeled toward support of politically radical movements. They were not prepared to tolerate older Americans, those relatively secure in their jobs and careers, who appeared more concerned about the alleged lack of patriotism of American young people than they were about the bleak future that this "Lost Generation" faced, nor were they able to identify with the lighthearted stereotypical college activities of the 1920s.

Lee Dover felt the need to voice particular concern about some ZBT members' romance with communism and the Soviet Union. "This writer feels that the 'Russian Utopia' has no place in American life nor on the campus," Dover declared in his March 1935 *Quarterly* editorial. "Jewish students would be more logical and philosophical if they would bend their efforts toward preservation of that which their ancestors sought and found in this country, rather than to ally themselves with forces which are directed toward the destruction of these institutions."

A sharp decline in the college football hysteria that had so recently gripped the nation was one symptom of the changing campus mood. Huge stadiums built in times of plenty now stood half-empty, and although the game would always remain important, never again would college football and its players enjoy quite the same exalted position. Whether it was lack of money to buy tickets, lack of spirit to cheer on their teams, or a realization that too much time spent in athletic practice came at the expense of acquiring more marketable skills for the job market, college students in the 1930s could not place the priority on football that they once had. They were more likely to be spending their extracurricular energy either studying harder or debating the merits of various alternative political systems.

The rebellious student mood and the spirit of rejection of college tradition was epitomized after an editorial in the *New York Times* that was especially critical of youthful radicalism prompted a countereditorial on April 27, 1936, entitled "Youth States Its Case," written by H. R. Byers, a student at Harvard University. The editorial followed the much-condemned formation of VFW chapters—for "Veterans of Future Wars"—by undergraduates at elite colleges who wished to ridicule veterans' organizations and to draw attention to their reluctance to be killed for nothing as they believed the World War I generation had been. The open letter was reprinted in the June 1936 *Quarterly* and extensively discussed in ZBT circles and indeed wherever college students gathered.

"I am a member of the so-called 'Lost Generation,' born during the World War and come to maturity during the great depression," Byers began. "I am a member of that generation which indulges in peace strikes . . . and which is able to pronounce the word 'communism' without hissing the last syllable." In contrast, the older generation had produced demagogues like Huey Long and Father Coughlin, World War I veterans who filched money out of the government, and state legislatures that had nothing better to do than pass bills compelling students to salute the flag and teachers to take loyalty oaths—thus setting the stage for "fascism and dictatorship." "I make no apology for our generation, for none is necessary, but I ask you in all sincerity, what is the matter with yours?" the Harvard student demanded. "You have a great deal more to answer for than the relatively trivial offenses cited." Referring to the Daughters of the American Revolution, who had called upon American youth to be more "patriotic," Byers responded with vehemence:

Don't they realize that youth have to be fed first? Do they think because we don't rush around waving flags and shouting "America is the best damn country on earth"; because we have anti-war strikes and form future veteran organizations to mock our elders who have made such a mess of things, that we are any less patriotic than those who trace their ancestry back to the Revolution? Or does it mean that patriotism and thinking do not mix? Our college generation is not that which is typified by the ukulele, the coonskin coat, the Ford covered with slang expressions, though the American Legion from its recent utterances, seems to think so.

He concluded: "I think I speak for my generation when I say that we are sick to death of platitudes and clichés, of flagwaving and heroic attitudes, of 'Red' scares and patriotism that is talked rather than felt, of Father Coughlins and William Randolph Hearsts, of Huey Longs and Dr. Townsends, of soothing talks and accusations, of political parties and political corruption, and all the other paraphernalia which are our unsavory heritage. No, Mr. Editor, it is not ours which is the lost generation. It is yours. We only ask that you don't take us down with you." (p. 6)

The Harvard House Plan and the Antifraternity Movement

Another, not unrelated peril of the parlous 1930s from the viewpoint of ZBT was a decided movement in higher education away from the expansion of fraternities and toward the establishment of various house, residential college, and more luxurious university rooming/boarding options. College officials were coming to fear that fraternities were too snobbish, exclusive, and divisive to be allowed to govern campus life so completely. They were too few in number and their "rushing" system too unwieldy to guarantee adequate care of large and more diverse student populations. Their intellectual, cultural, and academic standards were questionable. Most important, too many men had been fatally injured and the good name of the school disgraced in the seemingly never-ending stream of hazing incidents—a major factor in the steady attempts of state legislatures to wipe fraternities out of existence. Even college administrators who were themselves graduates of fraternities came to believe that it was unsafe to allow undergraduates to govern themselves. It appeared far better for the universities to gain control over this aspect of students' lives. An additional motivation was hope that income gained from room and board fees might accrue directly to the universities rather than to the national fraternities.

Thus, beginning with the nation's oldest and most prestigious universities, no longer would national fraternities (or their local equivalents) in college towns enjoy a virtual monopoly on the comfortable housing and feeding of American college students, while those not fortunate enough to be members were condemned to cheerless boarding-houses. The turning point came in April 1931, when ZBT observers noted with concern that the philanthropist Edward Harkness had just donated several million dollars to Harvard University to fulfill the president's plan of dividing the campus into houses on the English model, rather than allowing social life to be governed by the fraternities and clubs. The transformation of Harvard was quickly followed by the similar establishment of a residential college system at Yale and of an extensive dormitory system at the University of Chicago, financed by contributions by Julius Rosenwald. Fraternities limped on at Chicago, but by 1936 there was a consensus among ZBT leaders that the house system had effectively killed fraternities at Harvard and Yale; ZBT chapters at both of these schools had passed out of existence.

The new mood was summed up well by Dr. Henry Suzallo, president of the Carnegie Foundation for the Advancement of Teaching and in the past a strong supporter of the Greek system, in a frank speech, "Fraternity System Problems," that he delivered to the delegates of the NIC conference in New York City on November 27, 1931. In Europe, as he pointed out, the universities cared very little about the whole life of students as long as they passed their examinations. However, in America the universities and the public cared very much how students lived, and there was in fact no other educational system in the world that was so "finally and completely responsive to public opinion" as the American one. Fraternities could no longer claim that they were independent of the universities, Suzallo declared, and if they did not perform their proper functions within the system, then administrations were bound to either dominate or eliminate them. As fast as money could be acquired, he informed the assembled heads of national college fraternities, the gradual trend to replace fraternity life with residential college life would be accelerated. It was up to the fraternities now to work out a form of response that would allow them to survive in the new campus atmosphere. The sooner they acknowledged the trends, the more intelligently they could deal with the challenge and the less resistance they would encounter.

Business as Usual

Fortunately for Zeta Beta Tau, whatever challenges the fraternity system in general faced at the beginning of the Great Depression, there appeared to be no danger that their own group would become extinct. To a large extent the fraternity continued at first to expand and to prosper, and life went on much as it had before. Although many members were forced to drop out of school or leave the fraternity for lack of funds, others came to take their place. As to the grand tradition of study abroad and world travel, members such as Yale graduate Rollin G. Osterweis '30 were able to spend the summer attending Oxford University in England. "There are still a few who have transatlantic carfare," wrote Lee Dover in June 1931, describing how ZBTs would continue to gather on the most fashionable boulevards of Paris and Berlin. "Although it is reported that many of the transatlantic lines will, this Summer, run fewer vessels than usual between this country and European shores, nevertheless many ZBTs will meet in Montmartre and the Rue de la Paix or in Unter den Linden and the Kurfurstendammstrasse."

Scholarship

High scholarship was one ZBT tradition that did not cease with the Depression. In fact, Lee Dover expressed the belief that it was getting even better. When statistics were compiled for the academic year 1934–35, out of sixty-two member fraternities, Zeta Beta Tau overall ranked third in the country in its grade-point average. Other historically Jewish fraternities with equally impressive rankings were ZBT antecedents Kappa Nu (4th), Phi Sigma Delta (6th), and Phi Epsilon Pi (13th). On the level of individual scholastic achievement, ZBT could count not one but two Rhodes scholars during the decade. The first was James Goodfriend Jr. (Missouri '34), one of thirty-two American college students selected that year; the second, in 1936, was Leslie Alan Epstein of St. Louis, who had formerly been president of his ZBT chapter at the University of Illinois and at the time of the award was in his second year at Washington University's medical school.

Return of the *Quarterly*

By 1938 the worst of the Depression appeared to have lifted, and the *Zeta Beta Tau Quarterly*, which had ceased to publish between 1932 and 1935, had long since begun publishing regularly again. A list of proposed quarterly articles prepared by editor Lee Dover in 1938 indicated that Zeta Beta Tau members could still see the world as filled with choices, opportunities, and avenues to economic success. "Is it possible to be a ten-thousand-dollar-a-year-man anymore?" was a leading topic. Other questions in a similar vein followed, including "Should young men not subsidized by family fortune marry under thirty? What's better, business or a profession? Should college men return to their small communities where they grew up or establish themselves in the big cities? . . . What about the graduate who refuses to work for his 'old man' in the prosaic family business because his mind is fixed on the colorful and exciting life which he believes is provided in motion pictures, advertising, radio, or working for the Standard Oil Company in China, South America, etc.?" and "I want to be alive in the year 2,000—why?" And finally, in a reflection of the men's aspirations someday to end their dating days and settle down with the appropriate partner, "WIFE MATERIAL—Have American girls lost the 'princess' complex which afflicted their sisters during the golden years?"

Aside from such optimistic articles, evocative wedding announcements continued to make their appearance in the *Quarterly*, indicating that by no means all wealthy ZBTs had been wiped out in the Depression. These were at pains to indicate if the bride had attended a well-known "finishing school." At the end of the 1935 academic year, two of particular interest appeared: "Arnold G. Buchsbaum (Pennsylvania) is engaged to Miss Isabelle Hecht of New York City. Miss Hecht is a graduate of the Alquin School of New York City and Les Allières of Lausanne, Switzerland. They will be married this Fall. Arnold Buchsbaum is in the bond business at 25 Broad St. NYC." In the same column, members were informed that "Edward Lasker (Yale '33) formerly of Chicago and now of New York City, and Miss Carol G. Gimbel, daughter of Mr. and Mrs. Bernard F. Gimbel of Port Chester, NY were married on February 2, 1935 at Chieftains, the Port Chester estate of the bride's parents."

Father's Business versus a New Career

The old emotional conflict between fathers who wished their sons to enter the family business and their progeny who dreamed of striking out on their own, intensified during the Great Depression, although with limited economic opportunities probably fewer members were able to follow their dreams. It was for just such occasions that struggling fathers had prepared their sons for these takeovers, in the hope that they would never have to search for jobs or worry about providing for their families.

One ZBT, communicating anonymously, described in the June 1937 *Quarterly* how he was bored to tears after going into his father's business, thus reaching a goal chosen for him on the very day he was born. His college graduation gift had been a "nice big office with a carpet," two telephones, his father's blessing, and the expressed hope that he would succeed his father upon retirement in twenty years' time. Suddenly cast into the role of "crown prince," it was with shock that the son noticed people now called him "Mr." at every opportunity and asked if he had any orders ("The last time I was home on vacation they had all treated me like a kid"), yet he had none to give. All he was able to do was to kill time by writing, as he termed them, "silly letters." There was dissatisfaction with being in the shadow of his father and discomfort at the abundance of leisure time. Yet what else could he do? If he resigned and went to other fields that appeared more attractive, the father while saying and doing nothing, "would have suffered a broken heart." All the patriarch wanted at the end of his life was the knowledge that he had done well by his family, that his son would never have to feel the pinch of poverty or the struggle for life that his parents had passed through, that he would always enjoy a carefully planned and pleasant existence without want.

"Dad thought, no doubt, that he was doing the best thing for me," the son admitted. "*But what he forgot was the joy he experienced in building.* The sweetness of struggle and despair and the joy of light finally crowning his lifelong struggles. I, his son, was being spared that. To me it appeared that I, his son, was being robbed of it." For this ZBT member the solution had been to remain in his father's business but to soar beyond familial bounds by learning how to fly a plane. The father could never approve of such a hobby nor understand why his son wanted to do it, yet out of love for his progeny he would not prevent it. "Now, after a day at the store, I take the last hour of the day off and use the clouds as brooms to sweep the cobwebs away," the son concluded. "Dad, in giving me freedom, had allowed me to learn to live in other worlds than his. I like those of my own making better."

On to Texas and Washington, D.C.

By no means all ZBTs had the luxury of making such a choice; the majority were left scrambling on their own to make a living and explore new vocational options in a changing world. Willingness to resettle far away from one's home and to bring goods and services to relatively remote areas was one way ensure at least a modicum of financial success. ZBT's El Paso Alumni Club, formed early in the decade, was made up of such men who were willing to travel far in search of opportunity. One was a lawyer in private practice and the other, a Harvard graduate, was in his father's business. All other members were engaged in businesses that had probably been built from scratch. The head of the club was a graduate of Syracuse who was now a town grocer; two ZBTs from Penn were partners in a dry goods company, while a third Penn ZBT served as head of their advertising department. In Juarez, Mexico, just across the border, ZBTs from Penn, USC, and MIT, as well as from the Universities of Texas and Arizona, ran or managed stores, wholesale businesses, and cereal mills.

Another employment option for bright, ambitious college graduates, especially those equipped with law degrees or social work experience, was to head for Washington, D.C., and become a "New Dealer." Whether FDR's reforms were ultimately in the best interest of the country was yet in doubt in some quarters, but there was no doubt, as alumni columnist Jack Wagenheim put it in the June 1936 *Quarterly*, that the New Deal had been "a God-send for the American post-collegiate." The same social services that had been developed to cope with the problems of victims of the Depression were also providing thousands of new jobs for qualified workers, including, he noted, graduates who in years past might have headed for Wall Street or for jobs as corporate junior executives. In the spring of 1936 he counted no fewer than eleven New Dealers in Washington, with assurances that there must be many more. Leading the list was Harold Riegelman, who had been appointed special counsel to the Treasury Department in relation to the government's program on housing and mortgage finance. Other ZBTs were employed with numerous "alphabet soup" agencies, including the RFC, NRA, WPA, and SEC. One each worked in the Departments of Justice and Treasury, while two others worked as journalists.

Overall, Wagenheim found that nearly 100,000 college-trained men and women from every state in the Union were now in Washington, including former team captains, campus editors, Phi Beta Kappas, and indeed "the majority of campus leaders of the past ten years." Their housing was poor, consisting mostly of boardinghouses, and their work days were long, averaging from ten to twenty hours a day in some departments. Nevertheless, they felt "more like crusaders than wage slaves," and in any event, a lively social and educational life had sprung up to meet their needs in what had become for the first time a truly national city. The departments had developed welfare associations that maintained athletic teams, bowling leagues, bridge leagues, regular dances, and lectures—the very activities that a student might expect from a college union. According to Wagenheim, "The brand of basketball played in the Government League compares favorably with most collegiate competition"; one New Deal team could boast no fewer than five former varsity captains in its lineup.

In addition to carrying on with college-level sports and activities, a significant number of New Dealers appeared interested in furthering their education; the enrollment of George Washington University doubled between 1933 and 1936, and 90 percent of the student body was made up of government workers taking night courses. Wagenheim reflected on the implications this phenomenon had for predicting the character of the nation's future course. Though the New Dealers might leave someday and become business leaders, their Washington experiences would leave them forever changed; they would "definitely be more conscious of a social obligation than is the present generation of industrial leaders."

Expansion and Anniversaries

To the surprise of Lee Dover and the other officers, despite the economic crisis, applications to the fraternity were actually going *up*; in the 1930–31 academic year more men had been initiated into ZBT than in any other period of the fraternity's history. Indeed, across the board, a report commissioned by President Herbert Hoover found that two hundred American colleges and universities showed an increase in attendance. Why? Many who had means but formerly would have dropped out of college, ZBT's general secretary theorized, were staying in school, applying themselves harder to their studies, and even going on to graduate work. By doing so, members could both put off going out into a difficult job market and also gain the extra education and skills that might eventually put them ahead of the competition. Accordingly, ZBT's National Rushing Program was proceeding apace, and the addition of two new chapters—the University of Texas at Austin and Franklin and Marshall College in Lancaster, Pennsylvania—brought the chapter roll to thirty-four, with a charter granted to a new colony at the University of British Columbia in Vancouver.

The installation ball for Texas, held in 1931 at the Stephen F. Austin Hotel, was an especially grand event, as reported in the *Quarterly*. Two hundred guests from all over the state gathered for the occasion, which began at nine and ended with a midnight supper; there were several "grand marches and cotillions" during the evening, and all ladies present received party favors bearing the ZBT crest. Calls were also made for the establishment of a statewide association of ZBT graduate clubs. The organizers noted that there was cause for even more than the usual joy at the Austin installation. For many years, there had been no fraternity focus for the significant body of ZBT alumni who either originated in Texas and had gone to school elsewhere or who had moved there from other parts of the country in search of opportunity after their graduation. Now they were hopeful that those alumni who wished to be active in fraternity circles would have a chapter where they could apply their "ZBT love and interest."

Throughout the decade, other chapters were either installed or were able to celebrate significant anniversaries. In February 1936, a new chapter was installed at Miami University in Oxford, Ohio, and the photographs distributed pictured twenty-four young men, all in identical black tie, at a sumptuously laid banquet table. In 1936 the ZBT chapter at Ohio State (Nu) celebrated its silver anniversary, also with an appropriately sumptuous banquet and praises to the alumni who had helped to make the chapter flourish. A rhymed poem and toast presented by Robert E. Segal (Ohio State '25) and published in the March 1936 *Quarterly*, illustrated, incidentally, the group's Classical Reform Jewish orientation and the tendency during the Depression years for

Installation team at Miami University in Oxford, Ohio, February 22, 1936, prepared to welcome a new chapter into the national fraternity. Lee Dover stands center, holding their charter. "Charters are not mailed special delivery by the Supreme Council on wire requests," he once said, defending their arduous admission process. "The Fraternity permits only those young men who demonstrate that they can 'make the team' to establish its new chapters." Front row, left to right: Alex L. Siegel '26, president Cleveland Alumni Club; Dover; Thomas J. Reis '32; Walton H. Bachrach '17. Back row: Morris Effron '24, president Cincinnati Alumni Club; Charles F. Luft '31, president Columbus Alumni Club; Jac S. Geller '36, president of Western Reserve chapter; Robert S. Schwachter '37, president of Ohio State chapter; and Samuel D. Luchs '26, national fraternity historian.

wealthy non-German Jewish men to fight their way into the fraternity (the term "Litvok" refers to eastern European Jews from Lithuania, among the first non-German Jewish groups to reach any level of social respectability in such circles):

> Late Monday and the chapter is in session down below,
> The Litvoks fight the Germans; they can give 'em blow for blow.
> The kid that came from Cleveland is one that's hard to beat;

But golly me, he's blackballed; the reason is his street.
We ought to go to Temple more; we're slipping bad, by gosh.
Well Sunday next we'll send 'em half a dozen frosh. . . .
These are our college days, my lads, the days of ZBT
Days into weeks; weeks into years; and still blessed memory rolls.
The days at Nu, the days at State, the days that warm our souls.

(p. 44)

Conventions, as usual, remained the capstone of the fraternal year. The one in St. Louis, which ended on New Year's Day barely a year after the crash, was still deemed an unusually good "financial and fraternal success." Officers elected included Supreme Nasi Judge William S. Evans (CCNY '06), for his third term; Supreme Vice Nasi Rollin G. Osterweis (Yale '30; in 1943 he would be appointed an instructor in Yale's history department, becoming in 1968 a full professor in history and oratory); Supreme Gisbar (Treasurer) Herbert E. Steiner (Penn '14); Supreme Sofar (Secretary) Judge Benjamin J. Scheinman (Michigan '19); and Supreme Historian Jack I. Wagenheim. The fraternity now numbered more than four thousand alumni and an ever-growing number of alumni clubs, five of which had been chartered in the previous year: the Memphis Club, the Dixie Club of New York, the Little Rock Club, the Indiana Club of Indianapolis, the Capitol District Club of Albany-Schenectady, New York. In addition, the old Metropolitan Club of New York City had been successfully revived.

In the ever-important area of extracurricular activities, ZBT in 1931 proudly counted no fewer than thirteen varsity team captains and nineteen varsity football players in its ranks (although, regrettably, only seven members overall had made Phi Beta Kappa that year); the group included three captaincies in track and field and two college record holders (Lionel Weil of North Carolina in the 440-meter run and Myron Cohn of Union in the high jump). Members thrilled to the achievements of three promising football sophomores: Nat Grossman of NYU, Aaron Rosenberg of USC, and Sidney Gilman of Ohio State, all of whom appeared likely to make All-American before the close of their collegiate careers. As for student government, ZBT boasted fifteen class officers across the country, and the Supreme Historian noted, "Publications and dramatics continue to be controlled by ZBT's in nearly every college where we are represented."

The geographical expansion of the fraternity and the process of what might be called its "de-Newyorkization" were also proceeding apace.

ZBT was an increasingly national and even international fraternity, according to statistics compiled for its January 1932 directory. By that year, less than one quarter of the fraternity's 4,452 living members resided in New York City. Many had not been born or raised in New York but had migrated there after college graduation in search of the excitement and employment opportunities the city could offer. Other top-ranking cities for ZBT membership were Chicago, Cleveland, Los Angeles, New Orleans, Boston, San Francisco, Montreal, St. Louis, and Philadelphia. The Los Angeles contingent was growing the fastest of all; on Old Timers' Day, May 9, 1936, more than one hundred members turned out for a celebration at the Victor Hugo Cafe, the regular meeting place of the Southern California Alumni Club.

Not all ZBTs were limited to large cities, General Secretary Lee Dover pointed out with pride. Their members now resided in 47 states of the Union and in 530 cities, towns, and hamlets from the Atlantic to the Pacific coast and from the Canadian to the Mexican border, and everywhere they settled new alumni clubs were formed. ZBTs also were living abroad in Canada, British Honduras, Jamaica, China, Cuba, England, France, Mexico, Ecuador, and Palestine.

Fiscal Policy and Alumni Support

The relative stability of ZBT compared to other fraternities was in no small part due to the officers' foresight in establishing the NPEF (National Permanent Endowment Fund) on the eve of the worst years of the Great Depression. Every new initiated member and all alumni in good standing were required to contribute to the fund, which was also swelled by voluntary contributions. Between 1933 and 1937, the fund grew to $76,000.

ZBT's financial stability was also due to the consistent fiscal policy laid down by Lee Dover and the fraternity's treasurers. Other fraternities might cut or eliminate certain customary fees and take up local alumni collections to initiate poor but deserving pledges; other fraternities could admit men with shaky finances who might be forced to leave within two years. However, ZBT's Supreme Council, after brief debate in the fall of 1930, declared that despite criticism of high fees—especially the mandatory contribution to the NPEF—under no circumstances would *any* of them be waived nor any man initiated if a background investigation revealed that he was unable to give the fraternity four years of his full financial and moral support. Chapters were run on a share-and-share-alike basis, and anyone who could not contribute his share jeopardized the welfare of the entire group. If the man and his family were unable to afford the initiation fees, then he could not afford to become a member of Zeta Beta Tau. For those already members, financial delinquency for any reason had to mean expulsion from the fraternity.

Numerous ZBTs were thus forced to leave the fold, but the financial structure of the fraternity remained sound. At the thirty-ninth anniversary convention in 1937 at the Mayflower Hotel in Washington, D.C. (called "Reunion on the Potomac: A Capital Convention"), it was announced to the assembled crowd of almost five hundred that the NPEF had grown to over $100,000 and was increasing at the rate of $10,000 a year. That spring the University of Pennsylvania celebrated its thirtieth anniversary in a luxurious new home that the NPEF had helped to make possible; through a combination of NPEF and private donations from family and alumni, the fraternity had been able to invest close to a quarter of a million dollars to build it.

The year 1938 also marked ZBT's fortieth anniversary. According to the Bible, one officer wrote, forty years was one generation and also represented "a ripe age when a father and son can wear the same insignia through active membership"; hence, the choice of the 1938 convention motto: "A Generation of ZBT: Life Begins at 40!" There was no apparent letup in the numbers of alumni sons who wished to join the fraternity. Alumni ZBTs were so eager to serve the organization, even in a completely voluntary capacity, that the standing committees did not have room for them all. This led, in 1938, toward a move to require a completely new slate of officers on a regular basis in order to give everyone a chance to do his share. "We are confronted with the fact that there is available an annually increasing number of capable men who are eager to render service to the fraternity," the chairman of the nominating committee explained in advocating the change and insisting that it should in no way be construed as a reflection on the ability of the men who had served the previous year. "How to give them this recognition is a pressing problem. . . . We had to face a difficult problem and solve it the best we could." Nowhere in the related correspondence was there a hint of acknowledgment or pride that having too many alumni who wished to do service was not a problem that most other fraternities in those days would have been unhappy to have.

Conventions, Social Life, and Matchmaking

Zeta Beta Tau's glittering social life and the unending matchmaking associated with it, continued almost unabated even after the crash (some members took to referring to events as "B.C.," for "before crash," and A.C., for "after crash"). Such activities included active members, alumni, and extended friends and family. The New England Graduate Club, in sending out invitations to a 1931 summer weekend of fishing and boating on Cape Cod, attempted to make light of the worsening economic situation. "No marginal calls in the morning," the invitation read. "Don't forget—When better times are had, ZBTs will have them." On a Friday the thirteenth in April, the University of Missouri held a "Bad Luck Formal," making reference to both the date and the state of many of their families' businesses.

For the majority of members able to remain in college, "spring fever" took its toll; campus romances reportedly bloomed that year, with long waiting lines after dinner to use the house's telephone. Those who managed to graduate without being infected found themselves the object of attention of prospective matchmakers who wished to overcome the men's shyness in seeking mates or to otherwise help things along. One matron did not hesitate to write to Irvin Fane, ZBT's Midwest regional director, to request identification of all the young, unmarried members of the local Zeta Beta Tau Alumni Club in Kansas City; Fane promptly sent her back a list of sixteen names and addresses.

Members also frankly depended on the national fraternity for aid in meeting their romantic goals. A 1935 humorous feature by the ubiquitous A. D. Swartz, appearing in the fraternity's quarterly and titled "A Day at the Central Office" (in New York City), described affairs of the heart as occupying a good deal of General Secretary Dover's time, including the search for a judge to marry a couple who turned up at his door, answers to telephone requests from members who were spending the weekend in New York and wanted the names and phone numbers of women whom they could call for dates, and a decision on what to do about a member who every few days kept calling in, canceling, and then reinstating his engagement announcement to appear in the *Zeta Beta Tau Quarterly*. Similar difficulties would eventually lead ZBT and other fraternity magazines to the policy of printing only announcements of completed wedding ceremonies.

For reporter A. D. Swartz, the observed day allegedly began with opening the mail with a chuckle when one member requested Balfour, the fraternity's official jeweler, to send anklets to four different girls, all inscribed "With love to the only girl I love—Oscar." Other letters were from lapsed members or "old timers, ancient-vintage" deciding to "re-establish themselves in the good graces of ZBT after all these years"— the reason inevitably being, as Dover commented, a young marriage-able daughter or a son coming up for membership in some chapter. "Eventually," Dover remarked, "every ZBT man comes back."

The game of what might be called rating, dating, and mating was ev-ident in the collaboration between Jewish fraternities and sororities, particularly those occupying approximately the same rung on the social ladder. Wherever the Jewish fraternities went, chapters of appropriate Jewish sororities were sure to follow. Such was the case at the Univer-sity of Alabama in 1935, where Zeta Beta Tau had found no satisfaction in its complete acceptance by the "gentile social set" on campus, nor were its members willing to date women belonging to what they con-sidered to be a lower-tier Jewish sorority. Members longed for a more congenial group of women to come to campus, and it was for that rea-son that they personally invited Alpha Epsilon Phi president Elizabeth Eldridge to visit them in Tuscaloosa. It was in the Zeta Beta Tau chapter house that she held her meetings and discussed her plans, and the mem-bers cooperated so far as to give her a list of the young women they would like to see attending Alabama. "This list caused amusement in New Orleans" (the sorority's national headquarters), Eldridge later re-ported to her fellow officers, "for it read like a dance list or a house party or a debutante gathering. The Zebes know cute girls, if nothing else. . . . They will rush for us during the summer and when they make a rushing tour of the state for their own fall rushing, they will interview girls for us, persuading them to come to Alabama. They will guarantee the chap-ter that does transfer the best time any girls have ever had at Alabama."

Many ZBT chapter traditions, as collected and published by Lee Dover in 1937, in his *Manual on Chapter Administration*, revolved around social situations or events. For example, at Michigan and Ohio State, any undergraduate who announced that he was either engaged or "going steady" was "tubbed," or given a shower fully clothed (on occa-sion, "tubbing" could be done on a victim's birthday). Whenever a brother "pinned" a campus girl, it was customary for the entire chapter to go that evening to the beloved's dormitory or sorority house and serenade her. The University of Washington chapter made it a point to have regular exchange dinners and luncheons with other fraternities and sororities, whether Jewish or non-Jewish. The University of Southern California chapter stuck to a number of traditional annual affairs, including spring and fall house parties, swimming parties, sail boat regattas, horseback riding parties, and picnics. At the Cornell chapter, custom held that at house parties the first girl to arrive and the last one to leave was obligated to kiss every one of her hosts. At the University of Pennsylvania and several other chapters, an annual Ivy Ball Weekend was held. The house was turned over to female guests, and from five to eight o'clock in the morning following the Ivy Ball the chapter held a festive dance and breakfast for those who were still awake.

ZBT's social life continued to glitter with special brightness at convention time despite the Depression. The December 1930 convention in St. Louis included a formal supper dance, a luncheon party at the Anheuser-Busch Brewery, a dance at the Criterion Club, a formal fraternity banquet at the Coronado Hotel, and the annual formal New Year's Eve Ball at the Hotel Statler. In 1931 expectant convention-goers looked to Boston, where arrangements chairman "Wally" Walenstein reported receiving an encouraging letter from an organization calling itself Massachusetts Mothers of Marriageable Daughters. It read in part: "We are overjoyed at having the ZBT Convention once more in Boston [the last had been in 1916]. As the saying goes, we shall fatten the calf in preparation for the most stupendous stampede of eligibles since the days of 1916. Our contention is that Boston beauties cannot be rivaled . . . and not from a cultural standpoint only . . . their aim shall be to please."

The fraternity's copywriters, no doubt well trained in the art of advertising, bombarded members with convention rhetoric designed to break down the inevitable resistance at undertaking such a relatively expensive trip during a lean year. "Boston Massacre of Bad Times!" proclaimed the full-page convention ad mailed to members. They should not listen to the many wives who said, "'No convention this year, grow old along with me." "Offer the perfect alibi—carefully crossing your fingers—tell her it's the appeal of Boston's historical sights! Cultural atmosphere! Yankee Hospitality! Baked beans! That's luring you on—Make a B-Line for Boston, 33rd National ZBT Convention, Dec. 28, 29, 31—1931."

"What a treat is in store for the imaginative mind!" extolled another piece of Boston preconvention literature, which implied that the

Founding Fathers of the nation, who were so identified with the city of Boston, had nothing over a ZBT. "Wending your way down aristocratic Beacon Hill where the Cabots speak only to the Lowells and the Lowells speak only to God. Poke about the Old Burial Grounds, where lie the remains of a Paine, an Adams, a Hancock, and other ZBT's too numerous to mention." For the 1938 convention, the selling point was not cultural sights or ancestral prestige but the illustrious alumni that attendees could hope to encounter. "Meet the boys you've heard about," exhorted that ad for that year, "the famous tackle from '08, the editor of the annual of '19, the brother who roamed the second floor of the AEPhi house in '29!"

The years 1932 and 1933 had been lean ones for the fraternity, with the scale of convention entertainment noticeably reduced and the advertising rhetoric proclaimed only halfheartedly. However, it picked up again for the 1934 event in Kansas City, whose motto was "Kitty's Younger Sister Wants to Meet You, Mister!" Chapter members at the University of Missouri were urged to "recommend at least one or two local girls" as dates for visiting fraters. At the opening tea dance on Friday afternoon, members would be responsible for escorting their female guests to the function and seeing that every ZBT from out of town who wanted one had a date before leaving. Despite the elaborate social arrangements available to them, there were always some ZBTs who did not request them; they were coming, as the ads went, "Stag or Drag"—either alone, or "dragging" their wives along.

The 1936 convention in New Orleans, at which Cajun cooking and jazz music figured prominently, was billed as "Ze Best Time of Your Life" (an earlier slogan, which Lee Dover did not permit in the *Quarterly* more than once, was "A Perfect '36 in New Orleans!"). The festivities included seven dances, including the New Year's Eve Ball; a day at the races (Fairgrounds); and the attendance of the entire convention at the Sugar Bowl football game—in that year, Louisiana State University versus Santa Clara. The directors of the Washington, D.C., convention the following year also scheduled elaborate events, while they consciously strove to imbue the proceedings with the dignity appropriate to the nation's capital. Members were invited to return the following year to New York City, the birthplace of ZBT, to celebrate the occasion of its fortieth birthday.

Of all the conventions of the 1930s, that in December 1938, held at the Waldorf Astoria, was perhaps its grandest, its most joyful, and at the same time its most solemn. The record number of members in convention assembled that year had more than the usual reason to be grateful for the abundance around them and for the safety and stability of their fraternity. Only seven weeks earlier, on November 9–10, the murderous "Crystal Night" of Nazi Germany had shown with dreadful clarity the intentions that nation, the ancestral land of many ZBT families, had toward the Jews who still remained there.

Swing Music

Mixed dancing played a leading role at conventions and most social affairs, and with the advance of "swing" in the 1930s the music was getting ever livelier and more exuberant. "Swing music is one HOT potato that Americans, generally, and undergraduates, in particular, aren't letting go of," noted Mortimer W. Cohen in a March 1938 *Quarterly* article entitled "Beat It Out," which traced the history of the music from New Orleans in 1915, up the river to Chicago, and then out to New York City. "Like sex, swing is here to stay, and you can't do anything about it." In describing the music's background, Cohen also took the opportunity to initiate his readers into swing's accompanying slang language, which was making significant inroads on the American popular vernacular.

"Cats" was the basic term for swing musicians, and their own term for the music they played was "jive." Other terms players used for themselves included "brass-blasters, jive-artists, silver suckers, spooks, jigs, and pops." The language developed from there: "When the 'cats' are 'licking their chops' and 'frisking their whiskers' they are warming up to 'get hot, feel their stuff, get in the groove, go to town, or go out of the world,'" readers were told. "Musicians who are dead from the lips out are 'corn on the cob' or 'strictly union.' 'Icky' is Guy Lombardo. Non-improvisers are 'long-haired boys.' Sweet bands are 'long-underwear' gangs and their music is 'commercial, compromise, or schmaltz.'" Instruments had new names as well. A "cat" who watched the "suitcase" was not a porter but a drummer. A clarinet could be known variously as the "agony-pipe, wopstick, or licorice stick," while a trombone was termed "syringe, slip horn or push-pipe.'" The trumpet was referred to as "the plumbing," and a "gobble-pipe" meant a saxophone.

The identifiable dance steps available to convention-goers by the 1930s had also passed far beyond the waltz and the sedate fox-trot. Now those who were sufficiently athletic could indulge in "truckin,'" "shim-sham," the "Suzi-Q," the "shag," or "peckin' and posin'." Callers for steps in the group folk-dance tradition could proclaim "swing it. . . . Throw it down, son, throw it down. . . . Gather steam, brother, lay it on for the night, it's 'truck to the right—and truck to the left—and then double truck.'. . . Wham ditty, what a party, truck it low, boy, but truck it hot! . . . Esther, the Sal Hepatica!" (a patent medicine for stomach upset). "Now its 'walkin' in a circle.'. . . Then it's 'under the bridge and over the bridge.'. . . Now Suzi-Q—yea man, Suzi-Q all over! . . . Now it's shag brother, shag . . ."

Alumni and Awards

Throughout the decade, ZBTs took pride and a vicarious joy in the continuing achievements of its alumni and honorary members. The October 1930 *Quarterly* alumni columns carried to them the news that alumnus Judge Isidore Bookstein (Union College '12), had received the Republican Party's nomination for attorney general of the state of New York; also in New York public affairs, Herbert Lehman, who had been the lieutenant governor of New York when he was awarded the Gottheil Medal in 1931, moved up to be full governor of the state. ZBTs in the 1930s were also proud to claim Governor Henry Horner of Illinois, an alumnus of Champaign-Urbana who helped bring New Deal reforms to his state and who was reelected by a landslide in November 1936. When he died four years later, members recalled how he had frequently visited their chapter houses in Illinois and elsewhere and the honor they had felt in extending to him their hospitality.

Achievement also came in the world of entertainment, business, the arts, and the sciences. Other ZBT alumni of note in this period in various fields included David H. Dietz (Western Reserve '19), science editor for the Scripps-Howard newspapers and winner of a 1937 Pulitzer Prize; H. Stanley Marcus (Harvard '25), a native of Dallas who had entered the family business (the Neiman-Marcus Company) a year out of college and who had become a leading figure in Dallas civic and Jewish life; Louis G. Cowan (University of Chicago '31), who through the decade steadily advanced in the radio and advertising fields and during that time originated the well-known radio show *The Quiz Kids*. Other well-known ZBTs included William S. Paley (Penn '22), a member who had been president of his ZBT chapter and whose advances in the world of radio were increasingly coming to the world's attention. For

Herbert H. Lehman, then Lt. Governor of New York, receives the sixth annual Gottheil Medal at the "key" affair of "Old Timers' Day," in New York City on May 9, 1931. The fraternity's highest award, from 1925 on the Gottheil Medal was presented to the person who, in the opinion of a jury of editors from the Anglo-Jewish press, had done the most for Jewry the previous year. Lehman became governor in 1933. From left to right: Richard J. H. Gottheil, ZBT founder; Harold Riegelman, past president (Cornell '14); Lehman; and national ZBT president Herbert E. Steiner (Penn '14).

his fraternity brothers the peak of pride and identification came when a picture of the young and smiling Paley, as president and principal owner of the Columbia Broadcasting System, was featured on the cover of the September 19, 1938, issue of *Time*. Also counted by ZBTs as one of their own during those years was Dr. Abraham A. Brill, psychiatrist, psychoanalyst, and translator from the German of the works of Sigmund Freud. Brill (NYU '01, Columbia '03) had been a

*Broadcast pioneer and CBS president William S. Paley
(Penn '22), former president of his chapter, on the cover
of* Time *magazine in October 1938. That same month,
heralded as one of the greatest college football players of
all time, Sid Luckman (Columbia '39) appeared on the
cover of* Life *magazine; he eventually went on to play
with the Chicago Bears.*

member of the original ZBT society as a student and had left it behind
upon his graduation. However, he returned to the fold of the fraternity
in 1939 when, at the Old Timers' Day affair in New York City, the fraternity honored with its highest award for alumni achievement.

ZBTs were particularly well represented in the entertainment industry. A survey of the movie business in 1937 found more than twenty in
major positions, including Aaron Rosenberg (USC '33), former All-
America footballer and now first assistant director at Twentieth Century–Fox; Henry Berman (USC '34), an executive at RKO Pictures;
Robert Wasserman (Nebraska '34) at Columbia Pictures; and David
Weisbart and Oscar Hart (both USC '36) at Warner Brothers Studios.

The last was headed by Jack L. Warner, who had been initiated as an honorary member of ZBT soon after his son, Jack Warner Jr. (USC '38), had become an active member.

In the 1930s two of ZBT's most illustrious alumni held positions on the Supreme Court of the United States. Justice Benjamin N. Cardozo (1870–1938), descendant of a Spanish-Portuguese Jewish family that traced its ancestry to the American Revolution, was appointed to the bench in 1931 by President Herbert Hoover. Although the fraternity did not exist in his student days, he had been initiated into it as an active member in the early 1900s and had remained close to it throughout his life. Soon after he passed away in July 1938 (the *Quarterly* suggested that his black-bordered portrait be displayed in all the fraternity's houses), the position was filled by another ZBT Society alumnus—Felix Frankfurter (City College '02), a professor of law at Harvard. Not only was it a case, as observers noted, of one ZBT succeeding another; Justice Cardozo, while sitting in a lower court, had by coincidence performed the marriage ceremony for Mr. and Mrs. Frankfurter.

Legacies: ZBT as Family Affair

The matchmaking activity of ZBT went hand in hand with extensive and notable family involvement. Lee Dover's observation and warning to active members was to remember what a "closely integrated social group" they belonged to. To a greater degree than was imagined by the outside world, he wrote, "the relationship between the brothers of Zeta Beta Tau is similar to that which exists between blood brothers and endures for a lifetime. Through the years this relationship is extended to ZBT families." It was essential, therefore, that no man ever be initiated into the fraternity who did not have a capacity for friendship and fellowship and who would not be acceptable as a guest in the home of other members.

Indeed, though ZBT was officially a single-sex organization, its bonds continued to encompass not only the individual members and their business associations but their entire families—mothers, fathers, sisters, brothers, cousins, sons, grandsons, nieces, nephews, and other relatives. Sons of ZBTs were rushed years before they entered college, some receiving pledge pins as soon as they were born, and it was customary in some chapters to hold regular dinners for the female relatives of members, especially those attending the same college. These remained the obvious first choice for dating and marriage partners. "Would you want your sister to marry him?" was in ZBT, as in most college fraternities, a key question to be asked when deciding whether or not to pledge an applicant. Daughters were always potential partners, as one *Quarterly* birth announcement in 1931 indicated: "House Party Date: Mr. and Mrs. Milton S. Malakoff of New York City announce the arrival of Marion Sue Malakoff, a future candidate for all good house parties up State."

The alumni columns and announcements section of the *Zeta Beta Tau Quarterly*, the equivalent of the fraternity's "society pages," could be perused as eagerly by the women in members' lives as by the members themselves. In 1937 one ZBT wife wrote to the journal, infuriated that neither her husband's marriage to her, nor the birth of their daughter, nor her husband's appointment to a prestigious legal position had been reported in the *Quarterly*. The alumni editor replied to her in an open letter in the March issue: "Special Note to ZBT Wives and Sweethearts—If that 'dope' you like (or love) won't send in notices of engagements, marriages, births, jobs, or honors to this magazine, send a scented letter with your ZBT news to 'Uncle' Jack Wagenheim c/o this magazine."

At some individual chapters, Mothers', Fathers', and Parents' Clubs provided opportunities for socializing with congenial adults at monthly meetings. In addition, they could serve as an important source of financial and material support, backing chapter house construction and renovations and providing much of the furnishings and interior decorations. In the case of the University of Missouri chapter, Nat Milgram, president of the Parents' Club of ZBT in the fall of 1938, was able to persuade sixteen fathers of members to pledge at least $200 to help build a new house there. Others donated from $500 to $2,000. Meanwhile wives and mothers in Kansas City devised other ways of raising money, including selling tickets to special dinner parties. Their efforts paid off eight months later when they were all invited to a cornerstone laying and house party on May 14, 1939. The invitation was headed: "Mother's Day: A Dream Come True for Me and You; A Real Home for Our Son."

The Rise of Nazism

If financial difficulties had been the only challenge that Zeta Beta Tau faced during this period, then observers might conclude that the fraternity had gotten through well. In the 1930s, however, the world economic depression was not the only challenge they faced. Not even the richest or most indulgent of families could protect their offspring from persistent anti-Semitism, the specter of Nazism rising in Germany, news of the most blatant Judeophobia in eastern Europe, and the shadow of an approaching war.

When Adolf Hitler ascended to the chancellorship of Germany on January 30, 1933, even Jews living in the relatively free land of the United States trembled. Nazi party activity and anti-Jewish propaganda were not unknown in their own country, nor had the quotas and vocational barriers against Jews ever disappeared. There could be no absolute certainty that these phenomena would not increase. For ZBT the 1930s marked the end of using the noble Hebrew title "Nasi" (pronounced NOH-si); neither the Americans nor the German refugee students who found haven in the fraternity's houses could bear to call their leaders by a name that sounded so close to that of their greatest enemy.

No matter how wealthy, well-mannered, or professionally successful ZBTs may have been, each one knew that his ancestral background made him a potential target. Therefore, the pressure always to be on one's best behavior, to keep one's head low, and to disassociate oneself from Jews who did not meet ZBT's social standards grew stronger. Anxiety, fear, and uncertainty among ZBT members was an inevitable result of these growing tensions. The fear was more than justified, for not only would American anti-Semitism reach new heights in the late 1930s and early 1940s, but shortly afterward the fraternity's members would be called upon to risk their lives in the century's second cataclysmic world war.

CHAPTER FIVE

"TROUBLES NIGH"

Zeta Beta Tau on the Eve of World War II

Jewish fraternity leaders of the 1930s had cause for concern and dampened enthusiasm. The challenges of quotas, restrictions, daily ostracism and harassment, nonrecognition of their organizations, job discrimination, and the actions of scholars who hoped to legitimize hatred through eugenics and various racial theories remained from the previous decade and intensified under new economic and political pressures. The effects of the Great Depression were not limited to the United States; most of the world, especially the German nation, was affected just as badly or worse. Forever after the historians would debate the greater or lesser role that economic factors played in the rise of the National Socialist state in Germany and the misery it subsequently ushered into the entire world. Yet even in the earliest part of the decade mature ZBTs were familiar with an ancient pattern: "bad times" anywhere were by definition not good for anyone, but they were almost inevitably a disaster for Jews.

As the familiar collegiate anti-Semitic pattern remained, so too did the traditional ZBT responses to it. As in the 1920s, a mélange of self-blame, internalization, "pro-Semitism," the "best behavior" syndrome, and contradictory calls for greater or lesser assertions of Jewish identity came forth from the fraternity's leaders and writers. At this point, however, there was a distinct change in the tone of their rhetoric. That of the 1920s had been tinged with a certain optimism, a sense that the ultimate redemption and happiness of all American Jews could be achieved through growing prosperity and the passage of time. By the 1930s, redemption was no longer the primary goal; damage control had replaced it. It was all to the good if faultless behavior and constant proof of one's patriotism helped to maintain one's self-respect and ultimately improved the lot of all Jews. However, in the eyes of many alumni the immediate responsibility of a ZBT member was to make sure that things did not get any worse than they already were.

Among the most deadly innovations of modern nineteenth- and twentieth-century anti-Semitism was its increasing emphasis on the concept of Jews as a "race." Ancient and medieval Jew hatred at least had allowed a theoretical escape through religious conversion. However, if Jews were truly a hereditary racial group, then their religious beliefs and practices made no difference. Many American Jews and ZBT members in the 1920s and 1930s, particularly those for whom religious observance was not a focus of their lives, internalized the concept and used the term freely even among themselves. "You must keep actively in mind the fact that your obligation to Zeta Beta Tau is not at all religious, but racial," warned Tulane graduate Morris D. Meyer in his address to the otherwise festive University of Texas chapter installation ceremony in June 1931, reprinted in that month's issue of the *Quarterly*. In his view the observance of Jewish laws and precepts was not the new members' responsibility; instead, the Texas chapter would do its duty by strict adherence to conventional campus standards of achievement and behavior:

There is no place in Zeta Beta Tau for religion, as such, and it is not anticipated that religion in its more general concept shall enter into any of your deliberations. . . . Your obligation . . . is primarily to uphold the racial standards that have been established by your ancestors and progenitors in years gone by, the benefits from whose accomplishments are still being enjoyed and glorified in you. The history of your race is an open book, upon whose pages are printed in gold, events and accomplishments which have been a blessing for humanity at large. . . . Whereas it may not be your fortunate lot to add to the glory and honor and distinction that has been acquired by your fraternity in the past, you may at least contribute materially to your fraternity's welfare and to your university and to your country by doing nothing that may reflect unfavorably thereon. (p. 5)

Keeping Low

Since a central concept of Nazism was that "International Jewry" allied with Bolshevism was attempting to dominate the world, the pressure to keep one's head low, not be seen as part of a group, to keep one's good citizenship above reproach, and above all to avoid drawing any attention to the Jews as a people became intense. The year 1935 was the second time that ZBT did not award its cherished Gottheil Medal to the person who had done the most for Jews and Judaism in the previous year. In the first case the lapse had been due to a temporary shortage of funds, which prevented holding a proper celebration, and was the result of an internal decision by ZBT's Supreme Council. In the second case the award could not be given because too many members of the Anglo-Jewish editorial board refused to vote "on the grounds that it would not serve the best interests of the Jewish community to make the award in these trying times."

When Felix Frankfurter was appointed to the U.S. Supreme Court in 1939, Harold Riegelman felt compelled to speak out sharply against Jews and fellow members who had cringed and protested that no good would come to them from a Jew who made himself so conspicuous. Frankfurter should neither accept nor be given the appointment, they believed, because this would only intensify charges that Roosevelt's New Deal was actually the "Jew Deal" and that, as Nazi propaganda would have it, Jews were seeking to control the world by dominating FDR's administration. If anyone truly believed this, Riegelman declared at their fortieth anniversary convention in 1938, the premises of anti-Semitism were being embraced by the very people it sought to destroy. "Is it bad business in these unsettled times for a Jew to make himself conspicuous by serving his government?" he demanded of the fraternity's members. "Is it not worse business in these or any times for a Jew to refuse a service which any government has a right to expect of every citizen?"

The new atmosphere of caution also caused adult attitudes toward student involvement in radical causes to become less forgiving and indulgent than they previously might have been. One of the pretexts of the Nazis in Germany for persecuting Jews, warned Philip Spira (Western Reserve '13) in an editorial entitled "Campus Reds," was that they were Communists. Less than one half of one percent were, he wrote, but these "made a lot of noise. The onus of the few, as is always unfortunately the case when Jews are considered, was attributed to all of the Jews and the chase was on." In his view, bad economic times could be no excuse for such irresponsibility nor for the rationalization that the Communists were the only ones truly fighting the Nazis and that in such times a "broad anti-Fascist front" was necessary. If Jewish students persisted in their political activities in the United States, there was no way to be sure that the persecution would not spread. "With the Silver Shirts and other emotional organizations springing up in this country ostensibly to combat communism here," Spira admonished his fellow members, "might it not be well for well-minded Jews to disavow, openly, any connection with that insignificant minority of them who rant red! Could not these few campus reds ignite a flame that might sear all Jews and cause them, in their innocence, to suffer the horrors of a rampant race prejudice! Should we scrap everything these reds' grandparents and parents came for because of a few years of Depression?"

The members of Zeta Beta Tau in this period, like Jews the world over, found themselves caught between the horns of an increasingly painful dilemma. In the face of such violent attacks at home and abroad, swift organization and vigorous action might seem to be the natural solution; but how could they organize and act as a group when doing so would play right into the hands of the anti-Semites?

Within the Jewish fraternity world, the dilemma found expression in another abortive attempt to form a national council of Jewish fraternities in December 1937. Active anti-Jewish hostility and harassment on the nation's campuses was increasing, and members everywhere shivered when that year a Nazi flag flew for several days above the roof of a Gentile fraternity at the University of Washington and the authorities made no move to take it down. However Pi Lambda Phi, Phi Sigma Delta, Phi Epsilon Pi, Sigma Alpha Mu, and Zeta Beta Tau, which had in fact led such an effort previously in the mid-1920s, were opposed to any unified plan of action. An executive secretary of this group went so far as to vow that he would not even bring the letter of proposal to the attention of his fraternity and that he would do everything in his individual power to break the conference before it even started. Others argued that they were already taking action and that such a council would only result in duplication and competition with the many Jewish communal agencies already engaged in the struggle. Furthermore, they were fearful that creation of an independent organization might ultimately lead to the exclusion of the Jewish fraternities from the National Interfraternity Conference. Without the participation and support of those fraternities the council could not survive long, and it soon disintegrated. Once again, the very conditions that this Jewish organization had been formed to mitigate led to its swift dissolution.

James Katzman, a 1919 graduate of Syracuse University who was unanimously elected as the Supreme President of Zeta Beta Tau in 1939, continually emphasized the need for his fellow members to maintain standards of honor and quiet, upright conduct no matter what misfortunes befell them. Regardless of wealth, family associations, athletic prowess, or future prospects, as he pointed out in his address to the forty-first anniversary convention in San Francisco on December 30, 1939, "no man has the privilege of wearing our badge unless he is a gentleman." The remark was but a prelude to a long, circuitous discourse on the roots of campus anti-Semitism and how ZBT members could best react to it, apparently prompted by members imploring their president and the fraternity as a whole to "do something."

A major source of the American problem, Katzman stated, was the congregation of "eager and deserving coreligionists" in universities that still held their doors wide open. This was a veiled reference to thousands of "student migrants" of eastern European Jewish origin, most from working-class New York families, who were evading northeastern quotas, stiff intra-Jewish competition, and steep tuition by fanning out to the state universities of the South, Midwest, and West. Since the 1920s the problem of these "New York Jews" had troubled the officials of upper-tier Jewish fraternities, though they rarely spoke frankly about it in public. As a result of such students, Katzman delicately hinted in the passive voice, "provincialism has been emphasized and with the advent in 1933 of a new world figure, preaching a doctrine of hate and falsification unknown to modern civilization, seeds of unrest have been sown; seeds that conceivably may contaminate the unthinking and the uneducated, but which should never find roots on a college campus. We must all lamentably concede the rise of anti-Semitism."

No one should be foolish enough to discount or minimize the problem, Katzman emphasized, but neither was he nor the fraternity in any position to become "overburdened" with it, despite the pleas of alumni. The individuals of ZBT would fulfill their responsibilities as they saw them, but as a group, ZBT could only intensify its long tradition of working for better understanding between it and the greater university community. More than that, he emphasized, they could not do. "It is not my intention here of going into a discussion of the Jewish problem other than this," President Katzman concluded. "In more ways than one, we can be our brothers' keeper.... Let it suffice to say, that where our membership observes the amenities, and the traditions of the community of which they are part; if they will be but themselves; if they will but walk with dignified self-restraint, they will at least help to alleviate, even if they cannot eradicate, this problem."

Lee Dover's Chapter Manual (1937)

All the Jewish anxieties of the era were evident in the written values that the fraternity attempted to transmit to its members. In this case, the general secretary's considerable powers of moral suasion did not extend only into the matter of ZBT's accounts receivable problem. His fraternal opus, *A ZBT Manual of Chapter Administration*, first published in 1937 and reissued December 1, 1941, barely a week before the Japanese attacked Pearl Harbor, was permeated with the principle that since all eyes were upon them, upright behavior, a low profile, and conformity with the strictest standards of gentlemanhood were essential for ZBT men. Parts of the regimen were not exclusive to ZBT and could be found in any mainstream fraternity, yet set against the background of anti-Semitic stereotypes the rules held special significance.

"There are certain conventions in ZBT which are taught to and observed by all undergraduates from the time they are freshmen," Dover wrote, in describing his fraternity's ideal. "They eschew extreme styles in clothing, and loud colors. They are quiet in voice and manner. Their table manners are unobtrusive and correct. In short, ZBT's are gentlemen." In the dining room, discussion between tables or the passing of food or condiments from one table to another were forbidden; in speech, "decorum and proper modulation of voices" was to be the guiding rule. No ZBT undergraduate was permitted to wear a mustache; the rule was strictly enforced and with "rare exceptions" observed in alumni life. For presentation to the public, the paper stock and color of chapter stationery had to be carefully chosen; all ZBT printed matter had to be "conservative," meaning no "glaring headlines and lavish use of modernistic black letters" nor anything "'gingerbready' or ornate in design." For years, aside from shots of conventional dances, Dover would not permit publication in the *Quarterly* of any photograph showing a ZBT in physical contact beyond a handshake with his young lady. Mention of women's names was to be avoided, he advised, and any necessary public references should be made "only in the most respectful of manners." For illustrations of ZBT parties, any visual evidence of liquor glasses rendered a photo unusable, unless they could be cropped out of the picture.

Pride in ZBT's wealth went hand in hand with a paradoxical desire to avoid drawing attention or risk arousing jealousy because of it. In a directive strikingly reminiscent of the sumptuary laws that generations of rabbis had laid down for Jewish communities in Europe and the Middle East, the general secretary also warned that no chapter should collect fees beyond what it needed to carry on programs in a "successful" manner, nor should any chapter, "regardless of the financial ability of the families of its members," allow its operations to become "de luxe or pretentious." ZBT chapters, he insisted, should operate along modest but adequate lines "and should provide no reason for their campus associates to consider them ostentatious."

The manual prescribed a detailed regimen of discipline and subordination for pledges, freshmen, and recalcitrant members designed to eliminate any temptation to deviate from upper-class American norms. For example, ZBTs were required to wear coats and ties each night at dinner and, on "dress" campuses, to classes as well. Coats and ties were also required wear for Monday night chapter meetings, in those cases in which the entire chapter, with the exception of the president, did not wear their ritual robes. At these, the patriotic singing of "The Star Spangled Banner" and the recitation of an appropriate prayer were customary. Numerous offenses, including "unmannerly" conduct in the dining room, showing intoxication in public at a university dance, and absence or tardiness from fraternity functions, carried the penalty of automatic fines or withdrawal of weekend privileges. A common ZBT custom known as "chairing" could also be carried out before adjournment of the weekly meeting. Under the heading of "Good and Welfare," any member could ask a brother to sit in a designated chair, usually at the front of the room, to receive criticism of his attitude, actions, or lack of activity related to the welfare of the chapter. In some chapters the entire membership sat in a circle and was "chaired" once every thirty or sixty days. The whole procedure, Lee Dover wrote, was designed to enable undergraduates to see themselves as others saw them, to realize that their actions were observed and subject to approval or disapproval by others, and to accept criticism "with poise and good humor and without resentment."

As in most fraternities, pledges and freshmen ranked lowest in a strict chapter hierarchy. First-year students were required to carry matches, offer newspapers and seats to older members, handle morning wake-up duties, answer the telephone, and run errands for upperclassmen. Personal service and forms of hazing in some chapters were still being held over despite the alleged elimination of "Hell Week." In most chapters cleaning the house was a pledge duty. At the University of Michigan, the ZBT shield over the door was to be polished by a pledgee each hour of the day for a specified length of time, and pledgees were required to polish all members' shoes every morning at 6 A.M.

ZBT did not invent the principles or traditions that allowed for such authoritarian treatment and intensive socialization of a fraternity's members. However, their vulnerable social position led them to take conventional etiquette and customs more seriously than non-Jewish fraternity members might have. That in public they tended to cling to their training with unusual tenacity was clearly cause for comment among outsiders, as in this item by a *Kansas City Star* columnist that appeared on August 3, 1936:

Members and Alumni of the Missouri chapter of Zeta Beta Tau were holding a rush party in the Ambassador Hotel dining room on a recent night. The place was air-cooled, but, nevertheless, in the weather it looked odd to see sixty or more men sitting dignifiedly around a table with their coats on. The only other guests in the room comprised a boy and a girl twosome, some distance away. Both halves of the date were more than surprised when two of the ZBT's walked up, addressed the girl and said, "We beg your pardon, but would you mind a lot if we took off our coats at our table?" Just a fraternity with manners!

From Reform to the American Council for Judaism

American Jews' vulnerability during those years also had an impact on their relations with the Zionist movement, the ideological cradle of Zeta Beta Tau. For some, the idea of a Jewish state represented security, pride, a haven, and a "normalization" of their people that would lead to the end of anti-Semitism. For others, the formation of a Jewish state was a danger that had to be avoided at all cost.

Conflicting advice on how the question of Zionism should be handled appeared in numerous issues of the *Quarterly* during those years. In part, the writings reflected the split that was taking place within the Reform movement, which had its ideological roots in Europe among mid-nineteenth-century German Jews. From 1906 on, Reform had been the Jewish denominational home of the majority of ZBTs. Among its adherents were to be found, ironically, the strongest opponents of the Zionist movement, those who felt that a Jewish state might bring into question American Jews' allegiance and threaten their hard-won status. In the late nineteenth century—particularly in the well-known "Pittsburgh Platform" in 1885—American Reform rabbis in their annual gatherings had soundly rejected the traditional concepts that the Jews were a people in exile and that their return to the Land of

Israel was the ultimate goal. References to these ideas were eliminated from the liturgy, and the concept of a Jewish "mission" throughout the world replaced it.

In addition to renouncing the idea of exile, the movement's leaders had declared the distinctive Mosaic law as incompatible with modernity. Emancipated Jews were instead expected follow Judaism's purely "ethical" precepts, seek social justice for all peoples, and do as little as possible to differentiate themselves from all other good citizens of their respective countries. As a result of these attitudes, determined acculturation and "keeping low," in both the secular and sectarian sense, became a part of the Classical Reform religion.

For many years, this philosophy appeared to serve its members well. By the late 1930s however, political events, internal pressures, and the increasing prominence within its ranks of rabbis with more traditional eastern European Jewish backgrounds were causing a major shift in the American Reform movement. So too was the recognition that without a home of their own, the world's gates were closed against hundreds of thousands of desperate Jewish refugees. In 1937 the movement's Central Conference of American Rabbis, meeting in Columbus, Ohio, adopted a "Neo-Reform" platform endorsing the concepts of Jewish peoplehood, Jewish tradition, extensive use of the Hebrew language, and full participation in the obligation of upbuilding Israel, and the adherents of Classical Reform rose up in protest. Protests increased in 1942, when a significant segment of the Reform leadership gave full endorsement to the goal of a Jewish state and recommended the establishment of a Jewish army to fight the Nazis.

Opponents to these changes within the Reform movement eventually withdrew and established an organization of their own in 1943, named the American Council for Judaism. Its basic tenets were that Judaism was a religion only and the idea of Jewish state was an anathema. Among the ranks of this new group could be found a number of ZBT members, particularly in the council's stronghold of San Francisco. At the same time, ZBT also included many members who were embracing the Neo-Reform ideas or at least were not violently opposed to them. The conflict between these two camps accordingly found its expression in the pages of the fraternity's quarterly.

In October 1938, Herbert Ahrend, editor of the *Quarterly*'s "Literature and the Arts" section, devoted his entire column to a new book by Rabbi Morris S. Lazaron, an honorary ZBT soon to become a founding member and vice president of the American Council for Judaism.

Entitled *Common Ground: A Plea for Intelligent Americanism,* the book took the traditional Classical Reform, anti-Zionist stance in its attempt to outline the proper response of American Jews to anti-Semitism both at home and abroad.

Vigorous and open fights against anti-Jewish bigotry were not the answer, in Rabbi Lazaron's view, nor were attempts to hide it or to escape through assimilation. Readers were counseled to get "proportion" and "perspective" on their problem and to cultivate an attitude of "balance, wisdom, and restraint." After all, the rabbi reminded them from a pre-*Kristallnacht* perspective, atrocities were happening in many countries all over the world, and the suffering of the Jews was only one in a long list of tragedies. In America the Jews were in fact gaining more friends than ever before, and despite events in Germany and elsewhere, he insisted, "we must not permit ourselves to learn to hate." Furthermore, the Nazi threat did not eliminate the individual Jewish obligation to take responsibility for one's behavior and thereby ensure the safety of one's fellow Jews.

Most interesting was his not uncommon assertion that Jews themselves were at least partly to blame for their troubles. Rabbi Lazaron urged his readers to shun Jews who did not live up to the proper code of behavior, for it was the "internal enemy," such as those Jews who owned nightclubs and dance halls and vaudeville shows and "put lewd advertisements in the papers," who were the real problem, as was the reality of Jewish overrepresentation in certain professions and especially among medical school applicants. (The latter had already resulted in several well-placed alumni of Jewish fraternities flatly refusing to write any more recommendation letters for seniors wishing to apply to law or medical school). The rise of anti-Semitism, he argued, only increased the need for Jews to intensify their patriotism and take scrupulous responsibility for their every action. "Let us not brook nor protect wrongdoing among Jews under any conditions," Rabbi Lazaron pleaded.

. . . Let us condemn those Jews who by their manner of living bring shame upon all Jews; not that there are no wrong-doers among other groups, but because as Jews we feel and must accept a special obligation. Let us approach intelligently the problems of integrating ourselves into American life. Let us make an effort through cooperation with existing agencies to distribute ourselves more equally throughout the economic pyramid. Let us see to it that in the conduct of our business we observe the highest standards of honesty and in our professions the highest ethical canons. Let us not forget that we are in an exposed position. One Jewish cheat or "chiseler," one Jewish racketeer or criminal, one Jew who turns a sharp, shady deal can undo the work of thousands who are honest and upright. (pp. 18–19)

It was Rabbi Lazaron's special list of "do's" and "don'ts" directed toward the American Jewish collegian that made his book of particular interest to ZBTs. "Don't hold in light esteem that which is characteristic of the American campus—'College spirit,'" he warned. "Don't ignore sports or extra-curricular activities. A big 'don't' is this: don't think too much about anti-Semitism. Try to get rid of the persecution mania we have. Be yourself. Be natural. Don't be apologetic for other Jews with the implication that you're different." On the "do" side, he suggested: "When you have established friendships with Christians, and by all means cultivate them, talk things over. Be frank. Be explanatory but not apologetic." Unfortunately for his readers, Rabbi Lazaron's book did not include instructions on how students could follow over one hundred pages of advice on a subject—anti-Semitism—and at the same time not "think too much about it."

With the outbreak of World War II the adherents of such views became smaller in number, but the intensity of feeling among those who remained only increased. Among these was Cincinnati columnist Alfred Segal, who strongly denounced Zionism and Jewish peoplehood in an article tellingly entitled "An American of Mosaic Persuasion," which was reprinted in the *Quarterly's* October 1939 issue, only a few weeks after the Nazi invasion of Poland. In Segal's view, the entire shift of the Reform movement toward Jewish distinctiveness was regrettable and unnecessary; and as for the goal of a Jewish state, he would not so much as raise a finger to support it. "I have been glad to observe the revival of Jewish religion that is being attempted, [but] I am quite tired of being run in circles hunting security in a Jewish state, or in a separate Jewish culture, or in other devices by which Jews might seclude themselves in a shell," he protested. "In these efforts Jews have succeeded only in convincing those who don't like us anyway that we are a separate people of alien spirit for whom there must be separate treatment." Segal himself insisted that he had no feeling at all of being part of a separate nationality or culture, and he would resent being considered an "émigré" from any Jewish state, just as he now resented being placed in a false position "by those who loudly lament the fall of the Jewish state they had in their dreams." He himself was a man who belonged to a certain religious group, an "American of the Mosaic persuasion and nothing else."

"Of course," Segal had to concede in the course of this journalistic protest, "there are those who are asking, 'Segal, do you think that, as a Jew you will be any the safer? . . . How safe were the Jews who liked to speak of themselves as Germans of the Mosaic persuasion?'" I am not thinking of being safe; I am thinking of what Jews can do to fulfill themselves as Jews and as members of the community of man." By taking on the role of a separate people or nationality, the Reform movement's Central Conference of American Rabbis and the Union of American Hebrew congregations were neither fulfilling their historical Jewish mission nor strengthening their constituents' security in any way.

Jewish Activity

Despite the prominence given to these sentiments, by no means were the majority of ZBT alumni to be found among the ranks of the nascent American Council for Judaism movement or the vehement anti-Zionists, nor did all of them take the "keeping low" ethos to the extremes of shunning any distinctively Jewish activity. Once again, the intense discussions on what their individual and fraternal Jewish identity should and should not be, regardless of the answers, proved that it was an issue of some importance to them. As a matter of course, ZBTs continued to enter such organizations as the B'nai B'rith lodges, temple brotherhoods, and the boards and chairmanships of community synagogues and fund drives, and also as a matter of course, many of their names could still be found in succeeding volumes of *Who's Who in American Jewry*. The articles and book reviews published in the *Quarterly*, the awards ZBT gave, the honorary members it elected, the public projects it undertook, the achievements of its alumni, and the individual contributions of members on the various campuses—all reflected a group of men who, for the most part, cared deeply about their religious identity and about the problems facing world Jewry.

Henry C. Segal (Ohio State '23), since 1930 the editor and owner of the *American Israelite* (the oldest Anglo-Jewish weekly in the United States, published in Cincinnati), took a common stance when in the June 1931 *Quarterly* he gently chided ZBT undergraduates for their lack of knowledge of Jewish literature and philosophy. "Whether it be through individual and group reading, discussion, Hillel Foundation activities, contact with rabbis and other living authorities, serve yourself now by delving into that Jewish lore which is rightly yours but lies untapped by so many college men," he warned. "Others who wore the pin before you passed this heritage by, were called to large positions of communal leadership after graduation and have had cause to regret the fact that they dissipated their collegiate opportunities to familiarize themselves with the traditions of their own people." Each ZBT, he urged, should listen to this appeal to study Jewish literature and philosophy while in college—"and when you are an alumnus, you will thank me (p. 12)."

Books of Jewish interest were regularly reviewed in the *Quarterly's* column, and as the 1930s continued and the situation in Germany deteriorated, their appearance grew more frequent. One of the most striking came in the fall of 1936, one year after promulgation of the anti-Jewish Nuremberg Laws in Germany. The book was *The Jews of Germany* by Marvin Lowenthal, which that year was one of the most eloquent and widely read books on the ancient roots and present suffering of the German Jewish community. None other than Arnold D. Swartz, whose humorous and satirical columns had delighted ZBTs for years, was the reviewer. In the case of Lowenthal's book, however, the usual sense of fun was gone. Swartz could scarcely contain his bitterness, anger, and sarcasm at both the Nazis and his fellow German Jews who had despised fellow Jews not of their own class and had failed to see the danger that Hitler and Germany represented to them.

"The greatest tragedy to this reviewer of the German situation," Swartz fumed in the December 1936 *Quarterly*,

was that time just before Hitler's election when our smug, self-satisfied German-American families—yours and mine—smiled knowingly and said, "Ach, Hitler isn't worrying about our German Jews—it's those verdammte Polacks we, as well as they, want kicked out of Der Vaterland." Have you ever listened in at a bridge or Mah Jongh Klatsch and heard Tante Debby say, "I certainly hate that Yiddish jargon—I despise it—where did that language ever start? Where did those kikes learn it?" The answer is they learned it in Germany from the south Germans. Do you have any recollection of remarks like this, "the Jew will never be hurt in Germany; that's the one country where the Jew is respected because he is, like the German himself, a super-mensch, far ahead of Jews anywhere else in the world." Do you remember your rabbi or your father saying, "What the devil do we Germans need Palestine and Zionism. It's all right for those Jews of Russia, but we Germans are better off in America or in Germany. They should have their Palestine, those *ostjuden*'" ["east-Jews," a derogatory term used by Germans to denote Jews of east European origin]. (p. 17)

All the Jews together should have fought for their rights, Swartz concluded, since German-Jewish immunity was a delusion and the only defense against bigotry was to fight for the liberties of all.

On the campus level, occasional ZBTs continued to serve as Hillel officers and student congregational leaders, and a few ascended to the rabbinate. In December 1940, Rabbi Newton J. Friedman (Western Reserve '28), wrote from Cleveland that the number of alumni, active members, and pledges in his congregation came to seventeen people. The previous year, he reported, he had inaugurated a ZBT Sabbath service at his temple on the Friday evening between Christmas and New Year's when the student segment of his flock were at home. The program was repeated in 1940, with ZBTs giving the sermons and reading the service.

Furthermore, despite frequent accusations that Zeta Beta Tau was inherently an "assimilationist" organization utterly indifferent to Judaism, ZBT's honorary members and alumni continued to be chosen and lauded for their Jewish communal contributions. At the fortieth anniversary convention in December 1938, for example, the fraternity initiated five honorary members—Judge Edward Lazansky, Ludwig Lewisohn, Cyrus Adler, Professor Morris R. Cohen, and Justice Felix Frankfurter, who had been a member of the original home fraternity while a student at City College. Among these only Frankfurter was a fervent Zionist, but all the others were key Jewish communal figures in one form or another. Five out of twenty-five members of the board of governors of the Menorah Association for the study and advancement of Jewish culture were associated with Zeta Beta Tau, as were six of the board of directors of the American Friends of the Hebrew University, an institution that since its founding had exerted a sense of fascination on the part of ZBT undergraduates. Similarly, the achievements of ZBT scholarship students each year at the university in Jerusalem, particularly those who were refugees from Nazism, were noted with great pride; and when Lee Dover included a copy of university president Judah L. Magnes's address at the close of the 1940 summer session, exhorting students and faculty to remain courageous in the face of encroaching war, the general secretary appended the words: "Carry on, H.U.!"

George Macy's Journey to Tel Aviv (1939)

One ZBT, former general secretary George Macy, went so far as to visit the new city of Tel Aviv in March 1939 (it has been founded thirty years earlier) in connection with his book publishing business. He promptly fell in love with the place and shared his thoughts with his fellow members in a two-part *Quarterly* article (in October and December 1939) entitled "A Day in a City of Jews." Macy described how he and his wife Helen had departed from Cairo with nothing but dismal expectations and had indeed found citizens who were obviously poor and plainly dressed and who would never have passed as "ZBT material" if subjected to the cruel eyes of the fraternity's undergraduates. But both had been shocked and thrilled at the fine architecture, courtesy, energy, health, beautiful children, high cultural standards, and pride that were everywhere evident in this first all-Jewish city in more than a thousand years. During its brief existence the Jews of Tel Aviv had managed to produce, under the most adverse conditions, an entire city, with businesses, art galleries, movies, a symphony orchestra that had twice been conducted by Arturo Toscanini, an opera, and two theaters. All members of its population appeared to hold their heads high as they participated in the miraculous building of the city with their own hands, and Macy found their spoken Hebrew in the streets to be as beautiful as any language he had ever listened to. It was at a Hebrew-language performance of the Ohel Theatre that evening the Macy was struck with the desire to share the pride he felt with his fraternity brothers:

How I wished, then, that I could have had some of my loving, my devoted fraternity brothers with me! For we are full of silly little snobberies; we look down on the man who has not learned to handle his knife and fork in the approved manner, we look down on the man who does not wear the right kind of tie. These little snobberies are only whimsical when practiced among most people, they are tragic when practiced among Jews. For the Jewish snob is sensitive to the disabilities which he faces through being born a Jew, and he is quick to place upon ill-mannered Jews the blame for these disabilities. I wanted more Jewish snobs to be with me that evening, to share with me the experience of looking down one's nose at other people, only to discover that unattractive people can be people of wonder, capable of giving delight even to snobs, capable of warming the heart and quickening the senses even of the less wonderful but smooth-mannered swells from Park Avenue. (December, p. 17)

That evening, Macy confessed to his wife that he would like nothing better than to live in Tel Aviv for at least five years and do his part to help make the remarkable city grow. She answered gently that the goal was unrealistic, that a man such as he would never be able to adjust to such a life. Yet he could not stop thinking about his visit or the feelings it had inspired in him. "This is MY race, the people who have done this are Jews," he wrote, marveling at their accomplishments. "How often I think now of those twenty-four hours I spent in Tel Aviv, a city of Jews! And how glad I am, when I think of that day, how proud I am that I am a Jew!" (October, p. 7).

The Death of Richard Gottheil

The recall of ZBT's deeply Zionist beginnings came with the death of Professor Richard Gottheil in New York City on May 22, 1936, at his residence at 271 Central Park West. An entire issue of the *Quarterly* (September 1936) was devoted to his memory, and it included a detectable degree of soul-searching and even guilt that the fraternity had ever departed from the goals envisioned for it by its beloved founder. It had been many years since Gottheil had served as Supreme Nasi or had daily contact with the fraternity, with the important exception of the chapter at his own Columbia University, where he taught until two weeks before he died; but there was no question that his loss represented a major blow to the fraternity. At the Temple Emanu-El funeral services, held on May 25 and conducted by Gottheil's former doctoral student, Stephen S. Wise, the pallbearers included Herbert Steiner, ZBT's Supreme President, and former president Harold Riegelman. As Gottheil had requested in a letter to Wise giving his final instructions, "my boys"—ZBT undergraduates—lined the aisle and served as ushers. Gottheil himself had never fathered children of his own, although there had been two stepsons from his wife, Emma's, first marriage.

"Dear boys of the Zeta Beta Tau," he had written to them all in December 1934, regretting that at the age of seventy-two his health would not permit him to attend the thirty-sixth anniversary convention that year in Kansas City. It was among the last communications he ever had with the entire fraternity. Gottheil expressed his hope that they would enjoy themselves and also his certainty that they would not forget that Zeta Beta Tau stood for more than just "a good time." His boys should think of Germany, of Austria, of Poland, of what they could do to help Jews there "get on their feet again." They should remember Russia, where Judaism was being "stamped out," synagogues were being turned into stores, and the holy Torah scrolls were being sold in junk shops; they should think of Galicia, "where our brethren live in rags and dirt and don't have a decent meal even once a week." What, he asked, did it behoove Zeta Beta Tau to do under these circumstances? "I shall not attempt to answer the question," he concluded. "I shall leave that to our own consciences. You must find it out, individually and as a group. Long live Jewry! Long live Zionism! And long live Zeta Beta Tau! Shalom! Affectionately, your old leader, Richard Gottheil" (p. 14).

The Roger Williams Revival and the Gottheil Medal

The response of individual ZBT members to Jewish crises at home and abroad, as well as their personal Jewish observance, seldom reached the levels that would have satisfied the fraternity's founder. This did not mean, however, that ZBTs ignored what was going on around them. Awards and public commemorations were another area where Zeta Beta Tau's officers and associated boards could express the fraternity's values in what they saw as constructive ways. Less than four months after Adolf Hitler assumed the chancellorship of Germany on January 30, 1933, the year's Gottheil Medal went to the National Conference of Christians and Jews. On June 9, 1936, the Supreme Council voted to revive the fraternity's 1920s tradition of honoring Roger Williams of Rhode Island as the first man on the American continent to preach absolute freedom of religious worship. Brotherhood Day, established by the National Conference, was chosen as the appropriate day of observance. This ceremony at Statuary Hall on February 21, 1936, in Washington, D.C., was arranged and carried out by Henry King (University of Virginia '23), president of the local alumni club, in cooperation with the Jewish Welfare Board and other organizations.

It was not a small affair. More than 250 persons attended the commemoration, and the program included music from the U.S. Navy Band, addresses by rabbis, pastors, and priests, a speech by Senator Theodore Francis Green of Rhode Island, the singing of "The Star Spangled Banner," and the final laying of a wreath at the base of the Roger Williams' statue. The proceedings were broadcast for thirty minutes over a local radio station. A similar program took place the following year on February 20, 1938.

As the decade progressed, each year the awarding of the Gottheil Medal to the person who had done most to aid Jews and Judaism during the previous year increased in the publicity and significance attached to it. In May 1936 the award went to foreign policy specialist James G. McDonald (1886–1964) for the role he had tried to play as League of Nations high commissioner for refugees from Germany. In those days, Nazi Germany was more than willing to allow Jews to leave and in fact strongly encouraged them to do so; the problem was that no countries, including the United States, wished to take them in, especially during a worldwide depression when millions of people were unemployed. Daily, thousands of Jewish refugees were being denied visas, shunted back and forth across borders, or virtually stranded on the high seas. Despite the best efforts of High Commissioner McDonald and others, the governments of the world could not be persuaded to make substantial alterations in their restrictive immigration policies. Holding his post from 1933 to 1935, the high commissioner had issued a dramatic letter of resignation, accusing the German government of planning extermination of the Jews and attacking the League for their indifference to the refugees' plight.

As reported in the June 1936 *Quarterly*, Harold Riegelman, in presenting the award, invoked "the agony of 500,000 souls degraded and oppressed because their birth failed to conform to a cruel and senseless definition, or because they would not yield in religion or politics to the demand of the Dictator." Although McDonald had not succeeded in his ultimate goal of rescuing all German refugees, his resolute action clearly served as an antidote to their frustration and fostered a hope that the conscience of an indifferent world would be thus awakened. Riegelman concluded:

I do not know what will be the fate of these bewildered, tortured outcasts whose homeland is home no more and who can neither long endure the lash nor soon escape its soul-searing sting. But the clear and authoritative declaration that their growing sufferings call for the friendly but firm intercession of other nations; that the failure of such intercession will constitute a danger to peace and a source of injury to the legatee interests of other states; that the problem must be tackled at the source if disaster is to be avoided; and that the protection of the individual from racial and religious intolerance is a vital condition of international security, cannot but quicken the peoples of the earth to an acceptance of their forgotten responsibilities. (p. 31)

McDonald, in his acceptance speech, humbly referred to his own sense of unworthiness in accepting such an award. During the period of his service, he said, he and his colleagues had done their best to aid tens of thousands of victims of fanaticism. "But the need was so great, and what we were able to accomplish so small in proportion, that we deserve no reward save that which comes from the knowledge that we did our utmost." Despite all their efforts, the prospect for the refugees had grown no brighter and their numbers had only increased. The former high commissioner (who in 1949 became the first U.S. Ambassador to Israel) thereupon took the occasion to stress the acute danger facing the entire world if the progress of Nazism was not stopped by democratic governments everywhere before it was too late:

The authoritarian state, with its doctrine of totalitarianism based on the conception of blood and soil, attacks not merely a single group or class; it is the uncompromising enemy of every group or individual who either cannot or will not fit into the pattern arbitrarily prescribed by the rulers. The most numerous victims are the Jews, but there are also tens of thousands of Protestants and Catholics who, having dared to follow their conscience rather than the dictation of party leaders, now suffer a similar fate. These martyrs for freedom of the spirit—silenced, imprisoned, exiled—are fighting more than their own battles. They are fighting yours and mine.

President Franklin D. Roosevelt accepts the Gottheil Medal from a visiting delegation of national ZBT officers in the White House, May 17, 1937. From left to right: Lee Dover (general secretary), Theodore D. Peyser (supreme secretary), Murray Levine (past president), FDR, Alvin T. Sapinsley (past president), Herbert E. Steiner (supreme president), and Harold Riegelman (past president). Photo courtesy UPI/Corbis-Bettman.

The defeat of the principles of religious and political liberty in one country weakens these principles everywhere. (p. 32)

For members and alumni of the era, the highlight of the award came on May 17, 1937, when a delegation of the fraternity's officers visited President Franklin D. Roosevelt at the White House for a twenty-minute private interview and the presentation of the tenth Gottheil Medal. "In these critical times your clear, ringing and repeated affirmation of the right of free speech, free mind, and free conscience is of far-reaching consequences," Riegelman told the president. Members later wrote eagerly to order imprints of a photo of the event distributed by the Central Office. The following year, 1938, the Gottheil Medal went to journalist Dorothy Thompson, who had been reporting from Berlin and Vienna since the 1920s and was one of the most outspoken critics of the Hitler regime.

Harold F. Grotta, supreme president, and ZBT "elder statesman" Harold Riegelman present the Gottheil Medal to Eleanor Roosevelt in New York, May 10, 1952. The following year, Riegelman would make an unsuccessful run as the Republican party candidate for mayor of New York. N.Y. Daily News Photo.

The Zeta Beta Tau Émigré Student Program (1935–40)

Zeta Beta Tau also joined with other Jewish fraternities and sororities, beginning with Phi Sigma Delta, in providing concrete help to approximately two dozen European Jewish students who would otherwise have been unable to continue their education. Through the efforts of the general secretary, a ZBT national committee of advisers, international student organizations, or simply local agencies, refugee student "guests" were chosen and given room, board, books, and spending money by individual chapters. The chosen students had usually amassed such brilliant academic records that it was not difficult for them to secure their tuition through scholarships or work with university faculties and laboratories. If the relationship worked out well, the student could be pledged as a full member of the chapter. ZBT's chapters at Cornell and at Franklin and Marshall were the first to "adopt" a refugee student, and others soon followed. The program continued from fall 1935 through late 1940, when the war and Nazi government regulations made further emigration impossible.

ZBT "guests" during those years included Walter Plaut of Berlin, a younger brother of Rabbi Gunther Plaut, who had arrived in the United States several years earlier and eventually became a famed Reform rabbi and biblical commentator. After the conclusion of his college days at Franklin and Marshall, Walter also went on to receive rabbinic ordination at the Hebrew Union College and enjoyed an active career as a Zionist, a participant in the Freedom Rides to the South in 1961 during the height of the civil rights movement, and a pulpit rabbi in Great Neck, New York. Other refugees hosted by ZBT were Siegfried Garborg of Berlin, a Ph.D. student in economics at Columbia; Ernst Linde, of Western Reserve, who had arrived at his German university one morning in 1933 only to discover that his name had been eliminated from the student list because he could not submit evidence for Aryan descent; George Klein of Prague and Gerard Newman of Vienna, students of engineering and philosophy who found haven at Ohio State; Julius Jonas, also of Vienna, who became a student of aeronautical engineering at Michigan; and Maurice E. Galante of Rhodes (at the time an Italian possession in the Aegean Sea), a guest of Miami University in Oxford, Ohio, who had been studying medicine at the University of Rome when Mussolini's anti-Semitic laws forced him to withdraw from the school.

Preparation for War

When German forces invaded Poland, home to approximately three and a half million Jews, on September 1, 1939, and the dreaded World War II truly began, the members and officers of Zeta Beta Tau knew that their preoccupations would now have to pass beyond preparations for the new school year. Although the United States did not officially enter the war until December 1941, few had any illusions in 1939 that their country could or should stay out of the war indefinitely. The members of ZBT's Canadian chapters were already in it. Students who had spent the 1930s involved in pacifist movements regretted, as did Wolfe Gilbert Jr., that during the Depression waging war against the wolf at the door had caused them to pay insufficient attention to the rise of Hitler. Now, they lamented, the young men of the world would be paying the price.

Lee Dover, in his editorial for the October 1939 issue of the *Quarterly*, assumed that the United States would eventually enter the war, and he took the opportunity to review, for those who had not been born at the time, the experiences of World War I in 1917 and 1918. Campuses had been turned into training bases, he informed them, and university and fraternity life as they knew it came to a complete halt. Classes were few and attended mostly by women, with most students and even faculty away in the various services. Some national fraternities had been unable to pick up the threads after the war was over, and only an enormous effort by a small group of older alumni had carried Zeta Beta Tau through a chaotic period. The conditions might not be repeated, Dover warned, but the history of that era established beyond a doubt the value and necessity for any fraternity to have a strong alumni body composed of men from every part of the country, "who in their undergraduate days adopted the Fraternity as a hobby and continue to work for it as one does for a love and engrossing avocation."

By October 1940 a large part of the "Who's Who among the Alumni" column was devoted to matters "military and miscellaneous." More than a dozen graduates of the McGill chapter were already serving in the Canadian forces in varying capacities, joined by a number of Jewish students from the United States who had become impatient with their own country's delay and had decided to go north to enlist. A quarter century later, ironically, Canada would become a preferred haven for students who wanted to get *out* of serving in an army; but in 1940, as the battle over the skies of Great Britain raged, it was the quickest and nearest place for a young American man seeking to get in. By the spring of 1941, Dover noted, large numbers of the fraternity's alumni had joined the armed forces almost overnight, and the traditional May "Old Timers' Day" celebration had been turned into a National Defense Ball. Uniforms were accepted as formal dress, army "buddies" who were not members were welcomed (an almost unprecedented concession in ZBT), and all proceeds went to benefit American soldiers and sailors as well as to war relief. The Supreme Council declared that all chapters houses located near army bases should open their doors to welcome soldiers, a move favored and encouraged by the War Department since it was hoped this would provide the men with "hospitality and wholesome entertainment."

Gradually, as Dover had described, normal fraternity and university life ground to a halt. House parties, conventions, social life, sports, and alumni fund-raising paled in the face of trouble overseas and a great national defense effort. The change was symbolized in 1939, when Irvin Fane, midwestern regional director of Zeta Beta Tau, found more trouble than usual in soliciting funds in order to build a new house for their University of Missouri (Omega) chapter. Increasing numbers of alumni refused to commit their funds to such a cause. With refugees in Palestine and the entire world in shambles, wrote one, the priority of "college fraternalism" did not rank very high, and he did not think the boys of Missouri needed a new house. Another expressed the same sentiment by taping a pill to a piece of paper and sending it back with a scribbled note. "Herewith attached," the alumnus wrote, "is one aspirin tablet which will in some measure alleviate the distress that I know this letter will cause you. I am sorry at this time that I cannot do more for you or for Omega." It was true enough that once Japanese forces bombed Pearl Harbor on December 7, 1941, and the United States officially entered the war, normal collegiate fraternity life almost ceased to exist. Chapter houses were taken over by the armed forces, and almost all the young men were gone, some never to return.

Nevertheless, the absence of parties and dances and rush weeks and Monday night meetings did not mean that the ties of Zeta Beta Tau had ceased, or that the fraternity had lost any meaning as more than one-third of its total membership exchanged their civilian coats and ties for service uniforms. Indeed, the contrary was the case. Never before was the need for friendship and fellowship so great as when these young men found themselves alone facing injury or death thousands of miles away from home. With their willingness to shut down all normal fraternity operations for the duration and instead throw every ounce of their organizational energy into aiding their soldiers, Zeta Beta Tau entered an era of practical fraternalism that would be recalled by members as one of the greatest in its history.

CHAPTER SIX

"WATCH O'ER US EVER"

Zeta Beta Tau in World War II

Normal Life

From the fall of 1939 through the spring, summer, and fall of 1941, while the World War II was already raging in Europe, it seemed almost possible for ZBT officers and members to busy themselves with their usual activities and concerns without being unduly affected by events overseas.

At the San Francisco convention, participants sampled the city's numerous nightclubs, visited the World's Fair grounds, and danced the night away at a New Year's Eve 1940 Ball at the Fairmont Hotel; a few flew to Pasadena the next morning to take in the Rose Bowl football game. The alumni clubs of Omaha and Kansas City, located three and a half miles from each other by car, carried on enthusiastically with their Sunday get-togethers at each other's country clubs and homes—including that of international B'nai B'rith president Henry Monsky, a ZBT honorary whose son and son-in-law had both been initiated as active members. The Metropolitan Alumni Club in New York held their regular Thursday afternoon luncheons at Paul's Steak House at 41 East Forty-ninth Street or the Cafe Royale at East Forty-third Street and Fifth Avenue; as usual they sponsored an annual "Going-Away-to-College" party for two hundred potential ZBT freshmen beginning school in the 1940–41 academic year. In October 1941 members thrilled to the news that Sidney Luckman (Columbia '39), considered one of the all-time star quarterbacks of American football, had just signed a new contract with the Chicago Bears that granted him one of the highest salaries in the entire National Football League.

At the national convention in Omaha, New Year's Eve 1940. The six-branched cande-labrum visible at center is the Louis Marshall trophy, awarded each year to the chapter showing the greatest interest in Jewish affairs. Man in collar is special convention guest Fa-ther Edward J. Flanagan, founder of Omaha's famed Boys' Town; to his left is Interna-tional B'nai B'rith President and ZBT Honorary Henry Monsky, father of Hubert Monsky (Nebraska '42). Founder Rabbi Bernard C. Ehrenreich stands fourth from the left.

Lee Dover, in his regular *Quarterly* editorials, commented with ob-vious pleasure on the apparent health of their fraternity. Over 1,000 of their living membership of 7,200 as of June 1941 were undergraduates, he noted, the majority living in thirty-one comfortable and well-furnished residences across the nation, nineteen of them owned out-right by ZBT. Among the more than sixty constituents of the National Interfraternity Conference (NIC), ZBT had ranked second that year in scholarship. Through that summer and fall, plans were being laid for the fraternity's forty-third anniversary convention scheduled for De-cember 28, 1941, at the Congress Hotel and the Standard Club in Chi-cago. Except for a "certain amount of simplification of some of the parties," the Supreme Council noted at its November 18 meeting, the program remained the same as usual, as did the tone of the advertising rhetoric. "DON'T WAIT! MAKE A DATE! FIVE BLITZ-FULL DAYS AND NIGHTS IN CHICAGO, THAT WONDERFUL TOWN! War declared on gloom with this Bang-up Program!" the flyers read.

Preparations for War

Still, as the references to war betrayed, the world conflagration and the desperate situation of Europe's Jews was much on their minds. Lee Dover's references to ZBT's organizational strength were not gratuitous; they were meant to impart confidence that the fraternity was strong enough to withstand the challenges that they knew awaited them. Many members were already in uniform, he noted, and their civilians were participating in the war effort. "Come what may," he wrote, "the members of Zeta Beta Tau will continue to do their part." At the San Francisco convention in December 1939, participants had also passed a resolution of sympathy "with all its heart and soul with the tragic plight of our Jewish brethren and other persecuted minorities in those lands where tolerance, justice, and the institutions of democracy have been crushed by the forces of tyranny and dictatorship." The customary marriage and engagement columns in the *Quarterly* tripled in size as couples rushed to tie the knot and to start a family while they still had the opportunity. There was no time to wait for elaborate weddings with flowers and bridesmaids and receptions planned months in advance. The engagement announcement of Zeta Beta Tau's favorite humorist summed up the matrimonial realities of those years: "Lt. Arnold D. Swartz, Miami (Ohio) of Pearl Harbor, T.H., to Miss Rose Cetlin of Haverhill, Mass., in August, 1941. Marriage will take place in either Los Angeles, California, or in Honolulu."

At campuses across the country a new mood of austerity was taking hold. Weeks before war was declared, ZBT's University of Washington chapter decided to contribute to the defense effort by ruling out corsages for their dates. In place of orchids, the members each gave $4.50, which would have been the cost of the flowers, to the Seattle Greater Defense Chest of the USO. At the University of Arizona, ZBT chapter officers inaugurated "war-time formals." Dances and events outside the chapter house were banned, thus saving on hotel rental. Simple buffet dinners were served in place of elaborate banquets, and in place of corsages, defense stamp books were given to their female partners. In taking such actions, ZBT men had the example of one of their most illustrious alumni to guide them. On November 20, 1942, William S. Paley (Penn '22), president of the Columbia

Broadcasting System, had announced at a special meeting of stock-holders that he proposed to slash his own salary by $122,000 a year.

Long before the bombing of Pearl Harbor, the fraternity and its members were in fact exposed to the effects of the war and not only in a direct military sense. After years of Depression the cutoff of supplies from abroad, combined with the gearing up for a wartime economy and personnel shortages, sent prices for food, fuel, service, and furniture soaring as much as 20 percent. Alumni who in normal times would gladly have given their time and money to the fraternity found themselves scrambling, unable to get the materials they needed for their businesses. In September 1941, Lee Dover warned that, to compensate, all chapters would have to increase their budgets and possibly their fees by at least 10 percent and be as thrifty as possible in their operations.

Chapter houses were still full, but more and more young men were streaming into the armed forces after graduation. By the fall of 1941, ZBT men were to be found in camps and naval and air corps posts throughout the country, and nearby chapters were urged to reach out and grant them hospitality. A photograph of a soldier in basic training appeared on the cover of the September 1941 *Quarterly*, and much of its space was taken with a detailed article by a ZBT soldier describing for readers what they might expect when they soon entered the service. In "A Selectee Speaks to Future Selectees" by D. Hays Solis-Cohen Jr., a private in Company F of the 115th Infantry, Fort Meade, Maryland, the author preceded his discussion of military life with a call for his readers to become familiar with the three basic documents that embodied the liberties they were about to fight so hard to defend: the Bible, the American Declaration of Independence, and the U.S. Constitution. Courage and strength of heart were needed, for even before men were sent overseas they were exposed to dangers and accidents during their training. Indeed, Zeta Beta Tau's first service casualty never left American soil. Jules S. Rosenthal (LSU '40) of Baton Rouge, Louisiana, two months to the day after he had received his commission as a lieutenant in the U.S. Army Air Corps, was killed by the propeller of his own plane while on duty at Brooks Field, Texas, on July 29, 1941.

At least eight ZBT army and navy officers and one war correspondent came under fire at Hawaii, Midway Island, and the Philippines when the Japanese attacked on December 7, 1941, including five at Pearl Harbor; all survived the bombardment. Among them was Morris C. Jacobson, an ensign on the USS *Northampton*; Robert F. Politzer, an ensign on the USS *Trenton*; and newly married marine lieutenant Arnold D. Swartz.

Immediate Reactions

Although the damage at Pearl Harbor was less than it might have been, the fighting strength of the United States was devastated by it, and the prewar influence of the isolationist faction meant that American preparedness was also not what it could have been. It took almost a full year for the Americans to reach their full fighting force, and until then it was not at all clear that they would be victorious. On college campuses across the nation, pacifist and communist movement activity quickly fell out of favor as students rushed to donate blood and take up roles in local Red Cross work and civilian defense. On the eastern seaboard the population feared enemy raids and hurried to buy government war risk insurance. The officers of Zeta Beta Tau's New York headquarters, in common with such institutions as the Metropolitan Museum, the Library of Congress, and others, decided that their most valuable records should be deposited elsewhere for safekeeping. Accordingly, copies of the names and addresses of the fraternity's members and other vital data were sent to Edwin N. Sommer, a former vice president of the fraternity, whose home in Omaha, Nebraska, placed him at almost the exact geographical center of the country. The fraternity's national officers could not yet know that this precaution would prove to be unnecessary.

In few American institutions were the effects of the war felt as keenly as in the colleges and especially in college fraternities, which had been filled with precisely the healthy, fit, and intellectually trained young men most prized by a nation's fighting forces in wartime. An immediate fear for some universities was that they might have to close their doors for lack of young male students, who were now liable to be called up or to leave of their own volition long before graduation, and for lack of great athletes to bring in the ticket receipts on which so much of their income depended. Fixed costs had to be paid whether or not students were there to supply tuition and play football. Accordingly, the atmosphere of desperation led to changes that would never have occurred in normal times. Northwestern University and Stanford declared that they would permit the entrance of high school juniors with outstanding records. Washington and Lee University, which since its founding at the time of the American Revolution had never admitted a female student, announced in January 1942 that the presence of women would now be welcome; and Franklin and Marshall, also an exclusively male citadel, announced that it would admit women that summer.

Thousands of colleges and universities petitioned the government without success for army and navy ROTC units, which would permit students to obtain their military education while pursuing academic subjects and thus be eligible for commissions upon graduation. Large state and private universities, which had had substantial ROTC units for many years, had less difficulty maintaining their student bodies, but even they suffered from the inroads of the war on their most lucrative athletic teams. Frantic coaches accepted freshmen for varsity-level sports and attempted various means to keep their best players on the campus, but as Lee Dover noted in March 1942, the "natural patriotism of the American student" had already cleared the campuses of a large number of outstanding college athletes. In addition, he observed, "the draft has claimed a number of the paid, over-age athletes formerly prominent in the campus scene and, if the war does nothing else, it will for 1942 at least, give college football back to the legitimate students." Housing presented an additional wartime problem; at schools located near large defense plants, rooming facilities that normally would have gone to students were being taken up by defense workers, leading to lack of space for even those students able to attend and skyrocketing rents for the few rooms that could be found.

Higher Education in the Cause of War

In the face of these difficulties, universities across the country rapidly adjusted their programs to the emergency, and indeed turned out to play a key role in the massive U.S. defense effort. Virtually all schools began to operate on a twelve-month basis, allowing students to complete their courses in as little as two years and seven months instead of the usual four years, ensuring a rapid and steady supply of highly educated and trained personnel to all service branches. Physical fitness training moved to the center of the curriculum, as did military and technical courses. Premed, medical, engineering, chemistry, and other technical students received deferments and specialized training; upon graduation they were either absorbed into war industries or commissioned. Military authorities and university administrations cooperated in forming special pre–officer training units, such as the navy's V-7 program. President William Mather Lewis of Lafayette College, himself a member of Phi Delta Theta, observed with wonder the "revolution" he saw happening on his own campus. Without any preparation, hundreds of his own and other schools' faculties were being called on to prepare the men of the army and navy for essential services. At Lafayette alone there was an air corps training unit (300 men), basic engineering (400), advanced engineering (150), trainees for West Point examinations (250), and the so-called area and language trainees, who were being trained in foreign languages for nine months and then sent overseas as administrators, interpreters, or intelligence operators. "We should have a great deal of pride," President Lewis declared in a speech before the officials of the NIC, "that it is due in great measure to the American college that the American Armed Forces today are the finest trained military body that the world has ever seen."

Preserving the Fraternity

When the Japanese attacked Pearl Harbor a scant three weeks before the traditional December convention was scheduled to start, the first impulse was to cancel it, as indeed many of their fraternal contemporaries did. Yet the Supreme Council voted to go ahead with the Chicago convention anyway, a decision they had cause to be grateful for later. No one could expect to participate in the banquets and dances with the same lightheartedness that had been customary in previous years. However, the convention's business sessions were precisely the last chance for national officers and chapter delegates from across the country to pass appropriate resolutions and lay their plans for getting through the war before they all scattered to the four winds. One immediate decision was that neither conventions nor elections would be held for the duration of the war, so all officers elected in 1941 would continue to serve with ad hoc replacements if necessary. This meant that Samuel R. Firestone (Ohio State '18), who assumed the presidency from James Katzman on January 31, 1942, carried that burden through the entire war and did not step down until 1946, although it was only the strenuous efforts of his colleagues and an outpouring of their regard for him that dissuaded him from resigning in 1944.

In the weeks following the convention, Firestone and Dover immediately set about taking the situation in hand, beginning with the issuance of regular bulletins and letters to the chapters. Their missives of January and February 1942 left no doubt that they had no intention of allowing the war to threaten either ZBT's existence or its solvency. On an individual level, both the general and field secretaries and the president encouraged the young men to keep up their scholarship and to stay in school as long as possible. Obviously, it would be difficult to think about next week's examination when a draft notice could come at any moment, they conceded, but a good education would prepare them well for the responsibilities that awaited and also make them eligible for commissions and opportunities for service that they might not enjoy otherwise. In addition, undergraduates were urged to put dollars and time aside to help their fraternity brothers already in the service by purchasing defense stamps and bonds, sending cigarettes, candy, and books, and opening their homes whenever possible for hospitality to ZBTs stationed nearby.

Maintaining the integrity of the organization was a top priority for ZBT's national officers. Members were urged to call an immediate meeting of officers, to prepare for an immediate depletion in membership, to rush high school juniors "and anyone else you can get," to revise chapter finances and create new budgets, to eliminate nonessentials, and to attempt collection of dues from alumni as a source of income. Preparation and flexibility, as well as unusual reliance on the local alumni, would have to be the order of the day. As Lee Dover wrote: "The Fraternity's front lines will have to be the chapters themselves, with their trustees acting as captains." Indeed, it was to a large degree the local alumni advisers who had "the future of ZBT within their hands," as Firestone remarked in his own communication to them. "However, being familiar with your accomplishments, I feel that it is safe with you." More than ever the Supreme Council depended on its alumni to be their eyes and ears, particularly in areas far from New York City. On the West Coast, authority passed for all practical purposes to the hands of Vice President Alfred F. Breslauer (California '20) of San Francisco, and in the south to Vice President Lewis Gottlieb (LSU '16) of Baton Rouge, Louisiana; both worked mightily to keep the fraternity intact in their part of the country.

The insistence on prompt collection of accounts receivable that had marked Dover's chapter communications throughout the Depression intensified as members steadily departed. The general secretary was determined that the advent of war should not lead to the sacrifice of ZBT's hard-earned fiscal integrity. Under no circumstances should chapters hold to the erroneous idea that payment of accounts was not necessary because chapters were going to become inactive soon anyway, he declared in his February 1942 bulletin to the undergraduate membership. Sustaining personnel would simply get smaller while fixed costs such as bills to outside tradesmen, mortgage holders, and so on would remain; and it would be difficult or impossible to collect from a man after he entered the service. Therefore, chapters should begin a concentrated campaign to collect every nickel owed to them immediately, invoking the influence of alumni trustees and parents if necessary. "No special privilege attaches to a college student about to enter the service," Dover replied to those who believed some extra sympathy might be warranted. "Every able-bodied man of the same age is either already in or will be inducted later and if all strove to avoid financial responsibilities for this reason the country would be in chaos. ... The Council will hold strictly to account any chapter administration which in any way, War or no War, impairs the reputation of ZBT locally and generally by non-payment of just chapter debts. War conditions will not be accepted by the outside world as justification for bad practices of this nature."

Antifraternity Sentiment

As had been the case during World War I, when the activities of American fraternities had been curtailed by government decree as being inimical to the defense effort, the entire college Greek-letter world found itself facing intensified attacks from those who had long wished that it would go out of business altogether. In 1943, when the armed forces began taking over fraternity houses for use by soldiers-in-training, forcing the remaining members to go elsewhere, the action caused influential newspaper editors, public individuals, and university administrators to declare that fraternities and sororities should become an "unregretted casualty" of World War II. Students were carrying academic loads too heavy and following schedules too rigorous to allow for such frivolities, these opponents believed; fraternities were nothing but "high-class country clubs" that were inappropriate on a good college campus at any time and especially during a war. Many claimed that college fraternities were by nature undemocratic institutions and that their principles and practices were antagonistic to the ideals for which the entire country was fighting. Faculties had never liked them because of the allegedly low priority fraternities placed on scholarship and because they suspected that some houses took part in organized cheating and plagiarism. Wartime appeared as good a time as any to deliver the desired coup de grâce. A more concrete concern was the reluctance college officials felt to entrust the running of the fraternities to the sixteen- and seventeen-year-olds who were coming to comprise their main active membership.

The undemocratic nature of Greek-letter life and the class divisions it brought to the campuses where it was dominant appeared especially objectionable in the case of the sororities. It had long been a truism among the men's Greek-letter groups that if a male student truly wished to belong to a fraternity, then a place could be found for him somewhere. However, for a variety of reasons, national sorority chapters were far fewer, smaller, and more selective, a state of affairs that the National Panhellenic Conference (the female counterpart to the NIC) had fostered and encouraged, even where men and women were attending a college in equal numbers. Considerations such as family prestige, money, social grace, and an impressive wardrobe appeared to be even more important among sorority women than among fraternity men, and the possibility of being left out altogether was far greater. Each year the broken and humiliated hearts of young college women, as well as scattered rumors of alleged suicides and breakdowns among those who did not get into the sorority of their choice, grew more and more conspicuous and drew increasing public attention—including unwelcome newspaper and magazine exposés, novels, and Hollywood films.

Fortunately for the anti-Greek forces, the sororities were also the weaker link in the Greek-letter chain because of their smaller size and the relative lack of financial and political clout permitted to their alumnae. It was thus easier to get rid of them. In one celebrated case, the surprise "killing" of Stanford's sororities sent a shock through the Greek-letter world. In the spring of 1944 the university's administration abruptly announced that the charters of all nine of its sororities would be withdrawn on July 1 and their houses absorbed into a single-tier university residence system.

Nowhere was the unilateral action of outright charter withdrawal taken in the case of the men's fraternities. Nevertheless, the entire Greek world rose up in protest when, in the fall of 1943, Dartmouth College, the University of Oklahoma, and Oklahoma A & M announced that they were banning fraternities as a wartime measure. Fraternity apologists countered with letters and editorials stressing, among other factors, that brotherhood was never more needed than during wartime, that the contribution of fraternity houses was a financial blessing for the nation (expensive new facilities would have had to be built otherwise), and that it did not make sense to send young men to fight a war abroad for freedom only to deny them the cherished right of freedom of association once they returned home.

Wartime Challenges

Generalized antifraternity sentiment, however, was not the worst problem that Zeta Beta Tau and dozens of other college fraternities faced. Simply getting by and keeping their organization alive on a day-to-day basis was a struggle for the students and alumni who were determined not to let the chapters die. Chapter rolls not only became smaller, with a resulting drastic fall in income, the remaining members were also much younger than usual and required more supervision.

Yet many of the older alumni and local chapter advisers who normally would have seen to their needs were too involved with new war-related responsibilities to spare time or money for ZBT. William S. Paley (Penn '22), for example, had taken leave from CBS to serve with the Psychological Warfare Bureau in London and was helping to prepare Allied radio broadcasts to occupied Europe, while H. Stanley Marcus (Harvard '25), had left Neiman-Marcus to become a textile consultant to the government's War Production Board in Washington. A myriad of other noncombat alumni were either working around the clock in war-related enterprises or putting all their energy into keeping their normal businesses intact. The alumni who did choose to carry the burden of the fraternity on their shoulders assumed a heavy load. In addition, it was not only those of near undergraduate age who were being called to the armed forces; Supreme Council positions had to shift constantly as older alumni, including fifty-one-year-old Harold Riegelman, entered various branches of the service and could not attend the traditional monthly meetings. For those who did attend, twice fraternity business had to be conducted in total darkness due to blackout tests.

Assorted technical difficulties also intervened. Shortage of personnel and materials and new federal taxes everywhere affected routine business. Insufficient numbers of workers remained to sort and deliver mail, to drive delivery trucks, to make plumbing or house repairs of any kind. Most freight space on trucks, planes, and ships was taken up with war needs, leaving less room for civilian goods, including the millions of letters and packages crossing between servicemen and their friends and families back home. Difficulties with the latter meant rising postage, more restrictive postal regulations, and the innovation of

"V-mail," in which letters were photographed and shipped on rolls of microfilm. Wartime transportation restrictions and fuel needs meant that shortages and rationing of gasoline and coal were soon to develop, and through the spring of 1942 chapters were urged to buy and stockpile their coal immediately for fear that nothing would be left if they waited until the winter. A severe paper shortage hampered organizational publications and caused ZBT's *Quarterly*—now renamed *The Zeta Beta Tau Duration News*—to be printed in tabloid form on newsprint with the tiniest possible type taking up every inch of space, which led members to remark that they almost needed a magnifying glass to read it. Paper came from wood, and every scrap of wood was needed now for the ships that American war factories were building as quickly as the enemy could sink them. Even the delivery of such mundane fraternity products as insignia, membership certificates, and jewelry was affected by the war; L. G. Balfour, the traditional supplier of these items, had retooled its factories, and 90 percent of its production was now dedicated to defense work.

The Army Takeover of Fraternity Houses

As the draft age fell, the enlisted reserves were called up, and the military authorities announced that they would be taking over university facilities, including fraternity houses, Zeta Beta Tau geared up to face the worst threats to its continuity. The takeover of all the chapter houses was not an unmitigated disaster in and of itself. In the event that insufficient numbers of resident undergraduates were available to help pay the mortgage, then the fraternity benefited from the maintenance and adequate rent paid by the army or navy, with the promise of returning the house after the war. Indeed, it was possible for undergraduates to see the situation with some humor. A cartoon appearing in the May/June 1943 issue of the ZBT *Duration News* showed an army officer standing on a porch facing a group of bedraggled college students with sacks and suitcases under their arms and their leader declaring, "Our Only Regret Is That We Have But One Fraternity House to Give to Our Country!"

The actual evacuation, however, provoked more anxiety than humor. ZBT could announce its national policy that every chapter should continue throughout the war with or without a house, that members should try to live together in smaller quarters, eat at least one meal a week together without fail, and hold the traditional chapter meeting as long as two or more ZBTs remained on a campus; but there was doubt among even the most fraternity-minded that the policy would work. In the eleven houses rented to the armed forces, students struggled to follow instructions on packing and storing rugs, drapes, furniture, pianos, fragile articles, bedding, the contents of the house-mother's room, pictures, trophies, mementos, and ritual paraphernalia. All loading and unloading of goods had to watched and supervised. By the terms of their contracts, storage costs were to be borne by the government, but it was the young ZBTs who had to go through the upheaval of dismantling their houses with their own hands and then being unsure of where they would go.

Joseph Sonken Jr., president of ZBT at the University of Missouri (Omega), described the last, uncertain days of their house in a letter written to the New York office the night before it passed into government hands on February 20, 1943, and members scattered throughout the town: "Omega had a so-called 'Last Supper' Wednesday evening in which all of our present twenty four men participated," he reported.

Although deep down it was a sad occasion for all concerned it was good to know that Omega could still have contact with all the sorority houses on campus. . . . Although all of the boys are faced with many problems they feel for the chapter and I am confident they will not fail you, our alumni, or any of our fine traditions. . . . I had better close this letter since I have no place to sleep tomorrow. I am going to room with Rich Roberts and Bob Cohn and we intend to stay at the hotel over the weekend at least. You can reach me at the same address since I have placed all our mail in general delivery where we can pick it up. I will notify you immediately upon permanent settlement. With kind regards. . . ."

Similarly, the Kansas City Alumni Club, at one time among the liveliest in the fraternity, could barely muster the strength to celebrate the traditional Old Timers' Day. There were no army camps in the vicinity and almost all the alumni were gone, reported regional director Irvin Fane (Missouri '26), whose ZBT papers are today preserved at the American Jewish Archives in Cincinnati. However, he wrote, "you may rest assured that we will have some kind of get-together, so that the tradition will be kept alive."

Throughout the next year and a half, Lee Dover, the local trustees, and the regional director kept up a steady flow of visits and correspondence with the remaining chapter officers, urging them to keep the chapter going, but soon its membership dwindled to nothing. On August 7, 1944, Lee Dover had to report regretfully that the last remaining member on the Missouri campus had graduated and left school. World War II had brought the existence of Omega chapter to an end.

When late that fall the army, true to its word, returned the house to the possession of ZBT, there were no young men left to live in it.

Muddling Through

The Missouri chapter did not remain inactive long, however. The alumni and chapter trustees donated funds to maintain the building and tide it over until, a few months later, two ZBTs returned and began forming the nucleus of a new chapter around them. The same happened with the six other chapters, which had gone down to four, three, two, one, and finally no men at all. The demise was only temporary, and the desire for fellowship and support amid war duties, along with the call of tradition, proved strong. Unlike other fraternities, not a single one of ZBT's chapters was permanently lost as a result of the war.

Indeed, outside observers could conclude that ZBT had passed through the storm well. Its financial base remained sound. Out of 8,500 living members, 5,000 were subscribers to the National Permanent Endowment Fund (NPEF), which continued to grow steadily. Throughout the war pledgings, mostly of sixteen- and seventeen-year-olds, continued, and as of January 1, 1945, the fraternity could count a healthy number of 435 active undergraduates as well as 129 pledges, out of a total living membership of 8,500. The fraternity even managed to add three new chapters in 1942: the University of Tennessee at Knoxville in April, the University of British Columbia in August, and the University of Kentucky in December. Scholarship remained high, with ZBT continuing to rank in the top five or ten out of fifty-nine NIC member fraternities. Social events and dances, oriented though they were to servicemen and their "buddies," continued to take place. The baby boom had commenced, and although each issue carried news of those who had been killed in battle, it also brought news of new life that had been or was about to be brought into the world. "We expect the Quintuplets sometime in November," wrote Private Roy Glickenhaus, a recent graduate of Columbia who was serving in France and was reporting his marriage of almost one year to Miss Carol Levy of New York in an optimistic letter written in September 1944. "Boy, I hope I get back in time to make the first act. Is it too soon to book the little lads for 1962 rushing?"

Amid all of his war directives, Lee Dover spared a moment in August 1943 to give alumni a gentle reminder that they should not forget to let their fraternity brothers know about such "vital statistics," which remained of great interest despite wartime pressures and responsibilities. "We must not forget that there will be a tomorrow in which the sons and daughters of ZBTs will play a great part," he wrote to them. "Therefore let us put them on the ZBT record from the very beginning. The baby sons of ZBTs are future members while the daughters will be the belles of Fraternity parties in 1960." True to this request, the *Duration News* described a steady stream of engagements and marriages among the servicemen, many to "war brides" met in small towns near soldiers' bases, usually in the southern parts of the United States or in England, Ireland, or Australia. Examples were Lieutenant Harry Shifman (USC '35), who in March 1944 announced his engagement to Miss Lesley Jean Freestone of Melbourne, Australia; and George Lemberger (Franklin and Marshall '36), who was married to Miss Betty Bass of Shandarragh Park, Belfast, Northern Ireland, on February 23, 1944, in the bride's hometown.

A Record of Service

The creation of new life was an act of affirmation in the face of massive death. By late 1944 more than three thousand ZBTs were in the services, equal to more than a third of the entire living membership (the exact number on ZBT's "service flag" on the day of final victory was 3,516), which was among the highest percentages of any existing college fraternity in the NIC. The figure included men in all branches of the army, air corps, marine corps, and navy, with many hundreds decorated for bravery in every possible category save the Congressional Medal of Honor. Though the vast majority had entered as enlisted men, ZBT quickly became, as Lee Dover noted, a "fraternity of officers"; the final tally of approximately 2,000 included, in the army, 1 general, 4 colonels, 19 lieutenant-colonels, 70 majors, 172 first lieutenants, and 412 second lieutenants; in the navy and coast guard, ZBT counted 19 lieutenant commanders, 75 lieutenants, 139 lieutenants junior grade, and 99 ensigns. Statistics had to be kept with special care, not only out of regard for ZBT achievement but because the Jewish Welfare Board required them in order to help refute anti-Semitic propaganda that Jews were weak and cowardly and were shirking their full responsibilities in the war.

The grimmest of these statistics was the fraternity's number of "gold stars"—those who had given their lives in the conflict. It stood at sixty-six in June 1945, with nineteen servicemen missing and eleven known to be prisoners of war: eight held by the Germans and three held by the Japanese. In the months and years after the war the number of "gold stars" grew as more news was gathered, bodies were found and identified, and many listed as missing or imprisoned were confirmed to be gone forever. The final toll rose to 105 ZBT dead by 1946 and to 121 ten years later.

How to properly memorialize these men became one of the first orders of business after the war. The decision, at the first Victory Convention in 1946, was to collectively award all of ZBT's war dead the New Orleans Trophy—the equivalent of a man-of-the-year tribute to the alumnus whose personal deeds and accomplishments in life's endeavors stood forth beyond all his brothers during the year for which the award was given. "Who . . . could possibly have stood forth to a greater degree than those who gave their lives to their country so that it might endure?" asked Harold Riegelman on the day he accepted the award on their behalf. These men, he declared, "stood forth above, yes, far above all of their living brethren for this year or perhaps any other year that this award has or may be given."

Each issue of the *Duration News* carried word of individual acts of heroism and survival. Private Leonard Ira York (Ohio State and Alabama '37) was under fire for almost three hours at Pearl Harbor yet managed to down two Japanese planes before being struck by a machine gun bullet. He survived and was awarded the Purple Heart. T/5 Marvin Browner (NYU '44) was captured by the Germans near Strasbourg and taken by boxcar with others to a prison near Berlin, where he stayed for five months until, on January 31, 1945, he was liberated by the Russians. Lieutenant Paul M. Krasne (Nebraska '41), was wounded in action in Buna, New Guinea; his company remained within shooting distance of the Japanese for forty-seven days, and he was the only one of four lieutenants of his company to come out alive. Lieutenant Herman S. Rosenblatt (Nebraska '34), of the U.S. Naval Reserves was awarded the Silver Star for bravery in action in the South Pacific; he had been a member of the Supreme Council at the time of his joining. By the spring of 1945 his ship was in Japanese waters. He described at length how they had supported the landings on Iwo Jima, the nature of the last desperate fighting near the Japanese Main Island, and the loss they all felt at the death of Franklin D. Roosevelt, who had been president for as long as any of them could remember. In the midst of the battle, however, the officers and crew of his ship, which included

FDR's own son, could not even stop to hold a proper memorial service. On April 21, 1945, Rosenblatt wrote to the *Duration News* (April–
June 1945):

I am still alive, which is quite an accomplishment in these parts. . . . Somehow or
other, there is nothing in my background which ever taught me to enjoy explosives.
. . . I can remember going without sleep in college for a couple of days or so but I
was enjoying it then. I can't say the same here—and the sleep for the past six weeks
has been running about three to four hours in twenty-four. . . . We were all terribly
saddened in the midst of all our fighting to get word that President Roosevelt had
died. The word came after a night air attack and it was my sad duty to awaken John
Roosevelt and tell him the news and to read the inspiring message Mrs. Roosevelt
sent us to give him. You probably saw it in the newspapers but if you didn't it
won't hurt to repeat it: "To James-Franklin-John—Darlings: Pa slipped away this
afternoon. He did his job to the end as he would want you to do yours." This settled any ideas that John might have had about trying to get home for the funeral—
which would have been an impossible accomplishment anyway. With but an hour's
sleep, he got up and went on with his work on our staff. We half-masted all our colors and went on with the war. (p. 16)

ZBTs who did not themselves bear arms found other ways to fight
heroically. Rabbi Earl S. Stone (Syracuse '35), one of ZBT's several
army and navy chaplains, went through the entire Tunisian campaign
with his unit, the Eighteenth Infantry, ministering to both Christians
and Jews, acting as a stretcher bearer to evacuate the wounded, and aiding in the burial of the dead. When continuous fire made formal services impossible, he advanced with the men under fire, sleeping in a
self-dug foxhole and talking to the men individually. The *Duration
News* also noted that, in the course of the campaign, a number of German soldiers had been buried by this "non-Aryan" chaplain. Dr. David
Handelman (Franklin and Marshall '33), had the distinction of being
the only man who was not of Scottish origin to serve with the famed
Gordon Highlanders during the war. A 1939 graduate of Edinburgh
University's medical school, he had elected to remain in Scotland and
to enlist in the Highlanders after the outbreak of the war, where he
served until being wounded in the evacuation from Dunkirk in June
1940. Thereafter he served in the British Army Emergency Medical Service in a hospital located in one of the worst and most continuously
"blitzed" areas of London; all of his personal papers and records were
lost when the hospital sustained a direct hit, although he himself remained unscathed.

Major Julien M. Goodman (Western Reserve '34), a young Cleveland physician before the war, and Capt. Marvin Pizer (Nebraska '36),
also a physician, were both taken prisoner by the Japanese after the fall

of Corregidor. Goodman spent almost two years fighting for the lives of his sick and wounded comrades interned at Luzon before he and five hundred fellow prisoners were pushed and locked into the coal bunker of a transport headed for the mainland of Japan on November 7, 1944, away from the advancing Allied forces. The prisoners were packed so closely that there was no room to lie down or even sit down, he later recalled, and during the five weeks of the voyage thirty-nine of them literally died on their feet. Goodman and the other members of the medical corps did what they could to obtain food, fresh air, and medicine for some of the sick men despite constant beatings from the Japanese guards. The physician himself survived the journey to the mainland and heard the herald of his freedom in the distant bomb explosion over Nagasaki; several weeks later he was home recovering in a Cleveland hospital.

Each issue of the *Duration News* also carried word of those who would not come back, of college friends and comrades who had met grim deaths in every forsaken corner of the world that World War II reached. Among them were Flight Sergeant Joseph Jacobson (McGill '39) of the Royal Canadian Air Force, who was killed in action over Germany in 1942, and Sgt. Stanley Kops (Penn '39) of the U.S. Marine Corps, who was killed in action at Guadalcanal September 14, 1942, and was awarded the Navy Cross posthumously for extraordinary heroism. Captain Jack Joseph (Columbia '40) was also killed in action at Guadalcanal, on October 22, 1942, and decorated posthumously; he was cited as the youngest marine corps captain on record. Weeks after Joseph's death, Lieutenant Arnold Swartz, visiting the Guadalcanal cemetery, unexpectedly noted the name of a fraternity brother and fellow marine and arranged for a Star of David to be placed at the head of the grave. Lieutenant Charles H. Herr (Penn '39), was wounded in Tunisia, taken as a prisoner of war to Italy, and died there of his wounds in February 1943. Lieutenant Irvin S. Weintraub (Missouri '42) was shot to death in a small town in Belgium by German soldiers as he attempted to leave his downed plane on September 8, 1944, two days before the area was liberated by the British. As soon as they could, the townspeople buried him with honor and sent snapshots of the ceremony to his parents. Greil Isaac Gerstley (Cornell '41) went down with his ship, the USS *Hull* in the South Pacific in December 1944. Prisoner of war Benjamin Henry Levy (Illinois '37) was also packed into the hold of a Japanese ship, as Julien Goodman had been, but unlike him did not survive; the ship was struck and sunk by American airmen on

The Supreme Council of ZBT at the national office in New York, October 1945, shortly after the end of World War II. The ZBT "Service Flag" at center indicates 3,240 men who served in the armed forces, more than one-third of the fraternity's living membership. Though most entered as enlisted men, by war's end more than 2,000 had risen to the rank of officer. Gold stars above represent casualties. Ultimately 121 ZBT servicemen gave their lives in World War II. Around table, left to right: Alvin T. Sapinsley, Nathaniel R. Roth, Richard Reiss, Roy S. Sampliner, Robert I. Cowen, Supreme President Samuel R. Firestone, James Frank, Jr., Lee Dover, Julius Mark, James R. Katzman, and Dr. Howard T. Behrman. In rear, left to right: Stanley I. Fishel, Robert E. Oscar, Barnet A. Tannenbaum, Irving W. Roth, J. Henry Waldman, Michael S. Weiss, Simon J. Hauser, David Seidman, Sidney Kaplan, Jack London, and Robert C. Lowenstein. Photo by Leslie Gross.

December 14, 1944. In the last, most desperate days of the Pacific war, Stephen Herschberger (Washington University '33) was killed in action on Iwo Jima on March 8, 1945; and Alfred L. Lyons (McGill and Vanderbilt '28) was lost on the USS *Pinkney*, hit by a kamikaze plane off Okinawa on April 28, 1945.

There were many more such deaths. For four years hardly a Supreme Council meeting passed that was not concluded with a moment of silence in memory of these men and the passing of resolutions of condolence to the bereaved parents and widows. Members wrote of their grief as they leafed through old college annuals, remembered cheering at football games together, and visualized their lost friends stretching out their legs before the fraternity's hearth. It was almost impossible for them to believe that they were gone. Prof. Richard Gottheil had been dead for more than nine years as World War II drew to its bloody conclusion, but his widow, Emma, by then eighty-four years old, felt compelled to invoke his protection against war's carnage when she requested that the following message to all ZBT servicemen be printed in the *Duration News*:

In memory of the one to whom you were so dear, I want to say that your brother, Lee Dover, is keeping me informed of your activities—of your devotion to our country and to humanity.

I am proud of you. May God Protect each one of you so that you will return to your dear ones. I am positive that in this fervent prayer my dear husband is in unison with me.

Emma Gottheil

May 23, 1945

Servicemen's Service

At the December 1941 ZBT convention, held three weeks after Pearl Harbor, it had not been difficult for the delegates to make the decision that all normal activities not essential to the preservation of the fraternity be suspended and that all their resources should go to helping their members in the services in whatever way possible. What precisely they *should* do, however, was not clear, and there were no other college fraternity examples to follow. The answers, the fraternity's leaders decided, would have to come from the servicemen themselves. Letters of inquiry were thus written to seventy ZBTs (at the time 10 percent of all inducted members), and the replies were emphatic. Those afloat or overseas longed for food delicacies as a relief from "army chow" and were well able to supply specific suggestions. They also craved cigarettes, newspapers, and reading matter of any kind. The armed forces were willing to help distribute packages filled with such "nonessentials" from home and family, despite the space they required in overcrowded supply ships, because the government authorities well knew what the packages could mean to a homesick soldier's morale and, by extension, to his fighting effectiveness.

As an antidote to the loneliness and isolation of military life, ZBT servicemen also desired word on possible social contacts and on one another's whereabouts. Among the millions of soldiers being transferred at a moment's notice from place to place around the world, far from civilization and away from news sources of any kind, a fraternity brother or a close friend in civilian life could be on the same base, ship, or island, but without some central means of communication there would be no way of knowing it. Nor could there be any way of knowing when, if the worst happened, condolences needed to be sent when one of their number was listed as either killed or missing. Those stationed in the United States also expressed a strong desire to know of a friendly and pleasant place nearby where they could spend the few hours of leave that they had.

Accordingly, on March 17, 1942, the Supreme Council passed a resolution bringing "Service Men's Service" (SMS) into existence, under an executive committee chaired by former Supreme President James R. Katzman. SMS quickly became the single largest activity of Zeta Beta Tau during the war and, for its more than three thousand men in uniform, the most vital and most appreciated fraternal privilege of their ZBT careers. Each serviceman, no matter where in the world he was stationed, afloat or overseas, was to receive regular shipments of eleven-pound packages that included such delicacies as cake, cookies, preserves, cheese spread, salmon spread, canned chicken, anchovies, candy, Nescafe, tea, chewing gum, and cigarettes (in 1943 government regulations lowered the maximum permissible weight of the packages to five pounds). They would also receive subscriptions to the Sunday *New York Times*, paperback novels, and a special "Get Acquainted Bulletin" in the *ZBT Duration News* listing the known addresses of all other servicemen, plus names and addresses of civilian hosts and chapter houses in all states of the Union, available and eager to extend hospitality to them. ZBT's Central Office also became a clearinghouse for servicemen's correspondence, both responding to their letters and printing excerpts of them in their newspaper for the general readership in a feature called "Service Men's Mail-Bag." "We believe and think you will agree, that no undertaking of our Fraternity will have more appeal to Zeta Beta Tau men," declared Katzman, in announcing the program and appealing for donations to keep it going. "While we can't begin to do all that we would like to do, no effort within our power will be spared, that would add to their comfort."

The logistics and expense of this operation were staggering, the pile of clerical work it required enormous. A separate department with a full-time secretary was set up at the national office, although the volume of work frequently overflowed the room and required the assistance of whatever other staff members or volunteers happened to be nearby. Pictures files and war records of every ZBT serviceman were kept, along with an up-to-date list of the ranks and addresses of hundreds and then thousands of them. Up to one third or one half of the entire list had to be changed each time the *Duration News* was published. Thousands of labels for food packages and books-of-the-month had to be prepared, all typed by hand, along with long subscription lists to the *Times*, orders to the suppliers, and thousands of new index cards typed and printed up, first alphabetically and then geographically. As the months and years passed, hundreds of letters from servicemen, expressing their thanks and describing their activities, poured into the office, and Lee Dover directed that as many as possible were to be answered individually. The letters were excerpted and printed either in the "Service Men's Mail-Bag" or in individual chapter newsletters maintained by civilian members still at home.

The letters and packages, along with the fraternal remembrance and concern they represented, were no trivial matter to men living in such difficult conditions and daily facing death. "I pulled into this godforsaken hellhole a short time ago after completing a six thousand mile journey in one of those doggone wooden splinters that they call subchasers," wrote ZBT Ensign Isaac H. Strauss (NYU '36) from Somewhere in the Pacific in January 1943. "If you can imagine climbing out of one of those things after not having seen fresh food in over a month, not to mention something like cookies, to find a perfect assortment of 'tasty, tempting, delectable morsels,' you can also imagine how I felt. Lee, that was a bright spot in an otherwise exceedingly black period. I don't know who made the choices, but he's my candidate for the Gottheil Medal and any other awards that can be given. . . . Knowing that you're not forgotten, which is an easy thing to feel out here, is worth going through six successive Hell Weeks. Thanks for that breath from home."

In July, Private William C. Wasserkrug wrote from Somewhere in North Africa that he had never before "been given to sentiment . . . but as I write this, I admit I am a little choked up. These last few weeks have been trying and all that keeps you going are memories and hope. Then today your parcel arrived after following me up to the front. . . . Realizing the sincerity in which you sent it makes me realize how fortunate I am." Lieutenant Robert J. Spiegal (Michigan '34) wrote from Tunisia: "It might interest you to know that the box arrived at the height of the Gafsa-el-Guettar operation, and believe me it brightened up my foxhole considerably, especially when the stuff was dropping all around and one didn't know from one minute to the next if that big one whistling down had your name on it or not." "They cry for things like that," reported Ensign Ernest F. Marx (Penn '40) from San Francisco after four months in the Pacific, describing how the newspapers and delicacies had been enjoyed and shared with his fellows. "If you could have seen the drooling mouths of the vultures that witnessed the unveiling, you'd realize just how much I appreciated it," wrote Lieutenant Ed Speier from the South Pacific, upon receiving his accustomed package.

"After a wholesome but somewhat monotonous diet of powdered this and frozen that, your assortment seems truly like manna from heaven," wrote Lieutenant Stanley I. Fishel, from Somewhere in the Atlantic. The *Times*, he noted, was also a blessing: "They usually come eight or ten together at a time, but months old though they be, they are devoured section by section from first to last page." Some had not laid eyes on an American newspaper in more than a year; they remarked that the *Times* brought back happy memories of lazy Sunday mornings long ago, when war was nothing but a date in a history book. Others commented that every newspaper was read until the "print came off the pulp" and that the papers and books were eagerly passed around to more than a hundred men until they simply fell apart. Captain Myron Sulzberger Jr. (Columbia '29), who in May 1943 was with the marine corps in the South Pacific, was less effusive in his praise but still acknowledged the *New York Times* subscription with thanks, "officially and unofficially."

It had soon reached the point where the arrival of a package from Zeta Beta Tau was greeted with joy not only by the intended recipient but by all fellow officers and crew who shared in the goodies, many of whom turned "green with envy," wondered why their own fraternities weren't doing the same, and expressed pleasure and interest that at least one Greek-letter organization had thought of providing such services. More than one ZBT member commented that, among their many benefits, the SMS packages were proving to be an expected boon to inter-fraternity relations. "In my unit are alumni of Delta Tau Delta, Phi Kappa Tau, Sigma Alpha Epsilon, and two local college fraternities," reported Sergeant Si Sachberger (Miami '40), in September 1942. "All of these men had a part in the consumption of my package and all of them 'willingly' adopted ZBT as their number two fraternity before I opened the cans. (P.S. What's the fee for members in such a status?)"

The opportunity for welcome recreation also resulted from the distribution of the "Get-Acquainted Bulletin" and the lists of homes and institutions, including all Alpha Epsilon Phi undergraduate and alumnae chapters, who were eager to extend their hospitality to any ZBTs who happened to be nearby. Soldiers stationed in Lexington, such as Leonard S. Malmud (Penn '45; he later went on to serve as a fighter pilot and captain in the army air force) reported enjoyable visits to nearby University of Kentucky and Vanderbilt chapter houses. As the only chapter of any Jewish fraternity at the University of Arizona in

1942, the ZBT house there reportedly became the social gathering place for all Jewish servicemen at David-Montham Field at the Tucson Air Base. When a dearth of live-in members threatened the house with closure, the women of Alpha Epsilon Phi decided to stretch their ration coupons and help maintain the house by sharing meals. Accompanied by their chaperone (as the national office insisted), the women joined their remaining comrades at the ZBT house twice each day and continued to open the doors of their own house for ZBT servicemen to enjoy informal dances and parties.

Reunions and recreation were especially welcome for the homesick men who had been sent overseas, some of whom used the "Get-Acquainted Bulletin" to contact fraternity brothers that they had not seen in years. Lieutenant Alvin T. Fleishman (Washington and Lee '41) wrote in June 1943 from Somewhere in the Pacific to report that he had located no fewer than eight other members of ZBT from various schools and that they had held "a unique 'Old Timers' Day' celebration. . . . It was a mighty nice gathering considering our location and circumstances." ZBTs stationed in Hawaii reported gathering themselves into an informal "Oahu Alumni Club." Private First Class N. A. Wertheimer of the Michigan chapter, writing from North Africa, noted that "we could almost have a Phi house meeting here"; four of the boys he had attended school with at Michigan were in the same city as he. In September 1944 Lieutenant Robert F. Rosensteil (USC) wrote that he had discovered fraternity brother Mike Naumann while on leave in Australia after having had a "very rough go," and they were at that very moment "drinking a bottle of Stateside stuff, drinking to Bob Arkush, ZBT, and all the wonderful arguments we had about housebills, mortgages, and all those tremendously important things of five years ago. Wish you were here." His companion finished the letter, writing that "we have been waking up the whole neighborhood with the old refrain 'Oh ZBT, we sing to thee' and 'The Golden Gate by '48.'" Private Joel L. Bohrer of NYU reported from Italy in September 1944 that he had managed to find nearby Frank Hefter and Mike Browner, also from NYU. "We were constant companions for over a month and the pleasure of our meeting would defy the written word," Bohrer wrote. "Fraternalism becomes dynamic to a degree that previously was unsuspected."

The SMS program made a favorable impression on members of other national fraternities, but more important for the future of ZBT was the impression it made on the servicemen themselves, who otherwise might have doubted the value of belonging to a fraternity in such unsettled times. In the aftermath of the war, many beneficiaries of the program became the fraternity's most loyal and hardest-working alumni. "I can't tell you how much all this means to us out here," wrote Ensign Richard E. Friedman, Berkeley, writing from the Pacific in April 1945. "My dad (Cornell '10) used to tell me that ZBT would always be more than just a place to stay when at school and I can see what he means now." Lieutenant Sherman R. Wiesen (NYU), wrote simply: "Thank you from the bottom of my heart. In the years to come, when the world is once more at peace, and with God's help I can be back to my old life, I shall always remember ZBT."

Seven months before Pearl Harbor the Supreme Council had followed a common college fraternity custom by calling for a song contest among its members, with prizes offered for first and second place. Nothing of too "serious" a nature was expected, for college songs were traditionally lighthearted, the favorite subjects being sweethearts, drinking, or simple expressions of loyalty to the organization. Throughout the first year of the war, the entries came in; and on November 24, 1942, the National Songs Committee announced the winning entry: "My Brother, Here's My Hand," written by Lawrence Gavenman '42, Norman Rips '44, and Norman Smeerin '44, all of ZBT's University of Nebraska chapter and all shortly expecting to enter the armed forces. Lee Dover prophesied that it would become a favorite among ZBTs, and indeed it was widely sung among them for the next generation. Published in the November/December 1942 *Duration News*, the song was unlike any other that ZBT writers had produced and went far to express the sentiment not only of ZBTs themselves but of all college men about to embark on what might very well be their final journey:

> The friends I love, I'll leave behind
> No truer men I'll ever find
> We've won and lost and yet we stand
> My brother, here's my hand
>
> And if this year should be our last,
> We'll ne'er forget the glorious past
> We've launched the ship, the course is planned,
> My brother, here's my hand.
>
> Oh ZBT you shall remain
> MORE HONORS YET YOU SHALL ATTAIN,
> Your future's bright, with courage stand
> My brother, here's my hand
> Take my hand, take my hand, take my hand.

CHAPTER SEVEN

"WITH OUR GLASSES RAISED ON HIGH"

The Postwar Years and the 1950s

By the end of 1943 it was clear that the course of the war had turned decidedly in favor of the United States and the Allies, although more than a year and a half of bitter fighting remained ahead. ZBT servicemen began to speculate in the pages of the *Duration News* and among themselves about where the first postwar "Victory Convention," at which they longed to be present, should be held. Suggested locations included Tokyo, Rome, and Berlin, but the consensus remained that any American city would do. What mattered most to them was that the victory and the subsequent convention take place as soon as possible.

Final Battles

The "end of the beginning" in Europe came with D-Day on June 6, 1944, when a mass Allied invasion of France placed millions of troops on European soil. By September the Allies forces had reached the edge of Germany itself, and the Battle of the Bulge in the winter of 1944–45, which cost the American forces more than 77,000 in casualties, exhausted Germany's reserves. Thereafter, city after city fell to advancing troops, the Americans from the west and the Red Army from the east. In April 1945, not long after the two forces had met at the River Elbe, Sergeant Richard A. Koretz (Michigan '33) was able to visit the recently liberated concentration camp of Buchenwald and give his fellow readers of the *Duration News* a full and chilling description of mountains of corpses and evidence of massive disease, starvation, and torture. No one was left in doubt about the nature of the enemy they had just defeated.

Germany officially surrendered on May 7, 1945, and the next day, May 8, was designated by the Allied Forces as V-E Day (for "Victory in Europe"). Accordingly, the ZBT Supreme Council meeting scheduled for that evening opened with an appropriate invocation by President Samuel R. Firestone. He expressed thanks to the Almighty for victory in Europe and hopes for an early and complete victory over Japan in the Pacific, where the war continued. At his request, all present stood for one minute of silence in memory of the men who had given their lives in the struggle just ended.

In the Pacific theater, the Japanese loss in March and June 1945 of the islands of Iwo Jima and Okinawa, each only a few hundred miles from Tokyo, spelled the end of any hopes the Japanese Empire might yet have held for victory. Yet so tenacious were the Japanese soldiers that some military experts were predicting that to capture the Japanese mainland would cost at least another year of fighting and a million more American casualties. Young Japanese pilots with only a few weeks' training, hardly enough to learn how to land their planes properly, volunteered by the dozens to join the dreaded kamikaze ("divine wind") units, where they willingly committed suicide by crash-diving their planes into Allied naval vessels. The end was forced upon them, however, on August 6, 1945: after weeks of deliberation, President Harry Truman authorized the dropping of the first atomic bomb on Hiroshima. Three days later, a second bomb fell on the city of Nagasaki. On August 14 the Japanese surrendered. Thousands of young American men stationed on ships throughout the Pacific, along with their families at home, could not help but give silent prayers of thanks.

With surrender came once more the ability of each individual to concentrate on his or her own plans and dreams, and these varied considerably. The fighting was over, but that did not mean that optimism was in order. The Great Depression was a recent and dreaded memory, and fears were widespread that the demobilization of soldiers and the end to wartime production would lead to a repetition of massive unemployment. Young men and women felt keenly the loss of months and years of their private lives and yearned to catch up as quickly as possible. "All of us hope that by the time we return to the States and to civilian life, industry will be able to absorb the largest percentage of the men released," wrote Sergeant Richard J. Lewinson (Penn '33) on August 21, 1945, in describing the goals of his fellow soldiers. "Some want a steady job; others want to go into business for themselves; some want to remain in the army; others want to get more education; they'll expect more from fraternities, wanting the fellowship but not the 'horsing around' of days past; also they will want to cram in as much and as quickly as possible so they can get out and start earning their way."

The eagerness of the ex-servicemen to catch up with lost years, as well as their reluctance to tolerate the "horsing around" of fraternity and general collegiate life, was one of their generation's most distinctive features. By the end of 1943 discharged soldier-students had already begun to trickle back to their campuses, and Lee Dover could report that in December of that year other fraternities had ceased to raise funds for servicemen and were instead concentrating their resources on postwar rehabilitation. Not long after, Supreme President Samuel Firestone appointed ZBT's own postwar planning committee.

The GI Bill

In the spring of 1944, Congress passed what was to prove one of the most important and influential pieces of legislation in all of American history: the Servicemen's Readjustment Act, popularly known as the GI Bill of Rights. Among other points, the bill guaranteed full education benefits to returning servicemen—funds either to begin an education or to continue one that had been interrupted by their country's call. Applying to the school, gaining admission, and keeping up one's academic standing were the responsibility of the GIs themselves, but the government was prepared to underwrite their efforts. Those eligible would receive up to $500 a year for tuition, laboratory fees, books, and supplies, along with a stipend of $50 a month if single and $75 a month if married. Opponents who complained that all this was an exorbitant waste of public money in coming years would live to see the GI Bill pay for itself many times over in taxes paid back from increased incomes and the enhanced productivity of American citizens.

"Education" was not limited only to college, although it was for its college benefits that the bill became best known. The original law stipulated "an elementary school, trade or technical institution, college or graduate school," a range of learning that suggests that some young American men entering the armed forces had hardly been able to read and write. A survey in December 1944 revealed that of 2 million veterans who planned to enter school on the GI Bill, 600,000 planned to do so at college level. The ZBT leadership took upon itself the responsibility of mailing a "Veteran's Guide" to more than three thousand servicemen in July 1944 in order to help to answer, *before* they came home, any questions they might have about the complex educational or other benefits awaiting soldiers on their return to civilian life. To reach the membership while they still resided at their current addresses was another motivation to send the pamphlet out as soon as possible. As the soldiers returned, the ZBT Central Office faced a clerical task of monstrous proportions in the need to reincorporate into its records the civilian addresses of over three thousand former ZBT servicemen, many of them daily shifting about the country.

Whatever educational course the former GI chose under the bill, the law ensured a virtual stampede of students, for it had to begin no later than two years after either discharge from the armed forces or the end of the war and could not continue for more than seven years afterward. Furthermore, early marriage and the desire to support a family were not the impediments for the young men that they might have been in the past. The GI Bill inadvertently contributed to the postwar baby boom (a phenomenon caused by several factors) by providing a financial basis for ex-servicemen to marry and begin their families immediately, rather than waiting until they had finished their education and entered the job market. At least forty thousand married male veterans took their wives and children with them to college in December 1945; and in the peak years of 1946 and 1947, when more than 2.5 million veterans were obtaining educations under the bill, the number of full families grew even larger. For generations after, this demographic "pig in a python" was destined to exert an inordinate influence on all phases of American politics, society, and culture. The nation's institutions of higher education would feel its influence with special acuteness when, eighteen years later, the babies began reaching college age.

Chaos on the Campus

The first group of students to attend school on the GI Bill began arriving on the campuses of the nation in September 1944, before the war had even ended. By then, ten of the eleven ZBT chapters that had relinquished their homes to the army had taken them back. At various times during the war seven of ZBT's thirty-four chapters had become inactive, but the influx of new blood had an immediate effect, and three of these—the chapters at Miami, Washington, and Arizona—resumed

The intramural football team of the Penn State chapter, fall 1947. First row, left to right: Robert F. LeVine '49, Herman Lotstein '45, Julian L. Eliasoph '46. Rear, left to right: Seymour Silver '48, Bernard Gordon '48, Melvin Jacobs '47, Nathan Kushner '49, Bill Levy.

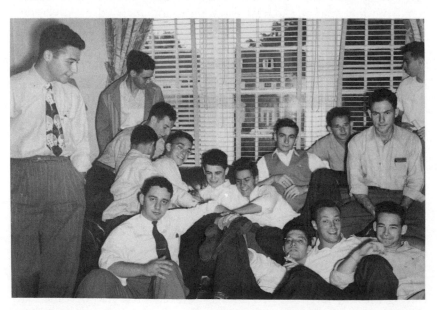

Afternoon in the living room—relaxing at the University of Alabama chapter house in Tuscaloosa, 1947.

ZBTs and their dates at an informal house party at Tulane University, 1947. Young woman at far right holds a package of "Lucky Strikes," among the most popular brands of American cigarettes during this period. Note that star over mantel is no longer the Jewish "Magen David." Fraternity members, left to right: Maury Bronstein '49, Sidney Cohen '45, Morey Sear '48, Albert Fraenkel '48, David Freed, Jr., '48, Adrian C. Benjamin Jr., '49, Robert Kahn '45, Henry Simon '46, Morris Scharff '48.

ZBT float with members of the Alpha Epsilon Phi sorority in Homecoming parade, the University of Florida, October 22, 1949. The figure of an alligator, Florida's mascot, along with the sign "Alligator Stew" appears on the float, suggesting that their gridiron opponent that day will be soundly defeated.

operations, with the others soon to follow. By the fall of 1945, the fraternity was planning its long-awaited Victory Convention in Chicago for December 28–31, 1945. President Firestone, in delivering an end-of-the-war address, noted that by all measures—membership, finances, chapter house integrity, cooperation of officers—the fraternity had gotten through with flying colors. All could approach the forty-fourth anniversary convention, he concluded, "with the conviction that ZBT has 'won its war.'"

In expectation of the resumption of normal college life, ZBT had already printed a new rush manual and was preparing for a steadily rising number of pledgings and initiations. The situation on America's campuses, however, was anything but normal, as the wartime famine of college students quickly turned into an unmanageable feast. The educational process had been interrupted for so long and the desire to get back to it was so strong that the numerical equivalent of four or five years' worth of male freshman classes hit the campuses all at once; and never in the history of American higher education had so many been accompanied by wives and children. Furthermore, ex-GIs were not the only ones interested in attending college. Aside from the encouragement of the GI Bill, American society as a whole after World War II awoke to the value of a higher education, to the point that more parents and young people than ever were convinced that a college education was not only desirable but necessary.

As a result, the nation's colleges and universities literally overflowed with students. The number of the nation's undergraduates, which had been under a million before the war, more than doubled to 2.4 million by the winter of 1947, and the "megaversity," with enrollments exceeding ten, twenty, or thirty thousand students, became common. Women, who had been sought after as students during the lean years, were now encouraged to forgo higher education and leave their slots to men. Alumni with teenage children were told to forget about their being admitted to the school of their choice; with first priority going to the veterans, a nonveteran would be fortunate to be admitted to his local state university. Classrooms, textbooks, apparatus, and teaching staffs were strained to the limit. Princeton's fieldhouse, with the addition of hundreds of cots, was turned into a dormitory, and Quonset huts bloomed overnight across the land. Undergraduates slept in hallways, gymnasiums, armories, GI barracks, and trailers. Students struggled to find any spot with a modicum of quiet and privacy that would allow them to study.

Fraternity chapters were caught in this crush as well. Their houses became filled to the bursting point but could not even begin to absorb this mass of student humanity, and National Interfraternity Conference (NIC) officials reacted with alarm to the possibility that all the values of fraternity life would be lost in such huge chapters. ZBT's Syracuse chapter began its thirty-fifth year of operation in September 1946 with over one hundred members—fifty of them ex-servicemen—and coped by renting outside rooms and introducing multiple "sittings" at mealtimes. The alumni corporation of the Ohio State chapter coped with a membership of over 150 men (all but 20 of them out-of-towners) by purchasing a second and then a third home and arranging for nearby rooming houses to be taken over by ZBTs.

Housing Shortages and Inflation

The inevitable overcrowding of fraternities was aggravated by a severe nationwide housing shortage in the years immediately after the war. For twelve million demobilized civilians to suddenly find places to live would have presented difficulties in any case, but because of the Great Depression and wartime conditions there had been virtually no civilian construction for more than fifteen years, and this lack made the situation critical. Now housing either could not be obtained at all, or could only be obtained at vastly inflated prices. At some universities students not pledged to a fraternity or sorority could not be admitted because there was no place to put them.

Not only was the price of housing going up; as Americans rushed to buy consumer goods, sharp inflation vastly raised the costs of food and services. A clothing shortage caused many an ex-GI to continue to wear his olive drabs on campus. The cost of food alone had leaped 25 percent, playing havoc with fraternity budgets. On some campuses, such as Ohio State, the entire Greek system coped by uniting into a cooperative buying organization and purchasing their goods together at bulk discounts. With the end of wartime ship construction, paper was once more available, but the cost of producing a publication continued to rise. In June 1947, Lee Dover, in apologizing for the declining size and quality of the *Zeta Beta Tau Quarterly*, pointed out that to duplicate the size and quality of their June 1941 issue would cost three times as much as it had then, and the use of cuts and letterpress would cost eight times as much.

Influence of Veterans

The postwar years brought problems on the membership front as well. Customs, traditions, and leadership techniques had been disrupted and had to be relearned. While excessive youth had been characteristic of members during the war, unusually advanced age became a characteristic afterward. Veterans, some of whom had been wounded in action, did not wish to tolerate the foolishness or the hazing that, despite constant attempts at regulation or elimination, stubbornly remained a part of fraternity life. Many had already faced death in battle and had no patience for preinitiation "tests" or "trials." In the years after the war they coexisted in chapter houses with teenagers much younger and more inexperienced than they; and although the younger ones benefited from exposure to more mature models, some tensions inevitably resulted. In addition, ex-soldiers found traditional rules about no liquor, gambling, or unchaperoned women on fraternity house premises ridiculous, and ZBT officials were unsure how to react when the inevitable "incidents" surfaced.

Nevertheless, none of these challenges mitigated the joy of ZBT's leaders that the period of greatest danger to their brotherhood seemed to have passed. Observers commented on the maturity of the veterans, the zest and seriousness they brought to the classroom, and the reality that the many who were married did not seem to be hindered in their studies at all. On the contrary, the support of wives appeared to be a key factor in their success. Magazine editors recommended that the degree of "P.h.T." (for "Putting Hubby Through") be awarded to these women who made homes out of huts and sacrificed so much to make the process work.

Time would heal the maladjustments of the academic years 1945–46 and 1946–47, ZBT leaders believed. What mattered was that the war was finally over, chapters had been revived, college enrollment was burgeoning, and ZBT was being presented with more potential members than it could possibly accommodate. The outlook for fraternities had never seemed so bright.

The Cold War and the Korean Quagmire

College enrollments continued to rise throughout the 1950s, along with ZBT's pool of potential members, but anyone who believed that the end of World War II would usher in an era of world peace was bound to be disappointed. Hardly had the ink on the articles of surrender dried before the threat of world conflagration loomed once more. Between the United States and the Soviet Union a cold war was on, and its earliest surrogate battlegrounds were Greece, Turkey, China, and the captive city of Berlin in the winter of 1948–49.

Uniforms did not disappear from the campus, as the authorities in Washington, D.C., announced an expansion of ROTC and military training programs. Members wrote letters to the *Quarterly* expressing their bewilderment and confusion at the developing arms race and constant threat of military draft and mandatory reserve duty over their heads. How could it be, they asked, that after having put in so much effort during World War II, their country seemed to be enjoying *less* security instead of more? The cold war became suddenly hot when North Korean forces crossed the Thirty-eight Parallel into South Korea on June 25, 1950, and President Truman, with the backing of the UN Security Council, sent first U.S. planes and then troops to the Asian peninsula. Korea was destined to become "the forgotten war" in the annals of U.S. history, but at the time fears were justifiably widespread that the conflict might widen into nothing less than a third world war. By the spring of 1951 fighting was in full force, with 90 percent of the troops originating from the United States even though the war was ostensibly a UN "police action."

In the postwar nuclear age the entire world was painfully aware of what the consequences could be if a single one of the world's growing stockpile of atomic weapons was actually used. Once more Lee Dover dispatched a copy of ZBT's membership lists and key records to Omaha for safekeeping. Once more students streamed to the local Red Cross to donate blood. ZBT's Supreme Council and alumni inaugurated Service Men's Service II and prepared for the campus conditions of World War II to be repeated, including the closing of houses and the need to store all their goods. Their best hope was that the government would allow undergraduates to finish their current year in school before drafting them into the armed forces. Chapters postponed improvements on their houses, for going into debt made no sense when the entire college system might collapse at any moment.

The morale of the undergraduates plunged, along with their scholarship. During the 1950–51 academic year, as the war in Korea continued, for the first time a significant proportion of ZBT chapters fell below the all-men's average. At the same time, drinking increased and appeared to some observers to have reached the level of mass alcoholism. "It seems that the boys feel that being drafted into the United States Armed Forces is inevitable and, consequently, are saying to heck with their studies and are looking for a good time at school," reported alumni trustee Roswell Messing, Jr. to the dean of men at the University of Missouri. "Ninety per cent of the 'bull session time' is occupied with discussions of being drafted into the Armed Forces. Some of the boys have taken the attitude that as long as they are going to get killed, they might as well have a good time now." The situation was the same for college students across the country; among themselves fraternity alumni officers discussed the possibility of getting parents to write letters to their sons, urging them to keep up with their studies and not to lose hope.

By the summer of 1953, after years of armistice negotiations, the guns died down in Korea, but not until almost forty thousand Americans had died and over one hundred thousand had been wounded. Civilian losses were estimated at four hundred thousand; Chinese and North Korean casualties exceeded one million. Barely another decade would pass before American citizens found themselves embroiled in yet another war in another Southeast Asia peninsula. In retrospect, the 1950s and early 1960s would be seen as among the most economically prosperous in U.S. history, and young fraternity men benefited fully from that prosperity. Yet all took place within the shadow of a struggle between two great powers, a constant international undercurrent of fear and anxiety, constant readiness for military conscription, and the threat of nuclear annihilation.

Expansion and Milestones

Although the impact of the cold war and the Korean conflict was inescapable, fortunately, it did not prevent the continuity of normal college and fraternity life. Indeed, the postwar years overall appeared to be healthy ones for Zeta Beta Tau, as the fraternity grew and expanded and celebrated a number of significant anniversaries. Its golden anniversary convention took place at the Waldorf-Astoria Hotel in December 1948, with four of the fraternity's founders present on the dais. At the appointed moment the entire convention arose as one to give them a standing ovation. In 1953, Lee Dover, Mr. ZBT himself, entered his twenty-fifth year of service and was feted at a surprise testimonial dinner

A pre-football game pep rally at Duke University in the fall of 1950. From left to right: Garry Goldstein '52 (by megaphone, leading cheer), Martin Sack, Jr. '53, Eugene Bernstein '53, Gilbert Person '53, Saul Strauss '52, John Rosenberg '53, Robert Getz '53, Maxwell Goldwasser '52, George Lustig '52, Samuel O'Mansky '52, Robert Fischell '51, Richard Watov '53, Henry Poss '52, Burnam Friedman '51, Marshall Novick '51.

Members and their dates at the annual Winter Formal of ZBT at Boston University, 1950.

Group photo at the 1951 Winter Formal of ZBT's University of Pennsylvania chapter. Champagne glasses barely visible at bottom and left were trimmed away when this picture was originally published in ZBT's quarterly. Executive head and editor Lee Dover strongly discouraged drinking by undergraduates on chapter house premises, and he would not permit liquor glasses or any evidence of "improper" dress or behavior to appear in any official ZBT photograph. (The original photo has written on the back in red pencil: "No liquor glasses—note trim marks.")

The kitchen crew at the Syracuse University chapter in 1950. Left to right: Gerald Leider '53, Robert Silverstein '52, Leroy Imber '53, Eliot Slater '51, Arnold Porter '52.

At New York University in May 1950, Alvin Kahn '50 stands to read committee reports at the traditional Monday night chapter meeting. At center, wearing the customary ritual robe and wielding the gavel, is chapter president Jerome Feinberg '50. Others, left to right: Albert Hartog '50, Mortimer Glotzer '51, Ralph Yanowitz '51, and Richard Zeif '51.

Newly elected officers of the Columbia University chapter on the steps of their house in 1952. From left to right: Robert Miller '54, David Shainberg '54, Maurice Sherman '53, William Frosch '53 (president), Robert Schaefer '54.

at Rosoff's restaurant in New York City. The festive occasion was attended by over sixty of his fraternity brothers, who sang chorus after chorus of "For He's a Jolly Good Fellow" as the guest of honor walked unsuspectingly through the door.

In an official report prepared not long afterward, Dover noted with pleasure how the fraternity had increased in strength since he had first taken his place at its helm in 1928. Since then, ZBT had grown from thirty to forty-five active chapters, the majority owning their own houses; its membership had grown from forty-five hundred to over seventeen thousand; and its endowment, the National Permanent Endowment Fund (NPEF), had grown from nothing to more than a half-million dollars. By ZBT's sixtieth anniversary in 1958, Supreme President Stanley I. Fishel noted that, despite its consistently conservative expansion policy, the fraternity's membership had increased by more than 60 percent in the previous ten years.

Social Life and Conventions

ZBT social activities continued to involve not only the undergraduates and alumni but all the members of their extended families. The list of weddings in the *Quarterly's* social columns consistently included the names of sibling sisters, daughters, cousins, and other female relatives. Married alumni who were active in the fraternity could not carry on their activities without the understanding, tolerance, and even cooperation of their wives. ZBT wives frequently became friends of one another through their husbands. Having ZBT sons in common drew fathers and mothers together, both to socialize and to give concrete help to their collective offspring—as in the case of St. Louis's Washington University chapter, for example, whose members began holding television-watching parties in 1950 with a new TV set given to them by their Mothers' Club. More than ninety people attended a Parents' Week End at Syracuse in the fall of 1953, enjoying an all-day formal at the Beeches Country Club.

Lee Dover had always made it a point that members and trustees should not minimize the importance of a "proper" social program. Zeta Beta Tau, he declared, was an adjunct to the higher educational system, but it was still definitely a social fraternity and would be judged by the excellence of its social affairs. In a bulletin to chapters and alumni clubs dated October 20, 1950, on the criteria for choosing

a convention city, the general secretary noted that ZBT's requirements went well beyond sufficient hotel facilities and a cooperative
staff. Any alumni club wishing to host a convention would have to
provide a statement "as to whether there are sufficient single young
ladies in the proposed city to provide 'dates' for out-of-town Convention delegates (100–200 girls—17 to 30) is required." "Maybe I'll
meet the girl I'm going to marry" was a key sentiment motivating unattached members to head for conventions, and it was not unknown
for happily married alumni to name their babies by some variant of
Lee or Dover to honor the man who had helped to make that happiness possible.

Whether members found their life's mate there or not, the hosts of
each convention city strove to devise a glittering program and, through
continued hyperbolic advertising, to tempt those members who needed
to make an extended trip to get there. The poster for the 1947 convention in Cleveland featured a drummer boy striking a huge drum fes-
tooned with dates of previous Cleveland conventions, along with cap-
tions suggesting that a ZBT convention ranked along with the nation's
most historic events: "Spanish American War: 1898: ZBT Founded!
President McKinley said, 'ZBT is what this country has needed since
1776!'" "The Year of the Income Tax Law: 1913: ZBT national Convention in Cleveland! First Time Outside New York!" "The Decade of the
Roaring Twenties: 1923: ZBT National Convention in Cleveland: Remember! Pop was there!" "The Year the New Deal Started: 1933: ZBT
National convention in Cleveland" "And now—ZBT's 49th anniversary convention in Cleveland! Fun Galore on Erie's Shore! Dec. 27
over New Year's!"

In December 1949 the convention took place for the first time in
tropical Miami, and the local committee was able to arrange an additional "Hang-Over Convention" in Cuba. After a formal New Year's
Eve ball and attendance at the Orange Bowl football game the next day,
ZBTs, whether "stag, date, or mate," could sail from Miami on the S.S.
Florida on January 2 and enjoy the delights of the city of Havana for an
additional week. In 1951, Zeta Beta Tau joined a national trend by introducing a beauty queen contest as an annual event; beginning with a
"Sweetheart Parade" the first night of the convention, all the invited
"dates" (each holding a numbered card) were evaluated and succes-
sively eliminated by a professional panel of judges until the final night,
when the "Sweetheart of ZBT" was crowned in a formal ceremony
along with four members of her "court."

Move to the Sunbelt

The 1952 ZBT annual convention in Seattle was the last to be held over the traditional New Year's Eve weekend. That of 1953 took place in Atlantic City in August, and from then on all succeeding conventions took place either over Labor Day weekend or sometime during the summer. Not all were set near beaches; the 1957 convention, which took place Labor Day weekend in Washington, D.C., was of a decidedly serious bent, as delegates visited national memorials and watched as Supreme President Stanley I. Fishel laid a wreath at the Tomb of the Unknown Soldier under the formal auspices of the Department of Defense. On the whole, however, warm-weather fun became the hallmark of ZBT and other fraternities' conventions in the 1950s. Such resort-type gatherings proved to be less expensive, less complicated, more enjoyable, and allowed alumni the option of scheduling extended family summer vacations around them.

The choice of Miami as the most popular of convention spots highlighted a decided postwar trend—the movement of the nation's population away from the Northeast and the Midwest toward the so-called sun belt. Before the war, tropical Miami had been strictly a winter vacation spot, but by 1946 more than fifty ZBTs were reported to be living there year-round, with new members arriving daily. Southern California, already well populated by the fraternity's motion picture colony in the 1930s, attracted ZBTs at an even more rapid pace. In the fall of 1946 there were over seven hundred ZBTs living in the area, with hundreds more arriving each year (the number more than doubled by 1955). The ZBT Southern California Alumni Club, with virtually every chapter in the country represented in it, was soon acknowledged as one of the largest and most active of the entire fraternity. There was no doubt, according to their 1946 convention advertising, that any member would like the greater LA area; "We're just afraid you'll like it so much you'll come out to live and we have enough people already" was the only warning. Over five hundred people habitually attended its annual ZBT Homecoming Ball held the night before the UCLA-USC football game, and the club held a regular program of parties, dances, business lunches, intercollegiate singing contests, fund-raising, and all manner of activities in cooperation with the local undergraduates.

The Southern California ZBTs were also notably active in fund-raising for Jewish activities. In October 1947, it was reported, a "highly

With the advent of air-conditioning and swifter methods of travel, ZBT and other frater-
nities began to switch their national conventions from the traditional winter holiday sea-
son to summer gatherings in warm-weather resorts. Here chapter delegates of Alabama
and North Carolina along with their dates take in the sun on the boardwalk of Atlantic
City in August 1953.

successful" dinner meeting was held at the Horace Heidt Restaurant in
Beverly Hills, attended by 125 alumni. They were addressed by Dr.
Abram Sachar, at the time national director of Hillel Foundations, and
Rabbi Jehuda Cohen (UCLA '30), Hillel's West Coast director, as part
of an effort to finance the bringing of twenty young displaced persons
from Europe and finding places for them in West Coast universities.

Alumni

The activities of the Southern California club were but one example of
a high level of ZBT alumni involvement across the nation. Of the
fraternity's forty-three formally organized alumni clubs, thirty-one carried on regular, well-attended programs. The Chicago Club enjoyed
over two hundred paid-up alumni members in 1948, meeting regularly

at the Standard Club. The Cincinnati Alumni Club revived after the war with a regular schedule of golf outings and country club activities. Although Detroit had only seventy ZBT members living in the area, fifty-four were paid-up members of the alumni club, an extraordinarily high proportion for any collegiate fraternity. Alumni clubs also sponsored luncheon tables at convenient clubs or restaurants in their cities, which were of special value to members recently out of college or those traveling to communities not their own.

Social gatherings were not the only activity of these active ZBT alumni; many put hard work into their local chapters, and Lee Dover continually referred to them as the "backbone of the fraternity." Despite the critical postwar housing shortage, in 1952 thirty-nine of ZBT's forty-eight chapters—twelve of them established since the end of the war—were able to purchase their own houses through their own local, nonprofit corporations managed by their alumni trustee-directors. The presence of mature alumni experienced in business and legal matters and willing to devote many hours of their time on a completely volunteer basis was essential to this success. Neither the NPEF (the fraternity's endowment corporation) nor the banks nor lending organizations of any kind would lend money to undergraduates for the purpose of purchasing or improving a chapter home.

Beyond securing the physical home and sometimes handling the actual mortgage payments, alumni directors frequently assumed the responsibility of helping the chapter in all its affairs. They secured the estimates and made contracts, they decided if the house was to be rented, and they were responsible for the purchase of new furniture and equipment. They also supervised the chapter's public relations and were the first to be consulted when any problems arose. Seldom if ever did these alumni trustees receive any payment for their services. On the contrary, their association with the fraternity cost them dearly in time, funds, and at times separation from their own nuclear families. What they derived from it, however, were the close and valued friendships with their peers, pride in helping the younger generation, and a deep sense of personal satisfaction.

"Big Men Off the Campus"

The *Zeta Beta Tau Quarterly* had always included news about alumni achievement, and as the fraternity and its membership matured, the lists grew longer and longer. Alumni achievement brought luster to the fraternity, permitted others to bask in reflected glory, and provided the constant comfort that being Jewish did not need to prevent a man from accomplishing great things.

In the 1950s the column "BMOC (Big Men Off the Campus): Letter Winners in Life" was inaugurated to feature prominent alumni. One in particular, William S. Paley (Penn '22), former president of his chapter, had been providing reading material for his fraternity brothers since 1928 when, six years out of college, he first bought CBS and its twenty stations for $300,000. By fall 1949, it was said, he owned 179 and an empire. As CBS board chairman and principal owner, he had already spent $2 million preparing for the day when the FCC (Federal Communications Commission) would allow the broadcasting of television in color. Radio and television producer Louis G. Cowan (Chicago '31) was the sensation of the broadcasting world in 1955–56, as millions of Americans tuned in regularly to watch *The $64,000 Question*, also on CBS. Aaron Rosenberg (USC '33) of Universal Pictures produced the box-office hit *The Benny Goodman Story* in 1956. Jerome Lawrence (Ohio State '37), who had been co-author of the Broadway hit *Inherit the Wind*, was about to open a new musical named *Shangri-La* on Broadway that same season. In his case, ZBT connections and devotion proved crucial; forty Ohio ZBTs had been among the backers of his earlier shows, and many were reinvesting their profits in the new venture. *Shangri-La* was soon followed by *Auntie Mame* (written and coproduced with Ohio classmate Robert E. Lee), which by the spring of 1957 was selling out to standing-room-only crowds. Norman Panama (Chicago '35), of the writing team Panama and Frank, had written and co-produced the Broadway hit *Li'l Abner*, while Robert L. Joseph (Syracuse '44) was responsible for the sell-out revival of George Bernard Shaw's *Major Barbara*.

In the field of sports, fellow alumni followed the college football coaching exploits of Sid Gillman (Ohio State '34), who had coached at Ohio, Denison, and Miami University at Oxford and in 1950 was leading the undefeated Army team. Dr. Joseph Alexander (Syracuse '21) was one of 105 chosen from thousands of players and coaches over a period of sixty years to be included in the permanent Football Hall of Fame at Rutgers University (the home of intercollegiate football). On November 13, 1955, in a special ceremony between halves of a Syracuse football game, Joe Alexander was presented with a plaque commemorating his election. The same evening, 350 friends and fraternity brothers, including 65 Syracuse undergraduate members, gathered for a testimonial dinner in his honor at the Hotel Syracuse.

Other alumni of unusually high achievement during those years included Joseph L. Eckhouse (NYU '28), executive head of Gimbel Brothers in New York, who was named as one of the country's highest paid corporation executives for the fiscal year 1948; Andrew Goodman (Michigan '28), president of Bergdorf Goodman; Harold Riegelman as always, who served for several terms as chairman of the New York division of the American Jewish Committee and was the Republican nominee for mayor of New York City in the fall of 1953; and Morris Marshall Cohen (Union College '24), who was sworn in as Justice of the Supreme Court of New York in 1955. Morris Cohen was no stranger to being honored by Zeta Beta Tau. More than a quarter century earlier the fraternity had selected him as its best all-around undergraduate.

Traditional Standards

If public service and achievement continued to be a prized Zeta Beta Tau tradition, so too did the ideal of the ZBT as the ultimate "gentleman"—no less a gentleman, and in fact even more of one, because he happened to be Jewish. Lee Dover and some of the fraternity's leading officers were perfectly aware that certain winds of change had begun to blow after the end of the war, but they did not rush to give in to them. Even as the college student population increased by hundreds of thousands and then by millions, Zeta Beta Tau continued to follow its conservative expansion policy, examining potential members with great care. In an editorial entitled "Wanted: Life Blood for the Next Fifty Years," written in 1948 on the fraternity's fiftieth anniversary, Dover warned that ZBT must continue to be as selective as it had ever been in the past:

The maintenance of standards has been the basis of ZBT's success during its first half century, and it follows that the continuation of our selective process will be necessary to maintain ZBT. No social fraternity of college students can be criticized of being snobbish, if it chooses only young men who come from excellent cultural backgrounds, who are of good character, who have a very good record in scholarship in their high or prep schools, who have a large capacity for friendship and who can afford the cost of Fraternity membership. This is ZBT's blood type, and every man, without exception, who is given membership in the second fifty years must meet these requirements. ZBT prestige has been built by maintaining high standards in membership, scholarship, friendship, public relations, good citizenship, restraint and modesty, and these must be maintained by the Fraternity.

That ZBT did not reach out eagerly to embrace all the opportunities for new chapters presented to it in the wake of the war was a matter not of concern but of pride in some quarters. "It is to be noted that ZBT's new chapters cannot be hastily organized and chartered 'sunflowers,'" declared the general secretary when queried as to why qualified new chapters were not being taken into the fraternity fast enough. "Charters are not mailed special delivery by the Supreme Council on wire requests. The Fraternity permits only those young men who demonstrate that they can 'make the team' to establish its new chapters."

In the 1950s the ideal ZBT member was still held to the same standards of behavior, culture, scholarship, social training, and gallantry toward ladies that had been widespread among America's upper classes twenty or thirty years earlier. These had been adapted to protect the good names of the both the individual members and of the fraternity as a whole—in large part, by disassociating Zeta Beta Tau from the negative stereotypes of Jews prevalent at the time. Social contact or association with other Jews of not so high a "type" was shunned. As for the members themselves, undesirable actions, habits, attitudes, and manners were to be continually brought to their attention and rooted out, as the eyes of the entire campus were upon them. In private, fraternity members had more freedom of movement, but in public their persona was to be guarded with great care. Into the 1950s the general secretary continued to stipulate that pictures showing ZBTs drinking liquor, romantically embracing women, or not properly attired in coats and ties (with the exception of athletic or other events requiring a special costume) were not to be reproduced in official ZBT publications. He advocated a good housemother for all chapters, ideally a "lady of culture" with social standing on the campus who could supervise help, preside as chapter hostess and chaperone at social functions, and discharge a myriad of other important duties with "efficiency, grace, and charm." Quiet speech and modulation of voices was to be the rule for everyone at all times; the cultural level of a chapter, Dover commonly said, could be measured by a sound meter in its dining hall, read in reverse.

At times some of these rules may have been honored more in the breach than in the observance, and the Central Office could usually depend only on the power of moral suasion to enforce them. Still, this was the tone that the ZBT national leadership chose to set; and for the alumni officers and large numbers of the fraternity's local undergraduate leaders, none of these norms or ideals, set in an earlier age, had lost their relevance.

ZBTs and their housemother around the chapter house piano at the University of Missouri in 1951. Left to right: Sherman Naidorf, '52, Martin Gross '52, Harry Berlau '53, Donald Kaufman '51, Albert Silverman '53, Mrs. A. Feltenstein, Stanley Stern '53, Myron Schultz '53.

Jewish Activity

Another Zeta Beta Tau tradition that remained intact at the beginning of the 1950s was its special role as a Jewish fraternity and the prominence in Jewish activities that it was taken for granted its alumni would achieve. Others within the community, including men who had themselves been former members of a fraternity, frequently hurled the epithet "assimilationists" against ZBT, condemning the intra-Jewish snobbery and undemocratic nature of the entire Greek system. Discrimination and exclusion of Jews from the mainstream of society was already painful enough, they argued, without adding the pain of exclusion from one's fellow Jews. Anti-Semitism practiced by Jews against other Jews was unconscionable and could only weaken the community. It had long been a common belief, besides, that Jewish fraternities were unworthy of the name since there was not the slightest Jewish content in their programming. All they did, critics charged, was copy the worst features of the Gentile groups and strive to blend into their surroundings by being as much like Gentiles as possible.

However, a review of the actual records reveals that the achievements of ZBT alumni in the sphere of Jewish communal life were far from inconsequential during the postwar years of rebuilding, renewal, and rebirth. Colonel Harold Riegelman, the epitome of ZBT alumni achievement as a war hero, public attorney, mayoralty candidate, and adviser to governors and presidents, was also a leading example of communal leadership. In the postwar years he also served as a high-ranking officer in the American Jewish Committee and as chairman of a $4 million postwar campaign conducted by the Hebrew University in Jerusalem to finance the first medical school in Israel in 1948. The campaign grew out of an urgent need to maintain the high medical standards that had so painfully been built up in the nascent Jewish state before the devastation of World War II. With a more than adequate supply of well-trained Jewish physicians coming from Europe, the university had not felt it necessary to expend resources on building its own medical school from scratch. However, the Nazi Holocaust had eliminated that source, and most of the Jewish physicians left in the new state were middle-aged or older. For this and other reasons, from then on, Israel had to be responsible for training its own doctors.

In B'nai B'rith, Frank Goldman (Boston University '10) succeeded honorary ZBT Henry Monsky as international president of the largest and oldest fraternal Jewish organization in the world, an achievement for which he was awarded the fraternity's New Orleans Trophy in 1952. In addition to serving on the board of governors of both the Hebrew University and the Jewish Theological Seminary, Goldman was one of the founders of the Conference on Jewish Material Claims against Germany, which successfully sought to obtain reparations for survivors of the Holocaust. When, in a well-known incident, a piqued President Truman refused to see Chaim Weizmann to discuss Palestine, it was Frank Goldman who got on the phone to Eddie Jacobson, a member of the Kansas City B'nai B'rith Lodge and a former friend and business associate of Truman's, and persuaded him to intercede. Jacobson ultimately helped bring about a historic meeting between Truman and Chaim Weizmann that was instrumental in securing early U.S. recognition for the new State of Israel.

In Europe, Charles I. Schottland (UCLA '27), who had been a charter member and first president of his ZBT chapter, served on the staff of General Eisenhower and as assistant director of UNRRA in Germany, where he was responsible for dealing with the care, rehabilitation, and resettlement of 5.5 million displaced persons. In February 1950, Governor Warren of California appointed him state welfare director. The winner of ZBT's 1954 Man of the Year award was George Alpert (Boston '18), a distinguished attorney who had been a founder and president of the board of trustees of Brandeis University since its establishment in 1946. In addition to such major figures, the columns of the *Quarterly* consistently reported news of ZBT alumni who served as synagogue and federation officers, as large donors to UJA campaigns, as heads of local B'nai B'rith lodges, and as leaders in a myriad of other communal posts.

Undergraduates played their part in the complex American Jewish communal scene as well; identification and leadership in this area was not limited to "mature" alumni. Hillel activity was one example. While on some campuses relations between the ZBT chapter and the local Hillel Foundation were filled with tension, through the late 1940s and early 1950s the number of ZBT Hillel presidents averaged between two and four a year, with many more reported as serving in lesser but important posts. In certain chapters, including Alabama and Penn State, the entire group joined Hillel en masse, was active in support of the annual UJA campaign, and took part in Hillel carnivals and competitions. Hillel president Seymour Glucksman (UCLA '48), in reporting in the *Quarterly* on his attendance at Hillel's summer institute, noted that five other brothers of Zeta Beta Tau were there as well: Howard Freeman '49 of Michigan and Eugene M. Schwarz '47 of the University of Washington (both presidents of their campus Hillels); Donald B. Kramer '50, vice president of Hillel at Washington–St. Louis; and Lewis Meisel and Bennett Kivel '49, vice president and cultural chairman, respectively, of the Hillel Foundation at the University of Florida.

Massive fund-raising for the United Jewish Appeal, which reached its peak in 1948, was another area where undergraduate ZBTs did their part. The Washington–St. Louis ZBT chapter provided autos and manpower for a citywide drive, provided ushers for a mammoth meeting of the St. Louis Jewish community in behalf of the UJA campaign, contributed its own funds, served in the top posts of treasurer and collections chairman, and composed what the local Hillel director assured the national officers was the most successful solicitation team in the city.

ZBTs also began to enter the rabbinate in noticeable numbers. In the fall of 1957 four young ZBTs were studying at the Hebrew Union College–Jewish Institute of Religion in Cincinnati: Floyd L. Herman

(Tulane '59), Michael A. Barenbaum (Chicago '58), Elliot D. Rosenstock (Cornell '53), and Stanley T. Relkin (CCNY '55). Older alumni already active in various pulpits in that year included Dr. Earl Stone (Syracuse '35), Dr. Robert I. Marx (Western Reserve '48), Robert A. Raab (Western Reserve '46), Dr. Albert Lewis (Western Reserve '34), and Dr. Felix Levy (CCNY '04), who had recently opened his own school for the training of rabbis.

Changes

Traditions and standards were important in ZBT, but it would have been difficult or impossible to maintain the standards of the prewar United States forever. The fraternity world was changing; the world of higher education in general was changing; the American economy was changing; the acceptance of a society legally based on divisions of race, religion, class, and ethnic background was changing. Although some of these changes may have redounded to the benefit of the fraternities, all of them tended to disrupt the established way of doing things.

One change was a growing antifraternity sentiment across the land that could no longer be ignored. From the dawn of the Greek system, fraternities had been accused of promoting discrimination, indifference to study, hazing, and drunkenness. As for the latter two, Zeta Beta Tau and the historically Jewish fraternities as a group had always prided themselves on the belief that they hazed less and drank less than other members of the NIC. However, in the 1950s and early 1960s the perception was that hazing and drinking within the ranks of ZBT were growing worse even as the number of boys who died in hazing accidents within the Greek system as a whole rose annually.

High scholarship, too, was no longer synonymous with membership in Zeta Beta Tau, nor was competent scholarship and even the minimum "gentleman's C" any longer the norm in the Greek system as a whole, a development that caused alumni and officers no end of distress. Careful scholarship and grade rankings had long been an American campus tradition, and the historically Jewish fraternities had always taken pride in placing well. Between 1937 and 1948, ZBT habitually ranked fifth among the constituent fraternities of the NIC, with a combined grade average far above the mean. For 1947–48, however, it slipped to fifteenth place, and the general secretary began extended communication with several chapters that had fallen below the all-men's average. Chapters were warned to raise their scholarship or to face disciplinary action, including social probation, and the national officers debated various ways to get their undergraduates to raise their grades.

In 1951, ZBT's national officers were appalled to be informed that one third of their chapters were performing below the mean and that on their respective campuses the chapters at Bowling Green and at the University of Chicago had placed dead last among all the other fraternities. That the problem of plunging scholarship was endemic to the fraternity system as a whole provided only scant comfort. At USC, for example, it was noted that out of twenty-nine chapters of national fraternities only five ranked at or above the all-men's average. In the 1955–56 academic year, NIC and administration surveys revealed that more than half of all the fraternity chapters in the entire country were performing below the all-men's average on their respective campuses. "How are the mighty fallen" was the sentiment of one officer, who worried that such showing was bringing the entire Greek system into disrepute.

In contrast with other fraternities, the collective grades of ZBT's undergraduate members still placed them near the top of the NIC rankings but only because the others were performing so poorly. As a rule, by the end of the 1950s and early 1960s in any given year more than one quarter of ZBT's chapters were judged to be doing substandard scholastic work. The decline was unprecedented within the fraternity.

Because of unwieldy student bodies, sharp variations in grading systems, and sheer exhaustion, the university administrations and the NIC gave up trying to compute the fraternity and all-men's scholarship statistics by the end of the decade. Nevertheless, the lack of concrete figures could not change the public's equation of fraternity membership with poor scholarship, for the historically Jewish fraternities no less than the non-Jewish ones.

Democracy in Education

Another major change in the postwar era that fundamentally affected the fraternity system was the advent of something approaching the true democratization of American higher education. A trend toward democratization and greater accessibility to a college education had become evident in the 1920s, when the percentage of young people receiving one had doubled. Still, college had not entirely lost its elite status, for not more than 8 percent of American youth aged seventeen to twenty-two actually attended.

As it turned out, the vast expansion of the student body that took place in the wake of the GI Bill was destined to last for the long term. The number of students did not contract when the last GI graduated; on the contrary, college came to be seen less as a luxury and more as a necessity, and the idea of entitlement to "financial aid," which had been almost nonexistent before the war, became a norm. University administrations ceased to put up more trailers and Quonset huts and rushed to build new, permanent dormitory buildings. The GIs who graduated were immediately replaced when the proportion of youth aged seventeen to twenty-two who entered college rose to 20–25 percent in the 1950s and past 40 percent in the 1960s. On top of the new popularity of college attendance lay the huge demographic bulge of the baby boomers, who were already reaching the campuses in the late 1950s and early 1960s in what some observers termed a "tidal wave of students" and "the college crush." State colleges routinely began to require higher admissions standards and higher tuition from out-of-state residents, and for the first time many colleges were receiving from five to ten times as many applications as they could accept.

By 1956 the U.S. collegiate student body stood at an all-time record high of three million, double the figure fifteen years earlier; and it was expected to double again, to six million, by 1970. Such a mass of students was too large to be assimilated into adult society; instead, adult society was destined in no small part to be assimilated by them.

Establishment of the Zeta Beta Tau Foundation, Inc.

Not only the size of the student body but the size of the students' tuition bills was skyrocketing, along with the cost of room and board. By 1950 the fraternity's leaders had decided to form a foundation to grant both scholarships and student loans so that no ZBT would ever have to discontinue his education because of financial difficulties. The Zeta Beta Tau Foundation was duly incorporated in 1952 as a not-for-profit, tax-exempt membership corporation. When its first scholarships were publicized to the undergraduates in 1954, the selection committee, headed by the foundation's first president, Harry Steiner (Columbia '18), was stunned by the number of applications and the high standards of need, scholarship, and "character" that all of them met. Most came from boys who were juniors and seniors and who, because of sudden financial reverses or unpredictable rises in cost, were unable to finish college without help. Clearly, Zeta Beta Tau could no longer assume that wealth and membership within its ranks were synonymous.

After the 1954 Miami convention every undergraduate was required to pay at least $5 to the foundation's scholarship fund (by the 1980s the amount had gone up to $10), and ZBT accepted a new fraternal responsibility. In time, the Zeta Beta Tau Foundation, Inc., developed separately into the charitable arm of the fraternity, accepting contributions from family and friends, maintaining special funds in honor or memory of chapters and individuals, dispensing loans and scholarships, and supporting leadership training programs within the fraternity.

Changes in Fraternity Membership Policy

In the course of the decade, Zeta Beta Tau was also forced to move, albeit slowly, away from its standards of extreme selectivity and an expansion policy so conservative that in the entire decade of the 1950s, while the general student body was doubling, the fraternity added only six chapters. National officers did not fail to note, to their great regret, that some petitioning chapters they had rejected had been accepted by other, competing fraternities and had evolved into groups that would have been a credit to Zeta Beta Tau. Wholesale admission of any applicant who happened by would never be acceptable to them, but neither did it serve the fraternity's best interest to maintain an attitude of exclusivity so impenetrable that no one new could pass through the door.

As it happened, much more than ZBT's high gentlemanly standards stood in the way of the fraternity's expansion. Zeta Beta Tau had been the first national college fraternity whose membership had been openly and officially limited strictly to Jewish men. Throughout the late 1940s and 1950s, attacks against that policy from both within and without the fraternity steadily intensified. All the changes of that era became focused on that one policy, and as the years passed, it became more and more certain that such a policy could not long endure.

CHAPTER EIGHT

"WE'LL BE BRETHREN OF ZBT"

The Sectarian Question, 1948–54

In the wake of World War II, fundamental ideological and political change was in the air across the entire country, not only on college campuses. ZBT had been born and had thrived as a Jewish fraternity, with membership limited exclusively to Jews. Through the years this had been one of its strongest traditions. Now this fundamental point was coming under attack, and the dispute all but tore the fraternity apart.

A confluence of social factors and historical forces were driving the change. Most important was the influence of the veterans who had done battle in war and who did not hesitate to do battle with their elders if a principle they believed in was at stake. In addition, the lowering of traditional social barriers during the war, the anger of minorities at not being granted full rights in the country they had laid down their lives to defend, the need to forestall Communist criticism of American racism, the growing need for academically and technically trained personnel no matter what their background, and an awareness of just how appallingly far racism and religious prejudice had so recently been taken all played a role. The 1954 Supreme Court decision in *Brown v. Board of Education* that the doctrine of "separate but equal" was inherently unequal and unconstitutional and the struggles of the civil rights movement were turning points. Educational institutions appeared the logical starting point for bringing about a more just society, and thus the cause of reform or outright elimination of college fraternities became a focal point of the general struggle.

College campuses were a reflection of the society of which they were a part, and strict social segregation by religion, race, and class, whether

A typical fraternity "rush" scene at the University of Minnesota, January 9, 1951. A freshman (at left, in armchair) is being informed of the merits of joining ZBT relative to other fraternities; the interview was also a chance to evaluate the candidate's acceptability as a potential fraternity brother. This photograph was taken by a member of ZBT's Twin Cities Alumni Club. From left to right: Leland J. Green '51, "unknown rushee," Robert N. Stone '52, Julius H. Klein '51, Israel Mirvis '53, Ronald M. Mankoff '54.

de facto or de jure, had almost been taken for granted in earlier periods. Social college fraternities in particular saw themselves as elite, selective, and intimate social organizations where members lived together, ate together, visited in each other's homes, and married among each others' relatives. In their view, careful discrimination was justified because every fraternity member, whether undergraduate or alumnus, was theoretically obligated to accept every other man who had ever been initiated into the fraternity as his own brother. Hence, it was crucial that criteria be maintained that would be accepted by all. Broken hearts and class divisions might result when an undergraduate was excluded from joining a desired fraternity, but few, including the excluded Jewish students, questioned the right of a social organization to set any criteria it chose for its members. It was partly for this reason that separate Jewish fraternities had been founded in the first place, and they no less than

Gentile groups prized the right to choose their own members. Among the sixty constituent fraternities of the National Interfraternity Conference (NIC) during the war it was estimated that at least two thirds, including several of the Jewish ones, had some kind of restrictive clause in their constitution or ritual, and in many of the rest the fraternity kept itself ethnically, racially, and religiously homogeneous purely by "gentleman's agreement."

This uneasy status quo on the nation's campuses began to break down under the strain of postwar social, political, and historical forces, when citizens of varying backgrounds organized and began a concerted attack on inequality and prejudice. Exposés of the social brutality practiced by Greek-letter groups became regular fare in the nation's media. Among civic leaders, journalists, legislators, and other public figures, long-smoldering antifraternity activism coalesced into a veritable flood of federal, state, and local legislation demanding that social Greek-letter groups prove lack of discrimination or get off campus. It was a sign of the times that the editors of the patrician *Fraternity Month* magazine fought back most vehemently against these opponents by claiming that their most important democratic right of free association was being violated and that the antidiscrimination movement was in fact a result of Communist subversion.

In some cases, what came to be known among ZBTs as the "S" question (for "sectarianism") served merely as a pretext for those who had long wished to abolish fraternities anyway for any number of reasons. In other cases, opposition was motivated by sincere desire for reform from those who saw the issue of unfair membership restrictions as a stab at the very heart of American democracy. The new accountability of America's colleges and universities in an era of rising costs played a role. Fraternities, opponents pointed out, were not truly private organizations. They were an integral part of an educational system supported in no small measure by tax dollars. Any student good enough to be admitted to a university had the right to full acceptance in all its facets, and fraternities had no right to set up artificial and arbitrary standards to differentiate among them. In the view of these opponents, not only the campus but the future of the entire country was at stake. Students, after all, were attending college and university to get an education, to graduate, and to become the future leaders of the nation. The social attitudes they imbibed while at school would surely influence them for the rest of their lives. Young people who in their most formative years had been taught to shun contact with those not of their background could not be expected to change very much as adults. How could a truly democratic United States emerge if prejudice was allowed to compose any part of the American college curriculum?

The "Amherst Edict" of 1948

Outside forces had attempted to reform or to eliminate fraternities for generations, but after World War II opponents were enjoying for the first time widespread success within the courts and lawmaking bodies as well as in the inner sancta of the nation's leading colleges. The pace was set by Amherst College, which in 1948 banned any fraternities with membership restrictions based on race, color, or creed. In 1953 the authorities of the State University of New York system voted to abolish national fraternities altogether. That was a special blow to the Jewish fraternities since so many of their constituency resided within the state; indeed, one of the reasons for the creation of a state university system in New York had been to make room for the thousands of Jewish students who might otherwise be denied a place in private colleges.

Throughout the late 1940s and early 1950s, in college after college, fraternities and sororities were ordered to open their constitutions and rituals to public view and reveal whether or not they had discriminatory clauses. Most of these cases attracted extensive media coverage. If the fraternities did have restrictive clauses and did not eliminate them within a certain deadline (the time usually given ran anywhere from one to six years), they could be severed from their national authorities, be expelled from the campus, or otherwise simply put out of business. If fraternities sought to expand by establishing new chapters on other campuses and could not state that their constitution and rituals were nondiscriminatory, college administrations politely informed their representatives that they would not be welcome.

An additional complication for the national fraternity authorities was lack of cooperation from the undergraduates themselves. Among both veterans and nonveterans, social attitudes tended to be far more liberal than among the alumni, and several undergraduate groups directly challenged their elders by pushing to eliminate the clauses or else actually pledging new members who did not meet the set racial or religious criteria. Jewish fraternities, in addition to the external opposition faced by the entire Greek system, suffered especially from sharp internal attack. In a pattern that would repeat itself later in the 1960s, both their undergraduates and alumni were notably more liberal on questions of social change than the population as a whole and even more liberal as a group than the youth of the Gentile fraternities.

Similar attitudes were held by the Jewish defense and antidiscrimination agencies, which were playing a major role in the postwar social transformation and continually pressured the Jewish fraternities to change their policies. Proponents of preserving ZBT's traditional membership rules could not easily press their case if it appeared that the organized American Jewish community itself did not want them to. Organizational pressure was especially strong from the American Jewish Committee and the B'nai B'rith Anti-Defamation League. Their ranks included several prominent Jewish fraternity members, who met with representatives of the Jewish Greek system continuously through the late 1940s and early 1950s to discuss this issue. It was one thing if Jewish college fraternities wished to follow a "positive Jewish program," they declared, but quite another to state categorically that no one but a Jew could become a member. How, these critics asked, could Jews in good conscience push for an end to restricted schools, corporations, summer camps, law firms, and country clubs while themselves discriminating against others on the basis of religion? Especially after the example of Hitlerism? And if the Gentile fraternities appeared slow to change to their ways, did it not behoove Jews, who supposedly embodied the prophetic ideals of social justice and whose destiny was to serve as a "light unto the nations," to pave the way by changing their clauses and rituals first?

However, the mutual removal of restrictive clauses, when it did occur, did not always work out to be the quid pro quo that Jewish supporters of the antidiscrimination movement expected. Nor did the new freedom and access to previously off-limits social institutions, achieved by attitudinal change and hard campaigning by Jewish organizations, always appear to be an unmixed blessing to national fraternity officers, undergraduate leaders, and especially parents. Certainly, American Jewish families felt some pride and pleasure that for the first time it was actually possible for Jewish students to be accepted into formerly exclusively Christian fraternities. However, there was a sense of resentment that Jews should have to make sacrifices in order to eliminate a situation that had been originated with Gentiles and a strong sense of doubt that, once they opened their doors to non-Jews, the non-Jewish groups would fully reciprocate the favor. Within a formerly all-Jewish house the relaxation of unguarded speech might disappear, and it was feared that the especially close ties of brotherhood, sisterhood, and intrafraternal marriage and friendship, so crucial to a scattered minority, would be irreparably damaged if Gentiles were admitted as well. Mothers of Jewish students in particular feared the total breakdown of barriers between the two types of fraternities. Many marriages, one such mother observed, were made in heaven; many more were made on college campuses.

In debates on the "S" question an important consideration was the ever-present dynamic of prestige and social desirability, which was based as much on subjective perception as on any objective, historically measurable reality. In the beginning, the Jews now being taken by the formerly all-Christian fraternities were the "best" students, the ones who would bring luster to any group—the best looking, the brightest, the richest, the best athletes. Fraternity officials from Zeta Beta Tau and other Jewish groups, as well as alumni and parents, continually reacted with surprise and concern to find that their leading pledging prospects had already been pledged to non-Jewish fraternities. Given a choice between ZBT and one of the larger, older, and more prestigious Greek-letter groups, it was natural for the superior Jewish student to be tempted to join the latter. But after all, the ZBT groups asked each other, what kind of Gentile would want to join a historically Jewish fraternity? So much hard work had gone into the cultivation of prestige, into selecting and training only the "best" members within their own sphere of influence. If forced to cease being Jewish and to open their doors to non-Jews, surely only the "residue" of the Christian students would join, and the size and character of their beloved fraternity would deteriorate.

The sectarian and racial controversy rocked the entire fraternity and sorority world for years, beginning in 1946 and continuing through the early 1960s, causing lines to be sharply drawn and friendships of long standing to be broken. In the end the new mood of the country and the relentless legal pressure against official bigotry of any kind proved to be too strong. Officials in the fraternity world realized that they were dependent on the universities and were there only by their sufferance. On many campuses, Greek-letter societies with discriminatory clauses in their constitutions were simply not allowed. Approximately half of the eleven historically Jewish fraternties and sororities still in operation at the time, including Alpha Epsilon Pi, were less of a target, as their constitutions had never had clauses limiting membership to Jews in the first place (their founders had never conceived that anyone but Jews would want to join). ZBT stood far more exposed, for it had been completely open about its membership restrictions from the very beginning. In 1953 and 1954, Sigma Alpha Mu and Zeta Beta Tau, the last two specifically Jewish men's fraternities, removed all sectarian clauses from their charters and rituals, thus ceasing to be officially Jewish. That they continued to be identified as Jewish fraternities and to some extent still are is evidence that one cannot so easily change the characteristics of an organization simply by removing a clause from a charter.

A Growing Movement

Within Zeta Beta Tau, serious debate on the "S" question began in 1948, the year of the "Amherst Edict." At that time, the preamble to its constitution still specified that only Jewish men were eligible for membership, and the initiation ritual included numerous references to He brew biblical and Jewish culture and responsibility, culminating with the vow: "I am a believer in God and the Brotherhood of Man; I am a Jew." Already the clauses were proving to be a serious obstacle to expansion. On campuses across the nation, college administrations, faculty, and a significant percentage of progressive undergraduates were no longer willing to tolerate, on principle, restrictions against any religion in any form. It did not matter to them whether such restrictions were legally specified, maintained by strong custom, or maintained by a majority or minority group.

At Zeta Beta Tau's golden anniversary convention at the Waldorf Astoria in 1948 the first piece of legislation on the subject, "Resolution #41," was introduced by delegates of the University of Chicago and passed. It called for a mail poll to be taken in the spring and fall of all eleven thousand members in good standing and for test votes of chapter delegates and alumni clubs to be taken at the upcoming December 1949 convention in Miami. As a result of the ensuing debate, by the fall of 1950, clauses restricting membership to Jews were removed from Zeta Beta Tau's public charter and constitution.

It was still impossible, however, for anyone but a Jewish man to go through ZBT's ritual. Only the public words had been changed; the private words, meant to be heard only within the limits of secret initiation ceremonies, had not. This type of subterfuge had become widespread in the Greek-letter world as a whole, since it allowed fraternities to claim they were nonsectarian in public while maintaining their traditional purity in secret. Such dissembling, however, could not last for long. Officers and members were understandably uncomfortable with it, and college administrations and state legislators would not remain fooled. Sooner or later they would demand concrete evidence that a fraternity chapter truly did not discriminate against anyone on the basis of religion, race, nationality, or creed.

Within ZBT, the movement to eliminate Jewish restrictions from the ritual and to make the fraternity truly nonsectarian gathered steam, as it did in other historically Jewish fraternities during that period. Members of the Supreme Council, in part because they were themselves so bitterly divided on the issue and in part because they wished to preserve some semblance of unity in front of the general membership, at first pledged themselves to neutrality. Heated debate and votes on the "S" question took place among the ZBT chapter delegates in convention assembled in 1950, 1951, 1952, and 1953. Each year the gap between the two factions grew narrower and narrower. By 1953 the final tally was twenty-five chapters in favor of keeping the Jewish ritual and twenty-two against. It was also in 1953 that Sigma Alpha Mu, a main competitor to Zeta Beta Tau, voted to remove all Jewish restrictions from both its constitution and ritual. This left Zeta Beta Tau as the last of the eleven remaining historically Jewish fraternities to officially maintain membership restrictions and the first among its contemporaries to be denied access to new campuses because of its allegedly discriminatory policies.

The Great Debate: August 28, 1954

After seven years of continuing debate, the issue came to a head at ZBT's 1954 convention, held in Miami Beach August 26–29. No other business matter on the agenda aroused such anticipation and apprehension, and no other debate was destined to be as long remembered. Discussion of the "S" question was scheduled to take place at the third business session, commencing at 9 A.M. on Saturday, August 28, 1954. It would be recorded on tape and immediately transcribed verbatim for distribution to ZBT men across the country who could not be present that day. "This is a controversial matter that has engaged the attention of the convention for the past few years," remarked Supreme President L. Reyner Samet as he opened the proceedings. "These discussions have always been conducted as brothers should conduct them, with dignity and mutual respect. I am sure that we will do it that way today." He thereupon introduced the resolution, submitted by the Columbia University chapter: "Be it resolved, that the Supreme Council be requested to adjust the ritual of the fraternity in such a way as to remove all actual and implied religious restrictions for membership into our fraternity." The ground rules were set that a prepared list of speakers for and against the resolution would alternate, each being allotted six minutes to speak.

Those Against

Among the first speakers against the resolution, Miles H. Friedlander (LSU '56) and Allan Resnick (North Carolina '56) both stressed their desire to share the bond of Judaism with their fraternity brothers, their fear that taking non-Jews would lower the overall quality of the fraternity and lead to problems in case of transfer, and their certainty that none of their Gentile friends could object to their belonging to a Jewish organization. Leonard N. Cohen (McGill '55) objected to assertions that ZBT had been founded as a Jewish organization only because Jews could not get into other fraternities. It had been founded for positive reasons, and its Jewish traditions were and should remain distinct. The resolution, he insisted, was nothing less than a "manifestation of Jewish inferiority," and he concluded his speech by quoting from the letter that Mrs. Richard Gottheil had written when donating a portrait of her husband to the fraternity: "The wish is that this portrait may be exhibited at each of your annual conventions so long as the pride in your Jewish heritage shall be the guiding principle for your great order which, please God, will be forever."

Stanley Relkin (CCNY '55), who would soon be studying for the rabbinate, admitted that the overwhelming majority of his chapter was in favor of the resolution and that he had been instructed to vote that way. However, his own feelings against the resolution were so strong that it was impossible for him to do so. To remove the words "I am a Jew" from the ZBT ritual, in his view, would be striking the heart from the fraternity. It was only as a Jewish group that they had achieved such a high position on the campus and within society. There was no driving need to admit Gentiles, and if ZBT did, he feared that within generations the entire character of the fraternity would change:

We could take a step forward in this liberal movement by removing this discriminatory clause. . . . But I doubt very much, seriously, that on my campus any Christian boy has been terribly hurt because he wasn't asked to become a member of ZBT. . . . If Columbia admits a few good Gentiles . . . next week, fine. But ten years

from now, half and half. In twenty years they have got the upper hand. I am not antagonistic against them. But . . . in 50 years ZBT could be completely Christian as a
fraternity. And maybe at a convention a suggestion would be made not to allow
Jews. I would hate to think that I would go home and say that I sat in at a convention that started the ball rolling, a ball that could well turn back on your own
grandchildren. It is something to think about. (p. 113)

Frank Fleischer (UCLA '55), who had been left without instructions
by his chapter, also objected to the notion that ZBT, which had been
founded because Jews had no other fraternity to join, was now discriminating against Gentiles. "How can a Gentile boy say that he has no fraternity to join?" Fleischer demanded. "That is a lot of hog wash. He has
all the fraternities in the world to join—millions of them." He further
joined with the delegate from City College in sharing his fears of what
would happen to the fraternity in the future if the resolution passed:

Picture yourself as an alumnus, say ten years from now. ZBT will probably be the
same then as it is today if this change goes through. Go on thirty, forty and fifty
years from now. You might be the outstanding Jewish leader in your community. I
am sure most of us will. Your fraternity will be ZBT. How would you like it to have
it known that your ZBT is now a Gentile fraternity? This could very easily happen
if we go through with this. . . . It's a trend because eight or ten other fraternities are
doing it. That doesn't mean that we should follow along on the bandwagon. We
must stand up and fight against it and keep our traditions as Jews and keep our
identification as Jews, as American Jews. We can do it. Let's not take the way out.
Let's stand up and fight! (p. 141)

As the debate continued through the hours, the speeches grew more
impassioned, although basic decorum and mutual courtesy were never
lost. "What are we marching forward to?" asked Stanley Horowitz
(Western Reserve '56), questioning that the move toward nonsectarianism represented progress. "We are like a killer marching forward to kill
his victim." Jack Zager (Vanderbilt '55) declared that he was not worried about his chapter being voted out of existence in 1957 or in 1960,
when the administration's deadline for removing restrictive clauses approached, "but in 1954, August the 28th, not by university officials but
by the brothers of ZBT in Convention assembled." Supreme Vice President Eli Fink (Washington and Lee '32) insisted that any changes that
had been made by the Gentile fraternities had only been for the purposes of expediency, that anti-Semitism had lasted for a thousand years
and was not going to be eliminated by removing a restrictive clause. If
all fraternities, regardless of origin, were requested to "demonstrate"
their compliance with a nondiscriminatory policy, then only ZBT
would suffer. "The non-Jewish fraternities to demonstrate their good
faith will be in a position to take the cream because that is all that they

will take—the cream of the Jewish boys," he insisted. "And the Jewish fraternity, whether it is ZBT or any other Jewish fraternity, will have to take—I will say—the clabber of the non-Jewish boys." Theodore H. Pinkus (Indiana University '55) spoke of ZBT's homogeneity as the essence of its strength and compared the situation to Prime Minister Chamberlain's 1938 appeasement at Munich:

Are we going to be Chamberlains at Munich or a Judas Maccabaeus in Judea? This is the day, gentlemen, this August 28th, Saturday, that can go on record as the Munich of the fraternity—the crucial hour of this fraternity. This crisis has not come from the outside, but has originated from within. . . . Your organization is the strongest in the field. Today you meet to choose whether to keep that national prestige or commit premeditated, outright suicide. . . . Vote for this change and you are going to speak for assimilation 100 per cent. . . . The very substance of your inheritance willed us by our founders is exemplified in the words, "ZBT, you shall remain. . . . With courage you shall take your stand. My brothers, here's my hand." But then it goes on: ". . . . If this year should be our last.". . . Gentlemen, this might be the end here and now, the dissolution of a monument to the Jewish religion built by sacrifices of those who came before. . . . For six years we have been threatened with suicide, but we ain't dead yet. Let's keep on living. (p. 154)

For several of the undergraduate delegates, their concerns lay less with the alleged detrimental effect nonsectarianism might have on ZBT's overall quality than with the discomfort it would cause to their religious life and what they saw as the inevitable hypocrisy of being theoretically open to everyone while still trying to maintain their Jewish traditions. "Can you imagine a Gentile pledge father coming into our house or your house and teaching the boys the rich, cultural Jewish heritage of ZBT?" asked Arnold Levitz (Kentucky '58), who stressed that their chapter recited prayers before every single meal, observed holidays, and attended temple regularly. "Can you imagine him at Yom Kippur. I can just see it now. . . . I don't want to see a bunch of hypocrites in our house. . . . SAM tried it on the campus this last fall. They went to the IFC to explain their setup. They wanted to be liberal. They wanted it open to everybody. They came there and said, 'Now, we are going to have kosher meals and observe all the Jewish holidays.' If that isn't hypocritical, I don't know what is, and I'm afraid that is what is going to happen to ZBT."

Those in Favor

Those speaking out in favor of the resolution stressed the need to be true to America's democratic values, the necessity of departing from the past, the certainty that changing the ritual would not fundamentally alter the fraternity's character, and most important, that not to become nonsectarian while all the other historically Jewish fraternities had would lead to the strangulation and death of their fraternity.

After seven years of debate, Kalman K. Marx (Cornell '55) pointed out that some of ZBT's best chapters had been told to get rid of discriminatory clauses or get off the campus. Theirs was the only Jewish fraternity left with discriminatory barriers, and these were rendering them stagnant. The demand that they be removed was not a spontaneous decision but part of a movement—a movement of reality to at last support the ideals of their American creed—and it was clear to all that the authorities had decided to accomplish this first through the educational system. "Remember, we are no longer living in the past," he warned his audience. "Tradition is a fine and wonderful thing, especially the tradition of the Jewish people. But we must remember that we should not hesitate to break tradition when that break is for the benefit of our people." Stanley J. Leiken (Michigan '55) pointed out that there were few things more important to a fraternity than its public relations and that to maintain discrimination within the ritual was to ruin ZBT's name and promote the worst types of public relations they could possibly hand out. If the fraternities did not remove discriminatory clauses themselves, he asserted, then the state legislatures, university administrations, and student councils would do it for them. Besides, how could they have fought so hard for religious tolerance for so many years and still maintain this kind of racial bigotry?

"No one wants to lose their religion and no one said we have to," commented Tom Hofheimer (Virginia '56), "[but] isolationism, segregation and narrow-mindedness are not American ideals. . . . It is only a question of time when sectarianism will be done away with. As college men we should be more progressive and more broadminded than others." John Newman of Miami University in Ohio asserted that the "antiquated policy of discrimination" should be done away with as quickly as possible. Already other fraternities were telling their prospective pledges that it was sheer folly to join a fraternity that would be dead in a few years, and Columbia and Cornell would have no chapters if they did not move immediately.

Aside from sheer survival, the principle of the matter was most important. ZBT, the proponents of the change declared, would be unfair to the very principles that constituted Judaism if it did not make the change. "White, Negro, Jew or Gentile, we must learn to live together in harmony and comradeship," Newman declared. "Gentlemen, we must progress, we must move ahead. Twenty-five years ago it was fashionable to remain a closed organization. This is not so today. . . . In changing our ritual, remember that none of the principles on which ZBT stands today will be disturbed. We shall retain the Jewish star, the Hebrew words and the biblical interpretations, and Jewish traditions will continue to permeate the entire fraternity. We can and must not wait any longer and I appeal to you intelligent individuals to step ahead for the good of your chapter, for the good of ZBT, and for the good of our country."

Supporters of the resolution castigated the arguments of those opposed as being overly emotional and unrealistic. "The point was made that fifty years from now, ZBT may be completely Gentile," countered Ronald Weintraub (USC '56) "To reduce that absurdity we might say, fifty years from now Sigma Chi may be all Jewish. I don't think we can project into the future and I don't think we'll become an all-Gentile fraternity. I doubt if my son or grandson will ever become Sigma Chi." (The name of Sigma Chi was habitually evoked by Jewish fraternity members because it was one of the oldest and most prestigious of Gentile fraternities, as well as one of the most openly Christian ones; its crest consisted of a cross and the Constantinian motto, *In Hoc Vinces*— "In this shall ye conquer.") David Hirsch (Cornell '57) denied that by becoming nonsectarian they would lose their identity as Jews. How could that be if they had spent eighteen or nineteen years being brought up in a Jewish family? No harm could come from getting to know Gentiles on a better basis, nor did it necessarily follow that Gentile members would be admitted under standards any different from those that had always prevailed in ZBT.

Earl Wiener (Duke '55), who had been instructed by his chapter to vote against the resolution, rose to address the floor as to why he had decided to vote in the affirmative. Most of the arguments heard that morning, he declared, had come from what might be called "alarmist" Jews. "They call those of us who try to put through this change anything from Judas Maccabaeus to Chamberlain," he chided his opponents. "I don't know how they forgot Benedict Arnold or Quisling. We have heard from the boys who, if you will excuse me, have used a kind of a Jewish version of McCarthy flag-waving. . . . One of my colleagues from a neighboring school even went so far as to say that if we put this change through that it will be the death of Judaism. Gentlemen, the Jews have survived a lot of things more serious than this question." By changing their ritual, he insisted, ZBT would not be weakening its religious identity but strengthening it by affirming the dignity of the individual and the equality of man, which were also important parts of its ritual. The fraternity would not be weakened one bit; "It will be as strong forty years from now as it is now and as it was forty years ago when our fathers joined ZBT."

Treasurer Bernard J. Moncharsh (NYU '44) reiterated the theme that the fraternity would no longer exist for their sons if the change did not go through. Already the great majority of their chapters were in imminent danger of closing. The handwriting was not on the wall but clearly printed throughout the country, throughout every institution and every organization of which any one of them was a member. No harm would come to their culture or to their Jewish traditions by making this change. Besides, it was not fair to say that up until that point ZBT chapters were free to choose the men they wanted. "There are men with standards as good as ours who are Gentile and who would probably make wonderful fraternity brothers," he pointed out. They were not knocking down the door to get in, yet they would welcome the opportunity to be asked. There could be no harm in welcoming them in turn: "They will only help us."

Turning Point: The Speech of Supreme Vice President Stanley I. Fishel

The impassioned debate might have gone on for several hours more, with the delegates equally divided between the two sides, had not the four key members of the Supreme Council who lived in New York City (L. Reyner Samet, Richard Graham, Bernard Moncharsh, and Stanley Fishel) decided to abandon their former posture of strict, official neutrality and switch to the stance of urging the undergraduates to pass the resolution. Supreme Vice President Stanley I. Fishel (Columbia '34) had formerly been, in public, among the most adamant that neutrality should be maintained; in private he was among the strongest believers that changing ZBT's membership policy would be a mistake. Chosen by Supreme President Samet to deliver the Supreme Council's opinion, he made an unscheduled speech lasting more than twenty-five minutes, explaining to the rest of the fraternity why concern for the very existence of ZBT had caused him to change his mind.

"We have faced up to the unalterable fact that ZBT's future lies in a constructive solution to the 'S' question," he began forthrightly, "and we believe that the only constructive solution is to change the ritual and to change it now. . . . We have no fears at all in the full responsibility of the offices we hold and the constitution we have sworn to maintain and defend, that any step such as this could mean the disintegration of the fraternity. Rather, we believe it is the only intelligent preventative of future disintegration."

Opposition to the change, he asserted, was coming mainly from two groups of chapters: those in the South who feared that dropping Jewish restrictions would lead to the pledging of Negroes and those, including some in the South as well, who were proud of ZBT's Jewish heritage and tradition and feared that any change would disturb their homogeneity. A review of the fate of other historically Jewish fraternities was enough to allay these fears. Fishel enumerated the ten other historically Jewish fraternities that were active on North American campuses that year: Pi Lambda Phi, Phi Epsilon Pi, Phi Sigma Delta, Sigma Alpha Mu, Kappa Nu, Phi Alpha, Beta Sigma Rho, Alpha Epsilon Pi, Tau Delta Phi, and Tau Epsilon Phi. Of these, only Pi Lambda Phi had started and remained a nonsectarian fraternity. All of these, with perhaps one exception, were national fraternities, and all had chapters throughout the South.

Since World War II, Fishel pointed out, each of these fraternities, one by one in convention assembled, had voted to revise its constitution and ritual so as to be nonsectarian. Some had pledged and initiated "two or three Gentile boys from here and there and less occasionally a Negro," and yet their chapters were still living harmoniously together; Pi Lambda Phi, Phi Sigma Delta, and Sigma Alpha Mu were still "flourishing, successful national fraternities recognized as being Jewish, proud to be Jewish and offering Zeta Beta Tau stiff and healthy competition on dozens of campuses." Zeta Beta Tau stood alone now of all the great national college fraternities of Jewish men as the single upholder of discrimination, indeed one of the handful in the entire National Interfraternity Conference, Jewish or Gentile, that still officially practiced and preached discrimination. "My brothers, I ask you, is it possible that all ten of our colleague Jewish fraternities are wrong and that we alone are right?" Fishel demanded. "Is it possible that all ten are out of step with the times and that we alone are in tune? Is it possible that all ten have sold their Jewish birthrights and that we alone uphold the great tradition?"

To justify preserving the status quo by conjuring up the "non-existing Frankenstein" of the "race question" was bad enough, but worse, in Fishel's view, was that the undergraduates did not seem to understand the consequences of voting down nonsectarianism one more time. More than half of their present chapters were located on campuses where they would not be permitted entrance were they trying to start up that year. As time passed, ZBT would find it difficult or impossible to expand, and if it could not grow, it would inevitably die. The Central Office had already received several petitions from potential chapters that they could not follow up on because they could not meet the local university's requirements of nondiscrimination. In another semester, surely one or the other of ZBT's competitors would be thriving on those campuses. Every second of delay was costing them dearly. In the period of postwar expansion, ZBT had been cut from consideration on new campuses as chapters of their competitors had been installed. If ZBT tarried on changing its ritual, it would end up being the second, third, or fourth fraternity of Jewish men on many a fine campus, instead of the historical first.

Those who proposed procrastination on the matter were not aware of how urgent the change was, Fishel warned. The deadlines given by the universities were growing shorter and shorter, and the bandwagon was beginning to roll into Canada as well, where their British Columbia chapter and no doubt soon their Manitoba and McGill chapters would be in danger. Only in the past few months the trustees of the State University of New York had summarily severed the national association of all their local chapters over the discrimination issue, and their right to do so was held up in court. ZBT did not have chapters at schools directly operated by New York state, but it did have chapters at Syracuse, Cornell, Columbia, NYU, and City College, all of which received some form of state aid. How long would it be before state legislators put pressure on them too? "As sure as we are all here this morning, ZBT will have to change for the public will not be patient," he admonished. "For, in the long run if fraternities do not eliminate discrimination, then the colleges and government authority will do so for them":

Whether we like it or not, the barriers to race, and religion are falling everywhere. We live in a time of great social sensitiveness and social irritability and fraternity discrimination is a cinder in the public eye. I hesitate to think that we in ZBT will make this change—and make it we inevitably must—only at the very last minute when we are forced to by the imminent loss of chapters. . . . With how much better grace would it be, how much easier on our conscience, if we joined the overwhelming majority of our colleague fraternities in the NIC and remove our discrimination at this convention of 1954. Must ZBT be last? ZBT has always prided itself on being first. . . . Don't put ZBT in the ignominious position of having a right to decide its own policies taken from it by collegiate or governmental bodies. Let us not be forced to do the right thing. Let us do it ourselves. (p. 143)

By changing the ritual now, he declared, they would be accomplishing three things: taking off the hook those chapters threatened with removal from campus if they could not prove nondiscrimination; satisfying the intellectual and moral desires of others not to remain part of a discriminatory fraternity; and finally, enabling those chapters that wished to go ZBT's "historic way" to do so completely. Certain chapters would continue to be 100 percent Jewish while others would be free to extend bids to an occasional non-Jew:

If our ritual is changed, your national officers have no fear that in the foreseeable future, if ever, will Zeta Beta Tau be anything else but a Jewish fraternity. Zeta Beta Tau will continue to represent the best of which Jewish young manhood is capable. The history of those of our great Jewish colleague fraternities that have become non-sectarian fortifies this opinion. They will always be recognized and accepted as Jewish because their brothers want it that way—are proud to have it that way. . . . I do not for a moment believe that if this ritual becomes law in time for initiations when colleges reopen this fall, that any of our chapters will go hell-bent to pledge large classes of non-Jews. Nor do I believe, conversely, that the doors of our forty-six chapter houses will be battered down by non-Jews desiring admission. I think we will go along pretty much as we have been for almost sixty years. . . . "I am a Jew" will come out, but Jewish ideals and Jewish traditions will stay in. (p. 144)

In so stating, Stanley Fishel read to the assembled gathering the text of the revised nonsectarian ritual, which included these words at the beginning of the ceremony: "As a pledgee, you have learned that in its origins, our fraternity was a brotherhood devoted to the attainment of Zion. In the year 1898 a number of Jewish college men met in New York and organized the Zeta Beta Tau Fraternity. Although with the passing of time our directions and interests have broadened, we, nevertheless, cherish and continue to revere and respect the historical Jewish traditions of our brotherhood."

In his peroration, Stanley Fishel delivered what was for many the most convincing reason that ZBT should remove any barrier to non-Jews who might wish to join their fraternity: the belief that it might lead to some small reduction of hatred in the world. If they were to become nonsectarian and adopt such a broad-based ritual, he asserted:

I think we will, for the occasional non-Jew we may initiate, do much to break down anti-Semitism. If he can live with us, I think that we, in turn, can live with him in complete brotherhood. For after all, Christianity itself and every one of its manifold denominations and sects is based on the law of Moses and the Talmud of Israel.

So, I have no fear that the Gentile of good faith cannot accept our ritual without any twinge of conscience, nor that we, in turn, cannot accept him as brother with any mingled feelings on our part. Indeed, I believe that the basic ideals on which Zeta Beta Tau was founded require today in this changing world the extension of our privilege of brotherhood to all college men who meet our standards regardless of race, creed, or color. (p. 144)

The Final Vote

After almost three hours of debate (the transcription of the session ultimately covered 221 typed pages), Supreme President Samet, in the belief that by that time all arguments had been adequately covered, had to ask those assembled whether they wished to continue discussion or to vote. Perhaps in equal weariness, the floor called for the question. "I wish to record my appreciation for the dignity and lack of personal animosity in which this highly controversial matter has been treated," Samet declared before calling the roll of ZBT's forty-seven chapters. "I, for one, am proud to be a ZBT today." He also reminded the gathering that while the decision of the convention would be taken into advisement, only the Supreme Council had the power to change the ritual; and until such time as they did so, the present ritual remained the law of the fraternity.

When the final vote was taken, those in favor of changing the ritual to make ZBT completely nonsectarian included NYU, Columbia, Cornell, Boston University, Ohio State, Syracuse, Illinois, Michigan, Virginia, Chicago, USC, Berkeley, Nebraska, Florida, Washington (Seattle), Arizona, Miami (Ohio), British Columbia, Penn State, Colorado, Rutgers, Maryland, Bowling Green, Manitoba, and Arkansas. Those opposed to the resolution included CCNY, Penn, Western Reserve, Tulane, LSU, McGill, Alabama, Missouri, Vanderbilt, Washington and Lee, Wisconsin, Washington (St. Louis), North Carolina, UCLA, Franklin and Marshall, Duke, Tennessee, Kentucky, Miami (Florida), Indiana, Michigan State, and San Diego State. Of the four alumni clubs represented that day (each entitled to one-third vote), Jacksonville opposed the resolution, Miami abstained, and both New York and Chicago voted in favor.

As expected, the overwhelming majority of ZBT's southern chapters opposed the resolution, while those of the Northeast, Midwest, and West Coast supported it, although there were several notable exceptions to that pattern. The final tally stood at 25⅔ for and 22⅓ against. Thus was the "S" question resolution passed by a bare margin of three and one third votes.

Adjournment

For many of those present, even those who had opposed the resolution, a wave of relief passed through them that at last one of the most divisive issues ever to face the fraternity had been settled. "Gentlemen, this discussion has been handled to my entire satisfaction and I am grateful and proud," announced President Samet at the conclusion of the session. "Tomorrow morning we shall continue with the rest of our business. Let us stop the cleavage that was, perhaps, present relating to the 'S' question and let's go back to operating the fraternity as fraternity brothers." To reinforce the ties of brotherhood, all present linked arms and sang "Here's to Our Fraternity." The following morning, at the final business session of August 29, Allan Resnick of North Carolina, who had found himself on the losing side, moved that the convention should go on record as voting for the "S" question unanimously. It was in the best interests of ZBT, he said, that no new friction be created by the question and that any friction that had been created was lessened. The motion was carried.

Just before adjournment of the proceedings, General Secretary Lee Dover, who had said not a word during the entire debate, attempted to lighten the atmosphere by a stab at humor. "I thought this was a remarkable convention," he declared. "We did a lot of house-cleaning here and cleaned up a lot of loose ends that have been giving us trouble for years. ZBT has nothing to fear whether it will be sectarian, non-sectarian, or co-educational." His remarks were greeted by laughter throughout the room.

Little did those assembled that day know what the next decade would bring or that, within less than twenty years, the national officers of Zeta Beta Tau would in fact have to deal with a serious movement among the members to admit women to their fraternity. In 1954 the upheavals and great social changes of the late 1960s still lay far away. At least for another college generation, Zeta Beta Tau would continue to exist much as it always had.

CHAPTER NINE

"JOYS AND GLADNESS"

Days of Glory, 1960–68

The Passing of Lee Dover

For more than three decades, through wars, depression, economic up-heavals, and the comings and goings of thousands of undergraduates, Leon David Dover had been as steady a rock as any national organiza-tion could hope for and the glue that held his fraternity together. Into the summer of 1961, his thirty-third at the post, he worked steadily on a new manual for chapter administration as well as a primer for new members, felicitiously titled *The ABC's of ZBT*. Time and poor health, however, took their toll, and it inevitably came to pass that "Mr. ZBT" was required to step down from active duty and to make way for a successor.

"The past is our heritage, the present is our responsibility, and the fu-ture is our challenge. Cordially, Fraternally, and Sincerely, Lee Dover" concluded his last report, delivered at the 1961 summer convention at the Edgewater Beach Hotel in Chicago to a visibly tearful audience. The Supreme Council, at its following September meeting, appointed in his place Barry D. Siegel (Bowling Green '52), a man who had served as as-sistant general secretary since June 1960 and who was destined to leave a mark upon the fraternity almost as enduring as that of his predecessor.

The venerable general secretary was not permitted to depart, how-ever, without due ceremony, nor was it expected at first that the frater-nity would altogether be denied the benefit of his wisdom and experi-ence. The Supreme Council appointed Dover as the fraternity's first and only permanent national vice president, while in Chicago the con-vention delegates unanimously voted to designate the following year's convention in New York—the first to be held in the birthplace of ZBT since 1948—"The Dover Convention."

Observers noted that the ZBT's sixty-fourth anniversary convention in 1962 was similar in many respects to the previous "fabulous fiftieth." The prospect of honoring Lee Dover brought out many of the "old-timers" who might not otherwise have attended, making it one of the largest gatherings ever in the annals of the fraternity. More than five hundred undergraduates and alumni overflowed the banquet hall of the Statler Hilton Hotel on the night chosen to pay him tribute. "Never again in Zeta Beta Tau will it be possible actually to live our entire past in capsule form as it was on the night of August 30, 1962," reported Jack I. Wagenheim, describing the testimonial dinner. "The occasion itself . . . was to many present a reminder of what we were like in 1928 and how far we have progressed since." The dais, Wagenheim noted, was filled with "those whose names are part and parcel of our great tradition back to the turn of the century." There were no fewer than eight past national presidents of the fraternity there, including Rabbi Aaron Eiseman, an 1898 founder and president in 1901–02, who also gave the benediction; Arthur S. Unger (Long Island Medical '05), who had served in 1907–08; Ralph J. Ury (Union '11), 1913–14; Alvin T. Sapinsley (Columbia '08), 1914–15; Harry Steiner (Columbia '18), 1926–27; Harold E. Grotta (Virginia '33), 1949–52; L. Reyner Samet (Virginia '25), 1953–56; and Stanley I. Fishel (Columbia '34), 1956–60. Also present that evening was 1898 founder Louis Posner, who presented the fraternity's Man of the Year award to Lewis Gottlieb (LSU '16), himself a founder of the Louisiana State University chapter in 1911.

The honorable retirement of Lee Dover, however, was destined to last for a regrettably short time. A heart attack intervened on June 17, 1964, exactly one month after his sixty-fourth birthday, and his death four days later created a shock that reverberated throughout Zeta Beta Tau and the entire fraternity world. Funeral services were held in New York City on June 23, 1964; the interment took place in Forest Hills. Messages of condolence poured in from across the country, as well as expressions of sympathy to his wife Margit (née Hirst) whom he had married in 1950, and their young daughter Marleigh, who had been named after both her parents. The entire fall 1964 issue of the *Zeta Beta Tau Quarterly* was dedicated to him, and opened with a commemorative editorial penned by the man who had been charged with the duty of fulfilling his legacy:

The loss of Lee Dover marked the end of an era in ZBT. He was my mentor and tutor and I will be everlasting in my appreciation of all that he taught me of ZBT and the fraternity system. . . . They say that he was a "legend in his own time" and, indeed, he probably was. He was probably more responsible for the "image" that ZBT has in the world today than any other single person. He built ZBT in his own mold and that mold was highly successful. Our growth over these many years in chapters, members, prestige and reputation can be attributed to our beloved Lee. His name will last forever.

Margaret Rossiter

The loss of Lee Dover was closely followed by the departure of another personage who had become almost an institution within the ranks of ZBT. Since the academic year 1930–31 the national office had operated with the services and assistance of Mrs. Margaret Rossiter, longtime assistant to the general secretary, but in July 1964 her time too came to retire. In the early days of the fraternity she had handled virtually all the paperwork and bookkeeping necessary for the continuance of a national organization and often ran the office by herself during her boss's long absences as he traveled throughout the country. She also served through a major depression, a major war, a postwar period, two minor recessions, and an additional armed conflict. "Through all of these turbulent years she held the fort and effectively handled all of the many and varied tasks assigned to her," Barry Siegel wrote in his *Quarterly* tribute to her that fall. "More than one undergraduate chapter president was told off on bad management practices by 'MR.' While not admitting it, she could probably recite the esoteric rituals verbatim. The office is not quite the same without her."

In the Wake of Sputnik I:
Education in the National Defense

Barry Siegel, who had been active in the fraternity and its Supreme Council since his graduation, assumed the helm of Zeta Beta Tau delighted to inherit its mantle and determined to stand upon the shoulders of those who had preceded him. Of the many innovations instituted under his administration from the new national offices at the Statler Hilton Hotel, the first and most dramatic was a rapid increase in the speed of the fraternity's expansion. The internal culture of Zeta Beta Tau, as in several other historically Jewish fraternities, had always tended toward caution in bringing in new members; but with the explosive growth in the American campus population since World War II and especially in the 1960s, the time appeared ripe for a change of heart.

The influx of veterans on the GI Bill and the later demographic bulge of the baby boomers would by themselves have been enough to bring about major changes in American higher education in the postwar years. Other influences continually augmented these, assuring that university training became increasingly valued on both an individual and governmental level and that higher and higher percentages of young people in that age bracket would seek it. It was a telling statistic that at the end of World War II roughly 16 percent of college-age Americans were enrolled in institutions of higher education, whereas by the 1960s the proportion had risen to 40 percent; among American Jews the proportion was more than double that number.

International politics played a significant role in making this expansion possible. The scientific and technological challenges of the postwar world, which had already made a bachelor's degree almost the minimum credential necessary for any "good" job, became woven into the fabric of the cold war when on October 4, 1957, the Soviet Union inaugurated the Space Age with Sputnik I. The first satellite ever launched by man, it successfully assumed a steady ninety-six-minute orbit around the earth for months, steadily beeping all the while, until early 1958, when it fell back and burned in the earth's atmosphere. This unmanned capsule, weighing less then two hundred pounds and measuring less than four feet wide, sent shock and terror into the hearts of patriotic Americans, who feared that the USSR was outstripping them not only politically but in the quality of the scientific, mathematical, and linguistic training they gave to their children. The subsequent launching of eight more Sputnik satellites, each one larger than the last, and news that they had progressed to carrying and bringing back to earth a variety of live animals did nothing to ease Americans' discomfort. Clearly, the Soviets were preparing to send a man into space. Even worse than the competitive resentment this aroused was the alarm that, if allowed to gain full command of the heavens, the Soviets might use the opportunity to rain unimaginable destruction down upon the United States.

In the aftermath of Sputnik unfavorable comparisons between the rigor of the Soviet educational system and the allegedly indulgent and easygoing American one immediately entered public discourse. U.S.

schooling at all levels was blamed for this mathematical and scientific disgrace, and its strengthening, along with a massive increase in public funds dedicated to research and development of all kinds, rapidly became equated with the cause of national defense. In October 1958, exactly one year after Sputnik I was launched, NASA (the National Aeronautics and Space Administration) was established under President Dwight D. Eisenhower. Less than three years later, in May 1961, President John F. Kennedy's State of the Union Address called upon the country to land a man on the moon and return him safely to earth before the decade was out. Year after year the race to the moon, which did not stop even in 1967 when astronauts were killed in accidents on both sides, engaged the highest technical skills of the United States and the Soviet Union, and mathematics and physics gained new respect and importance in the minds of legislators and the general public.

Against the background of these events, student financial aid, which had previously never been a well-organized part of the higher educational process, blossomed. Few at first questioned the necessity for draft-eligible male students in good standing to receive deferments from service in the armed forces, and for many young men and their families the attractions of college and graduate school were considerably enhanced thereby. Leaders and newspaper editors across the country hailed it as "a wise investment in the future of our country" when the National Education Act of 1958, a direct result of the Sputnik controversy, made any college student eligible for substantial loans at favorable rates if he or she could show and maintain good academic standing, with special preference given to potential mathematicians, engineers, secondary school teachers, and experts in modern foreign languages.

The 1958 act was only a small part of an entirely new level of enthusiasm as the baby boomers approached maturity and Americans of all ages rushed to support the cause of higher education. "Student enrollment . . . is increasing at a pace which staggers the imagination," the young executive secretary observed in a 1965 *Quarterly* editorial. The American college population had doubled between 1952 and 1962 and was expected to double again by 1970. Despite the fears of many, no dreaded third world war surfaced to devastate the world and deplete the male campus population, though the establishment of the Berlin Wall in 1961 and the Cuban missile crisis in October 1962 raised tensions. Between 1957 and 1963 alone college enrollment increased from three million to four and a half million. New institutions, including junior colleges, were built, and older ones, bulging with record enroll-ments, rushed to expand their facilities and establish new branches. "Schools barely heard of ten and fifteen years ago, today have thriving enrollments of five, ten and fifteen thousand full time day students," Siegel wrote. "Schools not even in existence ten and fifteen years ago are today large, attractive campuses.... Many of our ZBT alumni today have sons at schools which simply did not exist in their own undergrad-uate collegiate days."

The Growth of the Greek System

The expansion of the collegiate population had been matched by an ex-pansion in the fraternity population. Between the 1957 and 1963 issues of *Baird's Manual of American College Fraternities*, more than a mil-lion and a half new members had been initiated into national frater-nities and sororities. The massive numbers hid the ominous fact that, in real percentages, the proportion of American college students belong-ing to fraternities was actually shrinking. Whereas chapter rolls of one hundred or more had been considered outlandish twenty years earlier, by 1966 no fewer than twelve National Interfraternity Conference (NIC) member fraternities could claim that distinction. Of these, Tau Kappa Epsilon counted 220; Sigma Alpha Epsilon, 180; Sigma Phi Ep-silon, 168; Lambda Chi Alpha, 160; and Sigma Chi, 142. Indeed, the majority of the other fraternities in the NIC had already far outstripped ZBT in their rates of growth. Siegel was not prepared to let his own fraternity be outdone. What sense did it make for Zeta Beta Tau not to take advantage of the same golden opportunity?

ZBT Expands

The pace was set in March 1962 when ZBT added three new chapters—Rensselaer Polytechnic Institute, Youngstown University, and the Uni-versity of Pittsburgh—in the space of twenty-one days, a new record that was noted with pleasure in the pages of the *Quarterly*. Even as chapters were added, Siegel and his growing staff of field secretaries criss-crossed the country to help students in rushing and to establish colonies in places ZBT had never gone before, including more parts of California and the Sun Belt, far away from the fraternity's birthplace in New York City. Long Island University, American University, and

On the porch of the first home of ZBT's Johns Hopkins chapter in Baltimore, 1958.

Washington and Jefferson College followed in close succession in 1963; California State at Northridge and C. W. Post in 1964; Marshall and Louisville in 1965; Parson's School of Design, Baruch College, Bradley University, and Queens College in 1966; Western Michigan, Adelphi, University of Hartford, Memphis State, and DePauw in 1967; and Westchester, Widener, California State at Los Angeles, University of Wisconsin at Milwaukee, California State at Santa Barbara, and Seton Hall in 1968.

Simultaneously with the establishment of new chapters came a renewed emphasis on activity for old city alumni clubs and the establishment of new ones. The custom of holding weekly or monthly alumni club luncheons, which had been allowed to lapse, was revived under Barry Siegel, who published luncheon locations and dates in the *Quarterly*; and he helped to add six more official alumni clubs to the fraternity's rosters, including one in Dallas, Texas. The Southern California club had easily been among the largest and most active of any in the fraternity since the late 1940s, but by the mid-1960s that of

Cleveland was counted as ZBT's most active, with more than seven hundred registered members.

By the winter of the academic year 1967–68, Zeta Beta Tau had grown to 65 chapters, 12 colonies, 52 alumni clubs, and 33,700 members initiated, up from 48 chapters and 20,000 members in 1960 when Siegel had assumed his post as Lee Dover's assistant. The chapters were well housed; both old and new ones regularly reported the largest entering classes of any Greek-letter group on their campus, and the aid of generous alumni, the National Permanent Endowment Fund (NPEF), and obtainable mortgages assured their relocation to comparatively spacious new homes or the renovation of existing ones. A growing staff helped to make the expansion possible, with the approval of the Supreme Council. "We've been able to provide direct service for and visitation to our undergraduate chapters and colonies to a degree never before experienced in the history of our fraternity," observed National President Justin R. Wolf in 1966 in praising their personnel. "I doubt that any other national college fraternal organization can equal us in this regard. . . . We intend to make sure that the talents and ability of this group of number one professionals are utilized to their full scope."

By the spring of 1968, Siegel's professional staff of assistants had grown to five people, including two assistant executive secretaries— Martin M. Halpern (CCNY '64) for operations and James E. Greer Jr. (Cal. State Long Beach '64) for services—and three full-time field secretaries, Louis L. Gadless (San Diego State '65), Joseph C. Schwab, and Jeffrey H. Auslander. Even these personnel were not considered enough to bring in new chapters and members with sufficient speed. At the end of the 1968 school year the *Quarterly* ran advertisements for resident advisers for chapters, preferably juniors or graduate students, who would transfer to chapters and colonies and work at building them up through administration, financial stability, and membership. The fraternity promised to provide them free room and board, one-half to full scholarship, and a small stipend.

Innovations

Other innovations besides rapid chapter expansion came during the term of Barry Siegel, beginning with his title. The term general secretary was changed to executive secretary. In 1958 the term "national" had replaced the term "supreme" in the names of officers (i.e., national president rather than supreme president) and the Central Office had become the National Office. Office technology was another instance of major changes. In an earlier decade, when cross-country U.S. mail was not fast enough, the telegraph was considered inconvenient, and long-distance phone calls were viewed as a prohibitive expense, enterprising alumni national officers with "ham" licenses had conducted fraternity business by short-wave radio. Membership lists, mailings, accounts receivable and payable—all had been managed with nothing but the hands and brains of the office staff, the use of a conventional type-writer, and occasionally the use of a mimeograph, rexograph, or addressograph machine.

ZBT technology took a leap ahead in 1967 and entered the world of electronic data processing by acquiring through an external company the services of the "360," a third-generation IBM computer, operated with keypunched cards, that was capable of generating each of the fraternity's required quarterly reports in all of eight hours. The Supreme Council had briefly considered purchasing its own large computer, rather than leasing time from someone else's. However, a study of the matter revealed that they could not afford the extra floor space, special air conditioning, and complex staff training that would have been necessary to operate it.

A Leaner Supreme Council

Expansion, modernization, and streamlining extended to every area of the fraternity's operation. In 1960–61, for example, the Supreme Council consisted of a president, nine vice presidents, a secretary-treasurer, eight elected members-at-large, eight appointed members-at-large, eight elected regional representatives, eight appointed regional representatives, and from three to seven past national presidents. No undergraduate members were included.

Such a large and unwieldy group was ill-suited to quick decision making, and an increasingly activist undergraduate membership chafed at the lack of national representation. Furthermore, the "private club" character of the council was reinforced by the long tradition of holding meetings the third Tuesday of every month except July and August in New York City. This location and schedule effectively cut off from participation anyone who did not live within easy traveling distance, leading to grumblings that a "New York clique" was controlling what had long since become a truly national and even international fraternity.

Gradually, throughout the decade, the number of officers was reduced, a smaller executive committee (later executive council) was
given responsibility for day-to-day management, undergraduate delegates were appointed, and national access was improved by holding Supreme Council meetings only four times each year in different geographic locations.

The Quarterly

The *Zeta Beta Tau Quarterly* and indeed all the fraternity's publications
were also revitalized under the ministrations of Barry Siegel, who had
had many years' experience in the field of public relations before his appointment as executive head of the fraternity. With the consulting aid
of a professional editor, old columns and features were revived, new
ones were added, and the circulation was increased well beyond the fraternity circle. For the first time, the *Quarterly* began to accept advertising, albeit under strict guidelines, and the executive secretary began
negotiations with other fraternities to form an advertising consortium
with a potential circulation of more than one-half million college-
trained fraternity men.

Siegel's specialty became the summer rushing, or "Back to School,"
issue, which shamelessly promoted the advantages of both his own fraternity and of the Greek system in general, in contrast to the aloofness
and restraint that had been so prized a part of the ZBT ethos in past
generations. The summer 1965 rushing issue, for example, had an unprecedented press run of more than thirty-five thousand copies—
twenty-five thousand sent to all members of ZBT, whether they had
paid dues or not, and ten thousand to high school seniors and their parents whose names and addresses had been forwarded by rush chairmen
from the sixty-three undergraduate units. Moreover, the guard of Lee
Dover's puritanical journalistic standards was let down with the winter
1964–65 issue, in which the *Quarterly* actually published a photograph
of members of the Cincinnati alumni group posing with a pair of Playboy Bunnies.

Social Life, Marriage, and Miss America

The fraternity was also forced to make a concession to a changing social
condition of the late 1950s and early 1960s—a steady drop in the age of
marriage. As always, engagements, marriages, and births continued to

fill many column inches in the *Quarterly*. One marriage of particular note in spring 1964 was that of Denver attorney Lawrence Atler (Washington and Lee '57) to Marilyn Van Derber, Miss America 1958. She was, in fact, the second Miss America to marry a ZBT; the first had been Bess Myerson, Miss America 1945, who had married Syracuse graduate Arnold Grant '27. What had changed was that more and more men and women were marrying while they were still in college, something that would have been almost unthinkable in an earlier age. For many women this meant dropping out of school, while for ZBT men it meant petitioning for release from the fraternity's Four-Year Loyalty Oath on grounds of financial hardship. By tradition each of these cases was supposed to be ruled upon individually by the Supreme Council, but by 1964 the phenomenon had become so common that undergraduates requested that marriage itself be sufficient grounds for release from the oath.

Conventions

Zeta Beta Tau's annual conventions were also partially transformed through the 1960s. The social side could be deemphasized somewhat, in part because students were enjoying more official day-to-day freedom in interacting with members of the opposite sex than they had been permitted in earlier years and ZBTs no longer needed to rely so heavily on formal dances as a way to get good dates. The popularity of traditional couples/ballroom dancing was also disappearing among the younger generation and with it the absolute necessity of having a female partner at any party or social gathering. While transacting the fraternity's business and voting on matters of policy had always been the raison d'être of the annual convention, under Barry Siegel and the national officers of the period, convention dates were deemphasized and new emphasis was placed on the annual Leadership School, where members learned fraternity management skills from a staff of specialists.

The character of convention locations also shifted during this period, aided by the increased accessibility of air travel. In the summer of 1964 the fraternity gathered for the first time not in an urban location but in the remote resort of French Lick, Indiana, and over the next years conventions were held in the equally remote Grand Bahama Island (1965, 1967) and Lake Placid, New York (1966). Such locations made the trip more affordable for undergraduates and, it was believed, provided fewer distractions and enhanced the atmosphere of brother-hood between the delegates. Those held on Grand Bahama Island proved especially popular, with hundreds of undergraduate ZBTs sailing together from West Palm Beach while alumni were flown in by charter. Registration rose steadily. Almost 300 ZBTs were present in Lake Placid in August 1966, and almost 350 were in the Bahamas in 1967. Barry Siegel reported with pride in the *Quarterly* that delegations were large—none fewer than two and some as large as eleven—and the numbers of chapter trustees and advisers rose along with those of the undergraduates. Not a single chapter went unrepresented. The 1967 convention, it was announced, was ZBT's twenty-second in a row with delegates from every undergraduate unit in attendance.

Not all of the "old-timer" alumni close to the fraternity were entirely happy with the changes that their new executive secretary had wrought. However, the youthful dynamism and enthusiasm with which Barry Siegel infused every aspect of his work for Zeta Beta Tau and the obvious beneficial results that he produced attracted the highest regard and devotion of many of the fraternity's undergraduate and alumni leaders. At the summer 1965 convention on Grand Bahama Island, Resolution #17 expressed this feeling in words that would be repeated at several more fraternal gatherings before the end of his days with them: "This convention acknowledges with boundless pride in and admiration for the Executive Secretary of the Fraternity, Brother Barry D. Siegel, and with heartfelt thanks expresses the hope that his unequaled fervor may long continue in the name of Zeta Beta Tau."

National Leadership

The executive secretary would not have been capable of so much without the support, encouragement, and backing of the alumni officers, who included a number of new faces in the early 1960s. Richard S. Graham (Cornell '37) had been elected national president at the time of Lee Dover's retirement and was reelected for two more terms. An executive of an investment firm, he had been vice president of his chapter in 1937, a chapter trustee since 1938, president of the Cornell Alumni Association in New York City, and president of ZBT's New York Alumni Club 1949–51 and had served continuously on the Supreme Council since 1948. He was immediately succeeded on October 1, 1963, by Jack London (City College '38) of Stamford, Connecticut, an attorney in private practice in New York who specialized in representing prominent personalities in the entertainment industry.

The first Alpha man to head the national fraternity since 1933, London had been president of his chapter in 1937–38 and, like several ZBT national presidents, had received the Julius Kahn Cup for best all-around undergraduate in his senior year of college. His alumni service to the fraternity had begun as early as the academic year 1941–42, on the eve of World War II and in the immediate aftermath of Pearl Harbor, when he served as ZBT's field secretary. In later years he would recall traveling the country and doing his best to persuade members that they would better serve both their countries and themselves by staying a few months or a year to finish their education rather than rushing off to join the armed forces as soon as possible. Through the next two decades he had served as an alumni club officer, a regional director, national secretary, national treasurer, and a national vice president since 1956. His inaugural speech to the 1963 convention set the tone that would mark his entire administration: a commitment to progressivism, a determination to make Zeta Beta Tau nonsectarian in fact as well as in theory, and a commitment to making the Greek system relevant to the problems of the age, lest it stagnate and die. "ZBT: a powerhouse of excellence" and "If it is to be, it is up to me" were oft-quoted mottoes that characterized the activist nature of his leadership.

Other national officers and Supreme Council members who guided the fraternity through the Barry Siegel years—among them a number of World War II veterans who had served with distinction and who had benefited firsthand from the Service Men's Service program—included Maurice Kantro (USC '37) of Beverly Hills; Edwin Gage (Michigan '31), who unsuccessfully sought to centralize the purchase of chapter houses by pooling individual chapters' assets in the National Office; Richard S. Simon (Michigan '43) of Pittsburgh, who had served as ZBT midwestern regional director; Jack I. Wagenheim (Virginia '30), a nephew of one of the original founders and a native of Norfolk who had lived in New York City since graduation and whose love of the fraternity led him to embrace the recording of its history as his avocation; Justin R. Wolf (Harvard '32), an attorney in Washington, D.C., who had been voted best all-around undergraduate in 1931 and who would succeed London as national president in the fall of 1965; Richard Cohen (NYU Heights '46) of Millburn, New Jersey; Leonard S. Malmud (Penn '45) of Wyncote, Pennsylvania, who served for more than forty years as a principal alumnus trustee of one of ZBT's most illustrious chapters; and Burton L. Litwin (Washington and Lee '51) of Scarsdale, New York, who would be elected as the youngest Zeta Beta Tau national president in history at the summer 1967 convention.

Sports

Through a time of much turmoil and social change, in many ways Zeta Beta Tau continued to follow until the late 1960s the same patterns that had been established in an earlier age. Prominence in sports still brought special pride to members, and the achievements of ZBT athletes were covered with eagerness in the *Quarterly*. Aside from the normal collegiate regard for sporting excellence, there still remained within the predominantly Jewish membership of the fraternity a feeling that their group held a special responsibility for disproving the ancient stereotype that Jews were not competent in athletics. For example, few sports fans anywhere could fail to be impressed when, in the spring of 1965, Sid Luckman (Columbia '39) then on the coaching staff of the Chicago Bears, was inducted into the National Football League's Hall of Fame.

The 1964–65 academic year was an especially banner one for ZBT sportsmen. Three members won individual sport national collegiate championships—Howard Goodman (NYU '65) in fencing; Jim Nance (Syracuse '65), who won the NCAA heavyweight wrestling championship for the second year in a row; and Michael Jacobson (Penn State '65) in gymnastics, who went on to win eight medals at the summer's Maccabiah Games in Israel. Among the ten U.S. basketball players also sent to represent the United States at the Maccabiah that year were three ZBTs: Talbot Brody (Illinois '65), Bruce Kaplan (NYU '67), and Ron Green (Vanderbilt '66), who played on an undefeated team. Impressive individual ZBT achievements were also noted in tennis, track, and swimming.

Scholarship

High scholarship was another ZBT tradition that showed stability through the mid-1960s. True, from the 1950s on, observers had noted a decline in general scholarship; however, under the watchful eye of Scholarship Commissioner Dr. Emanuel Saxe of the Baruch College School of Business and Public Administration (himself a son of 1898 founder Bernhard D. Saxe), Zeta Beta Tau appeared to be recouping its losses and doing well, compared to the other NIC fraternities. In spring 1962 the fraternity ranked sixth among fifty-nine member NIC fraternities, with ten chapters leading their respective campuses; in 1963, ZBT ranked seventh, with eight chapters—Washington-Seattle, Alabama, Duke, Washington and Lee, Vanderbilt, British Columbia, McGill,and C. W. Post—ranking first, and another eighteen ranking second or third. By spring 1967 twenty-nine chapters ranked in the top three of their respective campuses, and thirteen ranked in first place. In the summer of 1968, Zeta Beta Tau ranked fifth among all the members of the NIC for the second year in a row, and only 15 percent of the chapters were not performing at a level higher than the all-men's average.

The Gottheil Medal

The values of the fraternity's national officers and its general membership were continually reflected in the achievements it chose to honor through the granting of honorary memberships and annual awards. Among these the Gottheil Medal, Zeta Beta Tau's highest award, was no longer limited specifically to those who had done the most for Jewry in the previous year, but still tended to be given to those whose lives had touched world Jewish affairs in some way.

In 1960 the Gottheil award went to real estate developer Philip M. Klutznick, an alumnus of Creighton and Omaha universities. At the time he had been president of B'nai B'rith for six years, was also president of the American Friends of the Hebrew University, and was serving as general chairman of the United Jewish Appeal. On October 16, 1962, at a special ceremony held on the grounds of the United Nations in New York, Harold Riegelman presented the award to UN Under Secretary Dr. Ralph J. Bunche. Active in the UN since 1947, he was best known for his role in 1948–49 as a mediator in the Arab-Israeli conflict who had successfully brought about an armistice agreement. In 1963 the medal was awarded posthumously to Pope John XXIII, who had inaugurated a new spirit of tolerance and rapprochement between Jews and Catholics and who set in motion the series of events leading to the reforms of Vatican II in 1965. In 1966, the medal went to Morris B. Abram, of Atlanta, an attorney, civil rights activist, and president of the American Jewish committee. In 1968 he would go on to become the second president of Brandeis University.

Louis Marshall Cup

The Louis Marshall Cup, which had once been given to the chapter with the highest level of involvement in Jewish affairs, was now given to "the chapter which conducts the best program of inspiring interfaith brotherhood," a designation that did not rule out participation in Jewish ritual life. In 1963, for example, the award went to the Indiana University chapter, which had worked for two years to bring members of different religions into closer contact and to promote mutual understanding. The chapter wrote and conducted a special service at the campus's Hillel Foundation, designed to explain their religion to those from other faiths, and were joined by a congregation of over seventy-five students. They carried on exchanges with other fraternities, worshipping with members of Sigma Alpha Epsilon at their various churches and in turn inviting them to worship with ZBT at Friday night synagogue services. They also held the campus's first interfaith Passover seder at their chapter house and charged each member of the fraternity to invite a friend of a different religion to join in the celebration.

Alumni

Specific awards did not have to be allocated for the fraternity to show its pride in the achievements of its members who, they believed, had received some of their earliest experience in leadership and management within their ranks and who reflected well upon the group as a whole. Illustrious ZBT alumni featured in the pages of the *Quarterly* through the 1960s included Andrew Goodman (Michigan '28), still president of the Bergdorf Goodman department store on Fifth Avenue in New York and a leader in many charities; Dewey D. Stone (Boston '20) of Brockton, Massachusetts, who served as UJA chairman in 1960; Walton H. Bachrach (Washington and Lee '24), who thirty years earlier had written the "Who's Who among the Alumni" column for the *Quarterly* and served as mayor of Cincinnati in 1961; William Pereira (Illinois '30), featured on the cover of *Time* in 1963 as one of the foremost architects and city planners in the United States; A. M. Sonnabend (Harvard '18) of Boston, a president of the American Jewish Committee in 1963 and president of the Hotel Corporation of America; Irvin Fane (Missouri '28), former national officer and Midwest regional director, who was elected as chairman of the board of trustees of the Union of American Hebrew Congregations and in that same year launched a campaign to raise funds for planting trees in Israel to memorialize the late President John Kennedy; George Alpert (Boston '18), a former director of the New Haven Railroad and a director of the ZBT Foundation; and Bruno V. Bitker (Cornell '21) of Milwaukee, who in 1968 was appointed to Lyndon B. Johnson's President's Commission for the Observance of Human Rights.

Show Business

Of all the areas in which ZBT alumni chose to excel, none exerted more fascination upon the membership than the field of entertainment. ZBTs as a group regularly achieved renown through their creative work in that field, through collaboration with one another, and through obtaining backing and funding from other fraternity brothers who had excelled in the world of business.

Perhaps nowhere else was the alliance of talent and money more important than in the Broadway theater. In the spring 1962 issue of the *Quarterly* it was noted that Jerry (Gerald S.) Herman (University of Miami '53) had written both words and music for the Broadway hit *Milk and Honey*, a show in turn produced by Gerard Oestreicher (Columbia '37), who had sent Herman on a special trip to Israel to get background material. At the age of twenty-nine, the composer-lyricist had already written several shows and was destined to write several more. Playwright Jerome Lawrence (Ohio State '37) was widely hailed for his penning of *Auntie Mame* and *Inherit the Wind. Hello, Dolly*, Jerry Herman's second major hit, went on to win the Drama Critics Award, a Tony, and the 1965 Grammy award for song of the year. He then went on to collaborate with Jerry Lawrence in writing both words and music for his next Broadway musical hit, *Mame*. The spring 1966 cover of the *Quarterly* proudly featured the smiling faces of no fewer than four ZBTs who had made that hit musical possible: composer Jerry Herman, playwright Jerry Lawrence, director Gene Saks (Cornell '43), and Howard Teichmann (Wisconsin '38) of the producing agency. Jerry Herman and Jerry Lawrence together were named ZBT's Men of the Year in 1967. While scores of ZBTs had contributed to their shows through the years, *Mame* was most heavily backed by CBS chairman and former ZBT chapter president William S. Paley (Penn '22).

Television also had its share of ZBTs as writers, producers, directors,

*Show business was an important area of achieve-
ment for Jewish fraternity graduates and a field
where the intrafraternal network could play a crucial role. Pictured here are four ZBTs who helped
bring the musical hit* Mame *to Broadway in 1965.
Front and rear, left to right: composer/lyricist Jerry
(Gerald S.) Herman (U. of Miami '53), playwright Jerry Lawrence (Ohio State '37), director
Gene Saks (Cornell '43), and producer Howard Teichmann (Wisconsin '38). Scores of other ZBTs
backed the show, most notably CBS chairman
William S. Paley (Penn '22).*

and executives in various capacities. One scriptwriter in particular,
Jerry Friedman (USC '66) of Van Nuys, California, was destined to
participate in an especially enduring aspect of American popular culture. His photograph appeared in the fall 1967 issue of the *Quarterly*
with the notice that he was writing for the new television show called
Star Trek. He had already completed one script, shot in mid-August
and entitled "The Trouble with Tribbles," and he had contracted to
write another. He would eventually become well known to generations
of *Star Trek* fans under his pen name, David Gerrold.

The "Backbone of the Fraternity"

The vast majority of ZBT alumni did not become billionaires or produce great films or Broadway hits. They lived lives of conventional achievement, holding down jobs and businesses, tending to their professions, and raising their families. Nor did the majority evince a great interest in the fraternity after leaving school, although they might live with wives they had met through it and still socialize most closely with those who had been their fraternity brothers in college. A small group of dedicated alumni, however, who embraced the fraternity as their avocation, continued as in the past to earn the respect and honor of their peers by the long hours of volunteer service and personal funds they expended as alumni trustees, chapter advisers, conservers of chapter property and financial reserves, and legal directors of chapter property corporations.

Into the 1960s, alumni also helped to assure, through generous donations to the ZBT Foundation's scholarship program, that no ZBT would be forced to leave school because of financial inability.

Tradition and Stability

The attention and dedication of the alumni, as a counterpoint to the inherent transience of a campus population, helped lend stability and strength to the fraternity as a whole and to the individual chapters, which were able to celebrate significant anniversaries during this period. Tulane celebrated its fiftieth anniversary on March 14, 1959, with National President Stanley I. Fishel traveling to New Orleans for the ceremonies. In the 1960–61 academic year the NYU chapter celebrated its fifty-fifth continuous year, and Ohio State, LSU in Baton Rouge, and Syracuse all celebrated their golden anniversaries.

The entire preceding year went into planning the Syracuse weekend celebration on November 4, 1961. Over five hundred alumni, wives, and parents of undergraduates converged on the campus and the Hotel Syracuse to enjoy a weekend of home receptions, attendance at the Syracuse-Pittsburgh football game, a postgame party at the chapter house, and a semiformal dinner dance at the hotel, where, it was reported, the rounds of speeches were followed by active members and their dates both exhibiting and instructing others in the intricacies of a new dance known as "The Twist." National President Richard Graham noted in his speech that he had a personal interest in the celebration, since his own father had been president of the Cornell chapter in 1911 and had himself sponsored and installed the Syracuse chapter. In the same year, Penn State's chapter celebrated both fifteen years of continuous existence and the dedication of a new $175,000 chapter house.

As the years passed and chapters matured, other golden anniversaries followed, with the occasions marked by gala affairs and celebrations. The University of Virginia chapter celebrated its fiftieth birthday in 1965, while nearly one hundred alumni and parents joined the Alabama chapter for their golden anniversary weekend in the spring of 1965. By 1967, Missouri has passed its fiftieth birthday as well, and two chapters—NYU Heights and the University of Pennsylvania—were celebrating their sixtieth. Over 250 alumni and wives returned to Penn that year for a weekend of cocktails, dancing, parties, group attendance at the Penn-Princeton football game, and Sunday morning brunch at the Locust Club.

The presence of several of the original founders in the 1960s also lent a sense of stability to the organization, although by the late 1950s most of these "giants" in ZBT lore were passing on. When Rev. Dr. Aaron Eiseman died in the winter of 1965, two of the original 1898 founders remained alive—Dr. David Swick and Louis Posner, both of them regular guests and speakers at fraternity Old Timers' celebrations and special events. The founders and earliest members, however, had left behind a coterie of sons, grandsons, nephews, and cousins who had followed in their ancestors' footsteps and joined the fraternity themselves; and some of these younger members were the beneficiaries of end-of-life reminiscences by their elder relatives.

Jack I. Wagenheim (Virginia '30), an advertising account executive with the *New York Post*, especially benefited from hours of oral history given him by his uncle, Dr. Herman B. Sheffield, a founder and original patron of ZBT, whose interest in the fraternity only increased with age and fading eyesight. The ZBT veteran obviously derived pleasure from remembering the early days, and his pride was coupled with disbelief that such a small group had grown to such a large organization. Another frequent and favorite visitor toward the end of his life was co-founder Aaron Drucker, who, Wagenheim reported, had left the City College campus to fight in the Spanish-American War in 1898 and had probably been the first ZBT ever to bear arms for his country. After Wagenheim published an article in the winter 1961–62 *Quarterly* entitled "Recollections of a Founder: Dr. Herman B. Sheffield," he returned to his one-time avocation as ZBT's historian; in each issue he supplied reviews of events reported in their magazine decades earlier. Unfortunately, the younger generation within the fraternity was not long destined to enjoy the benefit of these insights. Within one month in the fall of 1965, three young ZBTs were killed in separate auto accidents, the worst string of fatalities in the organization's history. Among them was Michael L. Wagenheim (Virginia '66), Jack's only son, who at the age of twenty-one had just begun his senior year in college. The father's heart was so broken that he himself died not long after, at the age of only fifty-eight, in the spring of 1966. Father and son were buried side by side. "For we who knew and loved him, cannot really picture ZBT without him," wrote Barry Siegel in the *Quarterly* obituary. "So involved was he in our fraternity that his absence from the scene creates a void that in all probability can never be filled.

The "Legacy Problem"

As the fraternity matured, more and more ZBT second- and third-generation young men presented themselves for membership. The tradition of presenting a newborn baby son with a ZBT pledge pin was still alive in the 1960s. It was customary to speak of these as future fraternity brothers, as in a spring 1964 announcement that Martin F. Brecker (Franklin and Marshall '56) and his wife had been blessed with quadruplets on October 23, 1963. "Only one, however, is destined for ZBT," read the article. "The others are young ladies."

By long tradition, a "legacy," or descendant of an "old boy," was an especially prized addition to a prestigious school, club, or fraternity, cementing as it did the ties between the generations and strengthening both the emotional and financial support that a family was likely to give to the institution. For many ZBT fathers, grandfathers, older siblings, and uncles, there could be no greater pride than seeing their boy become one of their fraternity brothers. Alumni fearful of all the changes taking place in the world were especially eager to hold onto the tradition of assuring a place for their sons within the ranks of ZBT.

The legacy issue, however, was a flashpoint of intergenerational conflict. Undergraduates resented the loss of autonomy and frequently resisted taking legacies, to the point that being a ZBT descendant could actually be a liability. Alumni fought back by pushing through legislation at conventions that would make the initiation of legacies virtually mandatory. At the 1948 convention, for the first time resolutions had been passed agreeing that potential members who were brothers, sons, or grandsons of members be given special consideration and that the trustees be consulted before any decision to depledge them.

Through the years the thorny controversy over legacies continued and the attempted legislation grew more complex. By 1966 the problem was the subject of a two-page spread in the *Quarterly*, and the Supreme Council imposed on a resentful undergraduate body the categories of "prime priority" (for sons and grandsons of the same chapter), "first priority," and "second priority" legacies. Yet undergraduates continued to resist taking such legacies, citing real or imagined deficiencies in them. The National Office was deluged each fall with outraged telephone calls from fathers whose sons had not been pledged, and one alumnus from Houston was driven to pick up his pen and write an article on the subject, castigating the younger members for their misplaced selectivity and false pride. If they had known earlier what they knew now about their present-day fraternity brothers, he pointed out, they might have blackballed all of them. As it was, they should not reject good potential members for perceived problems that were entirely correctable.

Local Autonomy and Nonsectarianism

It would have been too much to expect that certain ZBT alumni would ever cease trying to influence undergraduates to take in legacies, regardless of their individual qualifications. However, the undergraduates did win a significant battle on the front of local autonomy. At the August 1966 convention a resolution was finally passed discontinuing the circulation of names of pledges throughout the entire fraternity prior to initiation and permitting any member anywhere to voice objections. From then on, chapters could technically take in anyone they chose, and no one but the undergraduates of the chapter itself would have the power of blackball over a potential member.

Democratization had penetrated only slowly into the field of ZBT membership selection. Gradually, Lee Dover's elaborate descriptions of the ideal ZBT from the 1950s were replaced by shorter and more succinct requirements, and the acute class consciousness of the fraternity eased. "ZBT alumni and undergraduates are urged to recommend sons, relatives and friends, anyone who is superior 'ZBT Material,'" Dover had announced in the summer of 1960, the last time he would be directing rush from the National Office. "This is now interpreted to mean: Wholesome and friendly young men, good students, freshmen likely to make their college grades and be eligible after one term for initiation, remaining thereafter for four college years." There were no dire warnings as in years past, although he did insist without being specific that "ZBT's admittedly high standards for membership must, and will be maintained." On the recommendation form, right after "Scholarship," appeared blank lines on which to rate "Financial Ability (very important)" and "Cultural Background (very important)"—the same categories and words that had appeared on ZBT forms for generations.

Now, however, the words smacked of old-fashioned snobbery and did not sit well with undergraduates and alumni, especially at a time when the civil rights movement was transforming the nation and such language was being officially rooted out everywhere. The objectionable words made their reappearance on the official rushing form in 1961 and 1962, after Barry Siegel had taken over as executive secretary, but by 1963, "Financial Ability" and "Cultural Background" had disappeared. The changes coincided with the final passage by the U.S. Congress of the Civil Rights Act of 1964 and the Voting Rights Act of 1965, which gave federal teeth to the effort to halt discrimination on the basis of race, color, creed, or socioeconomic condition. From the 1963 fall semester's rush onward, "wholesome and intelligent" officially defined ZBT material; the only other category listed was "academic standing."

An entirely new ZBT constitution was voted on at the 1967 convention. The product of several years' work, study, and experience, it concretized the new reforms in the makeup of the Supreme Council and in membership selection. In addition to clearly spelling out local autonomy, abolishing the national blackball, making council meetings more accessible, appointing undergraduates to key positions, and establishing an independent discipline board (so that the entire Supreme Council would not have to rule on every individual problem), the goal of nonsectarianism was made more explicit than at any time in the previous two decades. "The Supreme Council was ordered," read the account of the proceedings, "so that there be no misunderstanding, that it must avoid denial of admission based on 'race, color, creed or national origin.'"

A New Idealism: The "Credo of Zeta Beta Tau"

Idealism, a thirst for social justice, and a desire of the younger members to have their say over the actions of the older members made noticeable inroads on ZBT affairs from the early 1960s onward. Youth everywhere was on the march. When in January 1967 the occasion arrived for *Time* to choose its "Man of the Year"—the personage who had most influenced the world for good or ill in the previous twelve months—the choice was not a single person but "The Young Generation—Those 25 and Under." Not only did that age bracket nearly outnumber its elders, but as *Time* described them, they were more assertive, articulate, well-educated, worldly, and independent than any generation that had come before them. Protected by unprecedented affluence, reared in a prolonged period of world peace, armed with the tools of science and knowledge, the authors declared, with a combination of optimism and indulgence, "This is the generation which will land on the moon, cure cancer and the common cold, enrich the world, and put an end to poverty and war." In short, it was a generation with complete faith in its ability to solve the world's problems.

For ZBT members, a major turning point in the development of a strong organizational social conscience took place August 27 to September 1, 1963, at the sixty-fifth anniversary convention at the Jack Tar Hotel in San Francisco. The gathering coincided with the August 28 March on Washington where some quarter million Americans stood electrified as Dr. Martin Luther King Jr. delivered his immortal "I have a dream" speech. The convention was taking place at a time when the Greek system as a whole had been under attack for several years as out of touch and "irrelevant" to the burning issues of the day. As fellow college students including some ZBTs marched with Dr. King, rode with the Freedom Riders, risked their lives in the South, and embraced the cause of fighting poverty, oppression, racism, and injustice in all of the United States, it appeared too easy to condemn fraternities as a needless frivolity. What could they do, some members wondered, to convince those they respected that the fraternity and its values had something to contribute after all?

In the course of the convention a group of eight undergraduate representatives from as many chapters gathered to discuss the issue. The group was led by Columbia chapter president Donald Mintz ('64) and included chapter president James E. Greer Jr. (California State at Long Beach '64) as well as four alumni, including Barry Siegel, incoming national president Jack London, and incoming treasurer Richard W. Cohen (NYU Heights '47). In a series of meetings they drew up a special resolution that would answer their critics and articulate in the language of the day the relevance of fraternity. There were no expectations that the final result, Resolution #17, would provide anything more than food for thought for the members and a defense against their detractors.

Instead, "The Credo of ZBT," as it came to be known, so thoroughly reflected the spirit of the times that it became among the most popular items of identification for ZBT undergraduates. It was regularly published full-page with scroll artwork in the *Quarterly*, was printed on membership cards and much of their other published material, was memorized by pledges and picked up by other fraternities, and quoted and requoted by succeeding fraternity generations. "Whereas it has been the business of the 65th Anniversary Convention of ZBT . . . to re-evaluate the changing role of fraternity on the university level, and whereas we, the undergraduates of ZBT, wish to reassert the long-established principles of fraternity, be it resolved that this convention adopts the following Fraternity Credo," the resolution began:

We, the members of Zeta Beta Tau Fraternity, believe that the development of the individual as a responsible, mature member of society is the primary goal of the university today.

We believe that fraternity offers the university a unique, desirable, and successful means of achieving this goal.

In fulfilling the purposes of fraternity, we dedicate ourselves to the principles of:

I. INTELLECTUAL AWARENESS: Fraternity creates an atmosphere conducive to the expansion of the individual's intellectual horizons, the interchange of ideas within the academic community, and the pursuit of scholastic excellence.

II. SOCIAL RESPONSIBILITY: Fraternity requires the individual to commit himself and accept his responsibility to participate.

III. INTEGRITY: Fraternity generates a standard of personal integrity—a framework for the individual to maintain honesty, exhibit loyalty, and retain a sense of self-discipline.

IV. BROTHERLY LOVE: Fraternity inspires and expresses the interrelation of the individual with his fellows, his pride in the institution, and respect for the wisdom of its tradition.

In the aftermath of the convention, National President Jack London and other alumni officers chose the implementation of credo as their top priority in all ZBT programming, and its ideals lay at the center of the keynote speech made by the national president later that fall at the sixtieth anniversary celebrations for the Columbia chapter. Of all his recommendations, some were implemented and some were not, but a motto he used within the speech, "ZBT: A Powerhouse of Excellence," like the credo, entered the fraternity's lexicon and was used frequently in the decades that followed.

Social Service at Home

Social service projects were one cause embraced wholeheartedly by all segments of the fraternity, in a continuance of a trend that had begun long before the writing of the credo. In 1950 the alumni club of St. Louis had established an award to be given annually to the chapter demonstrating the best program in that area. Underlying the award was the assumption that ZBT members enjoyed the background and educational advantages that fitted them to become community leaders and obligated them to help those less fortunate than themselves. Also, aside from its value in building individual character and responsibility, nothing more effectively countered the uncomplimentary image of fraternities in the media than a good social service program. From 1963 onward, along with the new campus mood of progressivism and idealism, the emphasis on social service activity within the fraternity noticeably intensified. "The fraternity system has been maligned and misrepresented because of the follies of a few," declared Barry Siegel. "Let the chapters of ZBT be known for their good works."

The national officers and the Supreme Council consciously strove to find an appropriate national social service activity to be followed by all chapters of the fraternity. The first, chosen in 1965, was reading for the blind. The varied social service achievements of individual chapters were also highlighted in the pages of the *Quarterly* and at fraternity gatherings, and others were encouraged to follow their lead. The undergraduates of Rider College, for example, in 1963 completely renovated and painted the American Cancer Society's Trenton office, participated in three major fund-raising drives, and held two parties at the chapter house for underprivileged children. The Alabama chapter adopted nearby Bryce Hospital, the only public facility in the state for the mentally ill, as their cause after Alan Goodwin ('63) of Chicago took an interest in it and began to bring some of his fraternity brothers with him. With the shortage of trained personnel to care for its five thousand patients, by 1965 between five and ten members of the chapter visited on a rotating basis for two days each week to engage in athletic activities with patients, teach art classes, participate in ward parties, and clean up parts of the hospital under the direction of the staff.

The NYU Washington Square chapter maintained a special Social Service Committee that collected canned food for distribution to local charities, collected funds and distribution boxes for the Leukemia Society of New York, sponsored a Halloween party for orphans at the chapter house, and ran a toy donation project. The University of Miami chapter adopted a needy youngster in the Dade County area, provided him with clothing and financial aid, and welcomed the boy and his family as regular guests at their house. The entire Cornell junior class picked up a project started jointly by ZBT and Delta Gamma

Sorority—the total financing of the education of a teenager in the Central American nation of Honduras.

The "College and Why" program of the Brooklyn College chapter, a unique innovation among ZBTs, was honored with the St. Louis Alumni Club Award in 1965. Aware that their educational advantages were enjoyed in close proximity to public schools with a high drop-out rate, groups of ten members would regularly visit high schools and junior high schools in the Greater New York area to conduct auditorium presentations on the value of a college education, followed by small discussion groups. The program also included follow-up presentations with parents at PTA meetings, and at synagogue men's and women's clubs and a personal tour of the Brooklyn College campus for prospective students and their parents. In addition to these activities, the Brooklyn College members also joined with New York City's PAL (Police Athletic League) to teach children football, baseball, handball, finger painting, oil painting, and ceramics.

Social Service Abroad

After graduation, national and even international social service was a popular option among ZBTs as well, as it was among increasing numbers of college students. Fulbright scholarships in interesting parts of the world were one option for the more academically inclined, as in the case of Donald Mintz, (Columbia '64), the guiding spirit behind the ZBT credo, who went to work and to study Spanish in Venezuela after graduation (he subsequently graduated from Tulane Law School and in the 1980s unsuccessfully ran for mayor of New Orleans in 1990 and 1994).

The Peace Corps, established by President Kennedy in 1962, was considered an especially worthy and fulfilling path for a recent college graduate of high ideals to follow. The winter 1962–63 issue of the ZBT *Quarterly* carried an invitation from the director of the program, R. Sargent Shriver, to either contact the office directly or speak to their campus liaison in order to join the four thousand volunteers already in the field. Through the Peace Corps the United States aimed to send "some of its outstanding young men and women" to the developing nations to serve as teachers, engineers, nurses, coaches, and surveyors; to take part in community development work, and in general to provide leadership and knowledge. Several ZBTs who had joined the Peace

Corps after their college graduations were either featured in the
Quarterly's columns or published first-person articles about their experiences. One volunteer, Barry H. Levinson (Columbia '62) of Brooklyn, trained for twelve weeks at Oregon State University, taking intensive training in the Hindi language and agriculture. He departed on
December 1, 1964, for northeastern India to take part in a Peace Corps
attempt to improve local farming techniques and expand the yields of
crops and livestock. Eventually he settled on Kibbutz Ein Hashofet in
Israel. Stephen Dienstfrey (California State Long Beach '65) spent his
Peace Corps stint on the Filipino island of Malaybalay. Contact with
the outside world, he reported, was maintained by all of three flights
each week, which landed on the island's grass-field airport. Although
one lone movie theater in town showed English films on weekdays and
Tagalog-language films on weekends, Dienstfrey wrote, the most popular entertainment on the island was the Sunday afternoon cockfights.
The winter of 1966–67 likewise saw Robert A. Youdelman (Western
Reserve '63, NYU Law '66) serving as a Peace Corps volunteer in Bra-
zil, accompanied by his wife, the former Miss Karen Schneier.

The Vietnam War and Incipient Collapse

In the early to mid-1960s young Americans were to be found in developing nations all over the globe, but gradually the name of one nation
almost crowded out all the others: South Vietnam. Before the escalation of the Vietnam War in 1965, while the U.S. presence was still limited largely to military advisors, to visit the country and to work there
for a period of time was frequently viewed in the media and privately
among ZBTs in the most idealistic terms. In their view they were, after
all, helping to save not only the country but that entire area of the
world from being engulfed by the forces of communism.

Gradually, more and more graduates headed to Vietnam in various
capacities, both military and nonmilitary. In the fall of 1967 it was reported that Don Sider (University of Miami '54) was off to spend eighteen months in South Vietnam as a correspondent for *Time*; his wife
and three children planned to reside nearby in Hong Kong. In the spring
of 1968, by which time the number of American servicemen in Vietnam was approaching more than a half-million, another University of
Miami graduate and former Julius Kahn Cup winner, Stuart M. Bloch
('64, Harvard Law '67) was reported to be serving with International

Voluntary Services in Vietnam. His goal and that of his organization was to care for the thousands of refugee children rendered orphaned and homeless by the war. No mention was made, in the alumni columns or features reporting such activity, of the mounting casualties on all sides in Vietnam or of how bitterly divided the American people were becoming over whether the United States should be involved there at all.

This silence was part of a general inability to recognize or face the ominous changes that were taking place. There had been occasional warnings, voiced from time to time in ZBT publications and at special events, that despite apparent good health American college fraternities in general and Zeta Beta Tau in particular faced a serious crisis. Students' anger, sense of betrayal, and fear of what was happening in Vietnam were only the capstone of trends destructive to the Greek system as it had existed for generations. Critics cautioned that Greek-letter groups were becoming increasingly "irrelevant"; that elaborate college dormitories and eating facilities were rendering the Greek system virtually obsolete; that the fraternities' share of students was plunging despite a rise in actual numbers; that violent hazing and irresponsible student behavior was on the upsurge; that students would no longer submit to patronizing regulations of their personal, political, and sexual conduct; that the scourge of illegal drugs was dividing and destroying the student body; that students of all races and backgrounds would soon lose their patience at the glacial rate of real social change. Soon all these tensions would explode, and scores of campuses across the nation would themselves be turned into battlegrounds.

At first it appeared that the developing campus tempest might pass Zeta Beta Tau by. In the summer of 1967 the fraternity was, by all conventional NIC standards, in the pink of health, and field secretaries traversing the country to help with rush were not alarmed by the few real problems they encountered. The fraternity was enjoying excellent scholarship; active and dedicated alumni clubs; a fine record of accomplishment among its graduates; admiration of its publication by other groups; an ever-expanding, relatively well-housed roll of chapters; and the leadership of one of the most popular executive secretaries in the field. The number of undergraduate units and the numbers of men initiated into ZBT in the fall of the 1967–68 school year had in fact never been higher.

Few within the fraternity could imagine, as students returned to school that September, that Zeta Beta Tau was poised for anything but further achievement. It was not merely public relations bravado that caused Siegel to headline his summer 1968 rushing issue "ZBT: a 70-Year Success Story."

He could not know that the glory days of ZBT's existence were rapidly drawing to a close and that his fraternity was soon to pass through a period that might have killed his predecessor, Lee Dover, if he had lived long enough to see it. For some time there would be no stability, no droves of dedicated alumni eager to help younger college students, and no real expansion save that which came through a series of mergers, which were themselves indicative of disaster for the historically Jewish fraternities. Indeed, over a period of five lean years, ZBT would come perilously close to being no fraternity at all. Only the desperate efforts of men who would not let ZBT die ultimately pulled it through and allowed it to survive to reach its one-hundredth birthday.

CHAPTER TEN

"AND IF THIS YEAR SHOULD BE OUR LAST"

The Collapse and Revival of Zeta Beta Tau, 1968–78

The Deluge

The signs that not all was well with the American college fraternity system began to appear several years before the late 1960s and early 1970s, when idealism and hope evaporated for all too many American citizens. At that point, student radicals led by such groups as the SDS (Students for a Democratic Society) ascended to prominence, and dozens of the nation's campuses became engulfed in violent conflict as riot police and the National Guard were called upon to restore order. At several campuses the unrest became so great that carrying on normal activities was impossible; classes, final exams, and graduation ceremonies had to be canceled.

The millions of American babies who had been born in the years following World War II were now on the verge of adulthood, and the tendency of a significant portion of them was to rebel against everything the older generation stood for. There was power in their numbers, and their youthful grievances were many. Students' protests centered on race relations, a desire for greater ethnic assertiveness, the issue of "free speech," opposition to required courses, restrictions on their personal lives, the sexual revolution, their preference for private apartments over supervised housing, the use of illegal drugs, violent and corrupt electoral politics, and what they saw as the misplaced priorities of a political establishment that could spend billions to set two American men on the moon in July 1969 but could not solve the problems of basic injustice. Above all, the bloody quagmire in Vietnam, carried live and in color every evening into the nation's living rooms, aroused students' rage.

Already, through the 1950s and early 1960s, virtually none of the general changes in American higher education had favored the Greek system. The effects of Sputnik on American academic life had clearly been one factor. After Sputnik, a dean at Ohio State University recalled, scholastic conquest had become a "fetish," with math, science, and physics the "key to existence." More and more entering freshmen had their hearts set on graduate or professional school and failed to consider fraternities because they or their families believed it would harm their scholarship. Too many who did enter, he noted, were turning in their pins as juniors and seniors and moving out into apartments, contributing to the weakness and immaturity of the remaining leadership.

In vain did advocates protest that academic needs were a priority in a well-run fraternity; in vain did they protest that in a time of huge enrollments, large classes, and inaccessible professors, companionship, the skill of getting along with people, and the art of becoming a "gentleman" were more important than ever before. "We have grown, perhaps, a little overly serious in this drive to excel in the competition, particularly with the Russians," noted television commentator Walter Cronkite (Chi Phi, University of Texas '37 and husband to a Delta Gamma) at an interfraternity workshop at his alma mater. "We have almost let fun become a dirty word. I can't believe that at all. I can't believe that we can beat the Russians by imitating them. I can't believe that being as stodgy and as dull as they are, by lacking a sense of humor, by keeping our nose to the grindstone until it comes out the back of our neck, we are really going to win this race for men's minds, as well as the race in scientific achievement." *Fortune* magazine might publish surveys of more than 750 large corporations, as it did in the fall of 1967, disclosing that 70 percent of their officers as well as 71 percent of those listed in *Who's Who in America* and 76 percent of U.S. senators were fraternity initiates; the general public remained convinced that any apparent links between fraternity membership and high achievement were of no consequence.

Restrictive rushing regulations, including deferred rushing, required registration fees, and fixed schedules of visiting houses, along with the competition of modern dormitory complexes complete with rooms, meals, lounging areas, coffee shops, a full program of social activities, and even some classes, were wearing away the Greek world as well. By the 1960s the days were already long past when chapter houses basked in their relative autonomy, non-fraternity members were relegated to dismal boardinghouses, and the only competition for a coveted rushee were other, supposedly bigger and better Greek-letter groups. In the new age any fraternity's biggest competition was no longer other fraternities but the thousands of potentially good members who were declining to join fraternities at all.

As Orville H. Read, chairman of the board of directors of Delta Upsilon (Missouri '33), noted in "The Case of the Vanishing Rushee," reprinted in the ZBT *Quarterly*, the time had arrived for fraternities to do an "up-to-date market analysis." What sense did it make to shoot continually at the wrong target, to aim at one's friends "when the bushes are full of enemies"? "The rushing market today is far different from 30 years ago," Read reminded his fraternity brothers with brutal frankness. "Back in those days we had a great rushing advantage—fraternities were living in nice warm caves . . . and the independents were still living in trees." This permitted them to concentrate on only one phase of membership expansion, that of "sinking the shaft into any other fraternity in which the rushee might be interested. . . . We knew that our prospect wanted desperately to join a fraternity—he *had* to in order to get out of the rain! All we had to do was knock other fraternities out of the running." Today, their biggest competitors included "the great big, plush dormitory that offers all the physical comforts of the Hilton hotels and looks mighty good to many a freshman."

Alongside such dormitories built and maintained by a professional staff, Delta Upsilon's chairman wrote, the average chapter house, usually a converted private home, looked "pretty grubby" and could virtually never guarantee the member a single or even a double room. Three, four, or even more members to a room remained a common living arrangement in fraternity houses, and in the new era a man usually had to be willing to accept some personal discomfort and sacrifice in comparison to the dormitories if he wished to become a fraternity member.

In addition, even tougher and more subtle competition was presented by the widely circulated idea that fraternities were no longer important and were even harmful to education. Just as no salesman in the world could persuade a customer to buy a particular brand of color television set before first "selling" him on the idea of color television, Read declared, no specific Greek-letter group could hope to gain members without first overcoming this wide-scale "indoctrination" and then "selling" them on the advantages of fraternities in general.

The Prices of Nonsectarianism

The new conditions on campus, coupled with the civil and legal transformation the country had undergone since World War II, affected the historically Jewish fraternities with special sharpness. Strong communal and family support had always done much to offset the relative youth, small size, and poverty of the Jewish fraternities relative to the much larger, older, and better-endowed traditionally Gentile groups. However, by the mid-1960s an important basis for this support was fast eroding.

Hillel rabbis, the Jewish religious personnel closest to college students, voiced their concern that, with all students' needs being met within the beautiful new facilities on large midwestern campuses, it was difficult to entice students away for religious or other services and certainly not to meet the opposite sex. In the old days, the rabbis recalled at their fortieth anniversary annual conference in 1963, men and women lived in separate quarters, usually far from one another. Church or synagogue gatherings, aside from the religious sustenance they offered, had provided a socially sanctioned place in which to meet. Now, men's and women's wings were in close proximity, dining rooms and all other facilities were fully coeducational, and dances and social events took place right on the premises. Male and female students of all backgrounds, they noted, were thrown together from morning until night, a situation that promoted nonsectarian, interdenominational contacts among students and "undoubtedly results in a large increase in interfaith boy/girl social relations on campus."

Endogamous marriage had long been viewed by Jewish communal leaders as the bedrock of Jewish identity and the only possible means by which the tiny minority could perpetuate itself. For generations, this desire had been reinforced by the general environment. Gentile students for the most part had been reluctant to date Jews, and Christian parents would no more rush to accept a Jew as a son- or daughter-in-law than Jewish parents would spring eagerly to accept the reverse. In addition, expecting Gentile partners to convert to Judaism appeared neither realistic nor desirable.

The strict social segregation along religious lines that had so characterized American life had been a source of great distress, and American Jews had expended no small part of their organizational resources in combating it, but at least it had promoted endogamous mating patterns. And although the relations between Hillel rabbis and the historically Jewish fraternities had frequently been antagonistic, the rabbis could be sure that virtually all the fraternity members, regardless of their level of religious observance, were in fact Jewish by birth and would be dancing with, dating, and marrying primarily young women from the Jewish sororities or otherwise similar cultural and religious backgrounds. This fact alone had always guaranteed a minimum level of respect for historically Jewish fraternities from rabbis and communal leaders and frequently a maximum level of support from Jewish parents and extended families.

Now, the Hillel rabbis noted, these fraternities could no longer truly participate in Jewish activities, and a significant increase in interdating was taking place, particularly in the Jewish fraternities such as ZBT that enjoyed the highest social status. A heavy application of the skills of gentlemanhood and gallantry, along with lavish expenditures for exciting dates, could go a long way in winning over reluctant non-Jewish women, and Jewish members of the Greek upper tiers were proving all too eager to employ such tactics in an era of newfound freedom. This, along with the certainty that segregated fraternities in any case were a legal and social anachronism inimical to American democracy, brought about the final jettisoning of Jewish communal support.

Legal Challenges

Legal challenges to traditional methods of membership selection were also a constant impediment to healthy fraternity growth. By the early 1960s, most of the deadlines for achieving nonsectarianism that had been set in the 1950s were being reached, and the suspension or elimination of individual fraternities on grounds of religious or racial discrimination had become commonplace. The Civil Rights Act of 1964 and the Higher Education Act of 1965, pushed through Congress by President Lyndon B. Johnson in the aftermath of Kennedy's assassination, disrupted the Greek world by outlawing discrimination in the public sphere and linking the granting of federal funds to nonsectarian, nondiscriminatory membership and admissions policies. Fraternities might think of themselves as private organizations supported primarily by fees and the donations of generous alumni, but they were also part of the general college campus, which was becoming increasingly dependent on government funds. Also in 1964, fraternities and sororities, including several that were historically Jewish, were driven to make an unsuccessful appeal to the New York Supreme Court against the action of the State University trustees in forbidding national affiliation on campus on the grounds that national fraternities inherently promoted illegal discrimination.

Regardless of the undoubted benefits the entire country could enjoy

from such much-needed reforms, losing control over membership selection challenged the most basic organizing principles of fraternity
life. Furthermore, it was obvious to all that potential new members
would be reluctant to become part of an institution that not only was
increasingly perceived as unnecessary and harmful to one's scholastic
health but was also suspect in the eyes of U.S. federal and state law.

Student Protest and the Generation Gap

Estimates of the percentage of students who were true radicals, the ones
who actually organized and led the sit-ins, strikes and demonstrations,
ranged from 5 to 10 percent. Observers noted that the proverbial "Joe
College," interested in dating and football, was far from dead in the
1960s. Nevertheless, fraternities and sororities were viewed as being increasingly removed from the progressive trends sweeping the campus.

In a characteristic article of the age entitled "The Irrelevance of the
American Fraternity System," published in the November 1966 issue of
Fraternity Month magazine, Tom Charles Huston, a Phi Kappa Psi
member, spoke for many when he warned that fraternity members
were "completely out of touch" and would surely go under if they did
not become a more integral part of this new and exciting university life.
"Stokely Carmichael, National Chairman of the Student Nonviolent
Coordinating Committee (SNCC) may come to campus and urge the
students to burn down the administration building and the typical
Greek is off working on a Homecoming float," Huston declared with
disdain. "While American boys die in Vietnam, and student leftists collect blood for the Vietcong, Greeks go about their business in the same
manner as their predecessors did 100 years ago when all was quiet and
serene on the campus." No wonder many of the best students coming
to college were not interested in the Greek system. "These people want
to be where the action is," Huston continued. "They want to come to
grips with reality. They find the fraternity system irrelevant, and to an
alarming degree, they are correct."

Even as the influence of the Greeks declined, Huston wrote, fraternity members were sealing their fate by becoming increasingly isolated
from the university as a whole and turning most of their energy to
"inter-fraternity" activities, rather than seizing leadership in activities
that truly mattered on the typical college campus of 1966. "The real
action on today's campus is not found at the football game or the

Homecoming parade," he declared. "It is found in the Union Building where two students are vigorously debating the merits of American policy in Vietnam. It is found in front of the dean's office where students are marching to protest university paternalism. It is found in the classroom where the bright student does not allow a dogmatic assertion to go unchallenged merely because it is mouthed by a Ph.D. In short, something exciting is happening on today's campus, and for the most part, the typical fraternity member is not even aware of it."

If fraternities did not reform, Huston warned, the best students would join the radicals, disrupting every campus as the University of California at Berkeley had been disrupted for weeks and almost shut down in 1964. They would ignore the fraternity system unless fraternities became more "relevant," left the "Mickey Mouse trivia to the junior set," and turned toward meeting the challenges of the time. Politics and social concern, he concluded, were the major characteristics of the brightest students of the 1960s, and any system "which stifles, rather than encourages, these characteristics is doomed to stagnation." There was still time; it was up to the Greek system to "measure up to the confidence placed in it by those who love it, have worked for it, and look to it for leadership."

Time, however, was running out. Protest against authority was not limited to disagreement with the war but permeated every aspect of students' lives and ran counter to every organizing principle of fraternity life. Parents, church, synagogue, school, government, law enforcement—all were suspect. In sororities, at the most basic level, women refused to wear dresses and stockings, refused to wear their pins, refused to follow any rules or regulations, joined only because their parents forced them to and then quickly dropped out. They totally ignored alumnae officers' insistence that they learn the social graces and how to act like "ladies." Sex-segregated chapter houses were daily abandoned for coeducational dormitories and private apartments. College administrations, both because of student protest and their own weariness at trying to stem a flooding tide, gave up even trying to enforce parietals and dress codes.

For many students of those years, their most vivid college memories would not be their senior proms but watching on television the Chicago police turn their billy clubs on student protesters at the 1968 Democratic National Convention. Their greatest grief and rage would come not from lost loves but from a string of catastrophic assassinations and memories of six students at Kent State University in Ohio and Jacksonville State in Mississippi who lost their lives in May 1970 when national guardsmen shot into a crowd protesting President Richard Nixon's escalation of the war and the invasion of Cambodia.

Each new day and new development drove college students further and further from the traditions of the past. By 1970–72, on all but the most politically conservative campuses, jeans and workshirts had become the common uniform for both sexes. Homecoming events and sweetheart contests were but a memory. At such schools as Washington University in St. Louis, Arizona State, and Indiana University, students took the money usually devoted for such purposes and gave it to social service agencies instead. Commencement ceremonies were abandoned as well; students no longer bothered to attend, claiming that the speeches were boring, irrelevant, and nothing but empty rhetoric. It was easier to have one's diploma mailed. Being elected to a class office or honorary society had long been a prize for the members of any fraternity, but at some schools students did away with student government and honoraries on grounds that they were undemocratic or, again, irrelevant. Formal dating became a thing of the past, and the elaborate rituals that had governed it were discarded. In such an atmosphere of anger, rebellion, and revolution, it was not surprising that reports began to surface of fraternity brothers meeting and promptly voting their own brotherhoods of out existence. Of what use were frivolities like fraternities when there were so many other burning issues at stake?

Alumni who had suffered through the Depression and fought through World War II, including many fraternity members, were less than sympathetic to the excesses of student protesters, whom they viewed as spoiled brats and the products of a too indulgent and permissive upbringing. This "generation gap" did not augur well. Support and close ties among older and younger generations had been basic to the maintenance of a good fraternity. No such institution could long survive without the financial and practical help of dedicated alumni, on both the local and national level. Furthermore, a belief in the value of the nation's young and the necessity to provide them with a good education had been responsible for older citizens' willingly sending their tax dollars to help improve and develop American higher education. But now alumni, even those who themselves did not support the war and who sympathized with some of the students' goals, were shocked at their foul language, their apparent promiscuity, their use of drugs, their long hair and torn clothes, their disdain for every principle of good grooming and dress, their contempt for every form of authority, their charge that "the establishment" of older reactionaries was ruining the world and that the only way to change "the system" was to destroy it.

Alumni were particularly disgusted at the seeming inability of university presidents and administrators to react with sufficient force when students destroyed property, occupied university buildings, and created general mayhem. Columnist Jenkin Lloyd Jones, an alumnus of Phi Gamma Delta, reflected in early 1967—after riots had virtually shut down his alma mater, the University of Wisconsin—on his own less-than-saintly student days. They were the kinds of days that parents of the protesters had likely passed through, yet in his view nothing they had done could compare to what college youth were doing now. In so writing, he declared himself "a normally temperate man speaking for a host of tax-paying, tuition paying citizens":

In the softening mists of time, it is easy for us of the gray heads to build a halo around our undergraduate days. But it won't fit. We drank Dago Red in the basements of Little Italy. We stole alki from the stiff lab. We put double meanings on our Homecoming decorations. We liked dark parties and blind chaperones. We were even rebellious in a restrained way. We were angry and dismayed at the nation's economic derailment, and many of us, including me, cast our first votes for socialists. But it never occurred to us that all the values of civilization and religion were ready for the ash can. When we sinned, we sinned guiltily and didn't kid ourselves that we were heroically blazing new trails of human freedom. In short, we were not armored in total rationalization for gross misbehavior, which seems to be an ailment suffered by some of the current young. True, we were excused from some of the current pressures. . . . still we were up against elemental struggle. Many a promising lad departed at mid-term with the rueful admission, "finances,". . . and occasionally there was the sobbing phone call that Dad had blown his brains out.*

The child-rearing strategies that had been used on these young people also came under attack, as the writer went on to denounce the "zany theories of child psychology" of the 1950s that decreed that youth must be denied nothing lest it suffer the trauma of frustration. All it had created was thousands of affluent youngsters with "runaway adolescent egos" whose every whim and appetite became law. (Dr. Benjamin Spock's bestseller, *Baby and Child Care*, first published in 1946, was a particular target of such complaints.) Jones also denounced the paralysis of college administrations, who in his view had completely lost control of their institutions. How long would it be, he demanded, before college officials regained their function? "What American universities

*Jenkin Lloyd Jones, "Student Activism and the College Fraternity," *Fraternity Month* 34, no. 3 (Feb. 1967):15.

need more than cyclotrons," he concluded, "is presidents who are not frightened of swinging professors, and deans with enough guts to send a few delinquents home." In so writing, Jones was expressing the characteristic sentiments of numerous fraternity alumni who were repulsed at the developments on campus and responded by turning away.

Drug Abuse

Of all the developments that came to characterize the American college campus in the late 1960s, perhaps none shocked alumni more or did more damage to the coherence of the existing fraternity system than a burgeoning pattern of drug abuse, addiction, and dealing. Mind-altering substances had been available to humankind since the beginning of time, and the use of drugs such as marijuana, cocaine, heroin, opium, and morphine had been well known throughout much of the twentieth century, particularly in large cities. Never before, however, had drug dealing and use become so widespread and fashionable in the apartments, dormitories, and fraternity houses of American college students. Artists, writers, musicians, and intellectuals with large student followings publicly extolled the mind-expanding properties of narcotics and spoke of them as an essential aid to their creativity.

By the fall of 1966, administration officials and campus observers were speaking of a disease, a spreading epidemic that was being treated by police. Students who had been "turned on" to drugs during vacations at home were returning to school and introducing dozens and then hundreds of others to their use, some earning hundreds of dollars each week by selling to their new customers. Marijuana and heroin had now been joined by a host of newly available psychotropic drugs, including amphetamines ("pep pills") and barbiturates. For the first time, hallucinogens such as LSD could be cheaply and easily synthesized in a laboratory by anyone with a basic knowledge of chemistry. Students turned to the selling and using of these illegal drugs for the thrill of "experimenting" and through peer pressure; there was also a desire to thumb their noses at the authority of the law and to relieve the anxieties and tensions of troubled times.

While students of all backgrounds and living conditions were known to be using drugs, the fraternity and sorority, with its closed doors, inherent network of friends and connections, strong tradition of group solidarity and collective protection, social sophistication, and the higher-than-average disposable personal income of its members, was particularly fertile ground for anyone wishing to use or to distribute illegal substances. Across the nation, fraternity houses, including those of ZBT, began to earn for themselves the reputation of being "a good place to get your drugs." At the same time, the very qualities that made fraternities conducive to individual drug use also contributed to their fragility in the face of the 1960s "do your own thing" philosophy. Few things could shatter a brotherhood more quickly then bitter divisions between students who wished to use drugs in the privacy of their quarters and their fraternity brothers who objected and threatened to turn them in to the police if they continued. National officers of the historically Jewish fraternities were to note, from the perspective of later years, that drugs led to the demise of some of their finest chapters.

Indeed, any student community could be shattered by drugs, especially when students met serious injury or even death through their use, an event that could lead to despair on the part of deans and others charged with overseeing student life. In the fall of 1969 the ZBT *Quarterly* reprinted an open letter, under the title "Death on Campus: An American Tragedy," by the dean of students at Amherst College. It described an incident in which a visiting Harvard University sophomore, in the throes of an LSD trip, died by falling seventy feet from the roof of a dormitory.

Expressing his despair, lack of comprehension, and overwhelming sense of helplessness, the dean pleaded with his students to take responsibility for one another and to cease taking drugs or inflicting such senseless tragedy on others. "He was young and bright," the dean lamented, "too bright to surrender his life in the foolish madness lighting a generation." He did not become a dean, he continued, in order to watch

a generation of students pollute their sanity or distort their lives. . . . Words aren't adequate and deeds seem fruitless. More than ever students have taken on themselves the individual responsibility which shapes their lives in all areas. It should be so, but the judicious exercise of such responsibility demands wisdom. I see no wisdom at all in the growing and indiscriminate use of drugs. . . . On a beautiful Saturday afternoon which was itself a natural stimulant, why the need for some artificial or uncertain drug? And where were we all on that night or on any night and when will we awake for the need to replace a disinterested privatism with a sustained concern for the troubled person in our community? And why do we tolerate in our midst the profiteers of poison? And by what moral right do we pass into the hands of others substances which can threaten their well-being and even their lives? What in God's name is happening to us?

The Collapse of ZBT

The campus unrest and anger of the late 1960s and early 1970s harmed the entire American college fraternity system, leaving the officials of the National Interfraternity Conference (NIC) in a virtual state of shock. However, it hit Zeta Beta Tau, whose membership was still predominantly Jewish in 1968, sooner, harder, and longer than other groups. On the whole, the historically Jewish fraternities were younger, smaller, and less well endowed financially than non-Jewish ones. This made them more susceptible to crises. Many of ZBT's chapters that had been added to the rolls in the 1960s were of too recent an origin to have put down real roots or developed extensive alumni support systems, and they fell easily. In addition, Hillel rabbis noted at their annual conferences that Jews, who made up close to 10 percent of all American college students despite being only approximately 3 percent of the general population, were also disproportionately represented among campus demonstrators and protesters, to the point of making up anywhere from one third to one half of their numbers.

The traditional ZBT student profile hurt the fraternity as well. A background of wealth, high family education, involvement in current events, and urban sophistication had gone far to lend ZBT its special cachet, but these were also precisely the students who, with the support of their parents, were most likely to be opposed to "the establishment" and to turn away in disillusionment from old collegiate frivolities such as fraternities in favor of more "relevant" activities. They might not actually join student protesters out on the barricades, but neither would they devote their time and energy to chapter house activities.

The extent of the disaster did not become clear to ZBT national officers until after it was already upon them. Indeed, initiation figures had never been higher. In the 1967–68 academic year, 1,431 undergraduates were initiated into the fraternity, and in the fall of the 1968–69 school year, initiations reached an all-time peak of 2,707. The summer 1969 convention took place as usual on Grand Bahama Island, and as in years past the delegates passed a resolution of "boundless pride in and admiration for" their executive secretary. At least three new colonies were in the process of becoming full-fledged chapters, while the ZBT Foundation was giving away more money for scholarships than ever before. The prospect of merging with other fraternities that had years of tradition and a proud heritage behind them cheered those who believed that fresh blood would invigorate and strengthen their brotherhood.

Nevertheless, the portents of disintegration soon appeared. The first indication was plunging undergraduate membership figures. After the peak of 1968–69, initiations fell to 1,929 in 1969–70 and to 1,191 in 1970–71, and then they plummeted to 721 in 1971–72. At that point ZBT also hit its nadir in the number of viable chapters. Although two large mergers had brought the chapter roll to over 150 and perhaps 80 still existed on paper in 1971 (meaning that they had not officially been expelled, suspended, or disbanded or the house sold), it was estimated that not more than 40 Zeta Beta Tau chapters, primarily the older, more rooted ones, were still functioning that year. By 1970, after more than two decades of unanimous chapter representation at ZBT annual conventions, delegates from fewer than one third of the active chapters came to the gathering, now renamed simply "the annual meeting." At the chapter level, even where drug use was not a major problem, students lost interest in Greek life entirely and virtually overnight dropped out, deserted, or even disbanded their fraternities, leaving the houses empty. Those who remained behind tended to rebel against the authority of the national fraternity to a greater extent than in years past, angrily greeting visiting field secretaries with the assertion that "national" had done nothing for them, so why should they do anything for it?

Equally ominous was the fleeing of local alumni trustees who in years past had derived joy and personal satisfaction from their work for Zeta Beta Tau and had provided the younger members with priceless guidance and support. They now recoiled from the younger generation and turned away in the justifiable fear that they might be held liable for the consequences of the undergraduates' activities and unpaid debts. College students might come and go, and what was lost in one semester could theoretically be gained back in another. Without a solid base of long-term alumni support, however, no fraternity could long endure.

In more normal times, if a house were found to be a den of illegal or risk-prone activity or a particular chapter was failing to meet its obligations as a unit of a national fraternity, then suspension or expulsion followed by a fresh start might be enough to turn the situation around. But now too much was happening too fast, and even worse, the most basic operations of ZBT were crippled by critical interruptions in cash flow. Without initiation fees and without payment of room and board contracts, not only was the fraternity denied the income it needed to pay mortgages and rents and utility bills in its suddenly empty houses, but its very existence as an organization was threatened. More and more bank loans had to be taken out, while the capital of the National Permanent Endowment Fund (NPEF) and other endowment sources was eventually bled almost dry to pay for legal fees and basic operating expenses. Other historically Jewish fraternities, including ZBT's eventual merger partners, did not have any endowment or credit to fall back on at all. Salaries and benefits for the staff, travel and servicing, office rent, printing, postage, telephone—all were in jeopardy, and the daily news of disaster in the field brought no relief. Chapters were closing down faster than the staff could get to them; the fraternity was embroiled in a real estate nightmare and was being sued from every direction.

As a stunned Barry Siegel struggled valiantly to adjust to sudden changes in a fraternity so unlike that which he had known and loved, Supreme Council meetings became marathon sessions devoted not to setting policy or standards but simply trying to keep the organization's head above the water. And by 1970 the central leadership of Zeta Beta Tau was charged with handling the problems of not just one fraternity but three.

The "Antecedent" Fraternities: Mergers with Phi Sigma Delta and Phi Epsilon Pi

At first there was little reason to believe that anything but good would come from the joining of Zeta Beta Tau with two other fraternities of similar standing and background. Phi Sigma Delta, which had been founded at Columbia University in 1909 and had merged with Phi Alpha on April 6, 1959, ratified a merger with ZBT in the summer of 1969. In 1960, Phi Sigma Delta had celebrated its fiftieth anniversary with a series of eight festive banquets held throughout the United States. Its growth thereafter had been slow, with only seven new chapters added between 1961 and 1965. Still, throughout the decade the core of the fraternity appeared to flourish, with an active and idealistic group of undergraduate members and a roster of distinguished alumni.

As in the case of ZBT, Columbia and Penn were among Phi Sigma Delta's oldest and most important chapters; other unique and important strongholds were the University of Vermont, the University of Connecticut at Storrs, the city and University of Denver, and Rensselaer Polytechnic Institute in Troy, New York, whose graduates had gone on to distinguished careers in engineering and technology. Politically, the profile of Phi Sigma Delta as an organization was more progressive and less conservative than that of ZBT. Despite a strong historical Jewish identity, it had been one of the first fraternities in the late 1940s to place a clause in its bylaws specifically barring discrimination by race or religion, and by the late 1960s it had a significant percentage of non-Jews among its membership.

Traditional fraternal and generational ties, however, were, if anything, stronger in Phi Sigma Delta than in other groups. The fraternity was known in NIC circles for an even greater than usual prevalence of graduates who had gone into business together as partners or co-workers after graduation. Phi Sigma Delta could also boast many families in which two, three, or even four sibling brothers had followed one another without question into the organization's ranks. A leading example had been the Wolpaw family of Cleveland. Harry L. Wolpaw (Western Reserve '20) had gone from being president of his chapter to the fraternity's national president; his younger brothers, Meyer T., Dr. Benjamin J., and Dr. Sidney E., had all become active Western Reserve members as well.

As in the case of Zeta Beta Tau, Phi Sigma Delta graduates were also well represented in law, government service, social services, Jewish communal affairs, and medicine. Among the alumni in which "Phi Sigs" took special pride were publisher Walter Annenberg (Penn '28), who served on the board of trustees of the University of Pennsylvania along with lawyer and civic leader Morton H. Wilner '30, who had been captain of Penn's baseball teams in 1929 and 1930 and a varsity quarterback in 1927 and 1929. William A. Hyman (Columbia '15), who had been "Master Frater," or president, of his chapter, went on to a career in insurance and aviation law. Under the auspices of the Inter-American Bar Association and the United Nations he authored in 1965 the "Magna Carta of Outerspace," codifying laws that would govern the nations of earth as they reached out to the moons, planets, and stars of the galaxy. Arthur Levitt (Columbia '21), who in 1966 was reelected to his fourth consecutive term as comptroller of the state of New York, was invited to be the principal speaker at the 1965 convention banquet of the fraternity at the Waldorf-Astoria in New York City, where he praised Phi Sigma Delta's early commitment to nonsectarianism and to social responsibility. Robert Abrams, former Master Frater of his Columbia chapter, had been elected in November 1965 as the youngest member in history of the New York state legislature in Albany. Businessman and art collector Armand Hammer (Columbia '19) was frequently featured in their quarterly's pages, as was Joseph L. Mankiewicz (Columbia '28), who in 1963 had just finished directing *Cleopatra*, starring Elizabeth Taylor and Richard Burton. Attorney Arnold Shure (Chicago '29), who had helped to lead the struggle of the Jewish fraternities to save refugee students during World War II, continued as a major benefactor of his alma mater and its law school.

Through the decades, Phi Sigma Delta's Western Reserve chapter in Cleveland had specialized in producing famed rabbis and communal leaders such as prominent Reform rabbi and Zionist leader Leon I. Feuer. Rabbi Ronald B. Gittelsohn '32 dedicated the Jewish section of the Iwo Jima cemetery as a U.S. Navy chaplain during World War II and in 1968 was elected president of the Central Conference of American Rabbis. Alan J. Altheimer (Columbia '24 and a graduate of its law school) had served as national vice president and then president of the fraternity in the 1930s, going on to a distinguished career in Jewish community center work and winning a major award from the National Jewish Welfare Board. In 1968, Phi Sigma Delta graduate and past national president Leonard P. Aries (Chicago '37), a world-renowned specialist in human rights issues, served as national vice president of the National Conference of Christians and Jews, while Edward Ginsberg (Michigan '38), in the aftermath of Israel's Six-Day War, had just been named chairman of the United Jewish Appeal at its thirtieth annual national conference in Cleveland in December 1967.

Phi Sigma Delta graduates were well represented in the world of scholarship and the creative arts as well. In the world of advertising copywriting, the fraternity could claim Charles P. Roman (NYU '28), who had begun his career as a promoter for the mail order bodybuilding course of Charles Atlas and had authored the immortal phrase "I was a 97-pound weakling." The winter 1965 issue of the *Deltan* featured a profile of best-selling author Bruce Jay Friedman (Missouri '51), the author of such controversial novels as *Stern* and *A Mother's Kisses*, which dealt with a Jewish mother's all-consuming passion for her son. Professor Morton Halperin (Columbia '58), who had earned his MA and PhD degrees in international relations at Yale, had been doing research since 1960 at Harvard's Center for International Affairs and at the age of twenty-seven was considered one of the world's experts on China, especially important during the cold war years. Professor Sidney Goldstein (University of Connecticut '49) earned a PhD in sociology at the University of Pennsylvania and became head of his department at Brown University in 1963. In 1966 history and government major

Ronald Katz (NYU '67) of Missouri won the first Rhodes Scholarship in the history of the fraternity and the first one earned at New York University since 1928. In the annual NIC rankings, Phi Sigma Delta regularly placed even higher than ZBT, with more than 70 percent of its chapters performing well over the all-men's average.

The social idealism evident among many Zeta Beta Tau undergraduates in the early 1960s was equaled or surpassed within the ranks of Phi Sigma Delta. Joining the Peace Corps was a popular choice after graduation, with many such volunteers regularly featured in the fraternity's magazine, and in the summer of 1966 the University of Chicago chapter won special recognition for its program of tutoring young people who lived in the ghettos of the city's South Side. Among Phi Sigma Delta's best-known "radicals" was Phi Alphan Peter Yarrow (Cornell '58), who grew up in New York studying both violin and guitar, graduated from the High School of Music and Art, and majored in psychology. He contributed his talents as a performer to campus and fraternity life, singing and playing his guitar at house parties, rush events, and local clubs to the great enjoyment of his fellow students. After two years of solo performing, he joined with Paul Stokey and Mary Travers in the Peter, Paul and Mary trio. Their first singles, "If I Had a Hammer," "Lemon Tree," and "Puff, the Magic Dragon" (the last composed by Peter himself), took the group to the top of the charts. By the summer of 1966 the group had performed several times at the White House, during the Selma-to-Montgomery march of the civil rights movement, and at the memorial service for Andrew Goodman, a civil rights workers who had been slain in Mississippi in the summer of 1964.

As in the case of Zeta Beta Tau, there was little warning in the mid-1960s that Phi Sigma Delta was entering its twilight as a stable, independent organization. The year 1966 was the golden anniversary of both the Penn and University of Michigan chapters. At Penn more than five hundred undergraduates, alumni, wives, children, and girlfriends celebrated the milestone with a buffet lunch, group attendance at the Penn-Yale football game, two receptions, and a dinner dance. A large group of "old-timers" gathered at the fraternity house on the evening of Friday, November 4, for an informal reception, taking time to examine the doors and rooms where once they had slept. Two of the original founders, Emanuel Dreyfus and Samuel Konwiser, and the widow of a third were present, as were three trustees of the university (all alumni of the chapter) plus all the living past Phi Sigma Delta Master Fraters and former Grand Regents (as the fraternity's highest officers were known) of Penn's Phi Alpha chapter. A similar celebration was held at the University of Michigan, including a banquet at which National President Harold A. Levanne presented associate membership to Dr. Werner Landecker, a professor of sociology at the university who had come to the United States during the Hitler era under Phi Sigma Delta's refugee student program and had lived at the chapter home while receiving his degree.

The latter part of the decade was marked by a flurry of energy, reorganization, and dedicated but belated alumni fund-raising for the purpose of hiring a full-time professional staff and improving the fraternity's publications and services. Phi Sigma Delta and later Phi Alpha had been held together on the national level by the dedicated and frequently unremunerated service of Administrative Secretary Alexander "Babe" Lewin, who had devoted himself to the fraternity for twenty-two years before retiring in 1969, and Joseph Kruger (Michigan '26), who, in the midst of numerous other activities, served as national secretary, field secretary, and editor of the *Deltan* for more than forty years. In the fall of 1967, Lee I. Dogoloff assumed the post of Phi Sigma Delta's executive director while the new national president, Richard A. Wells, reached out to alumni, national officers, and undergraduates to revitalize all phases of national operation and begin serious efforts at growth and expansion.

Their efforts were not entirely without success. By the summer of 1968, Dogoloff was proud to announce the installation of three new chapters at Queens College, Seton Hall, and Cleveland State, along with a new array of fraternity programs and services. More than 125 delegates and guests attended the annual convention that summer, as plans were announced to celebrate the fraternity's sixtieth anniversary as an independent organization. By the time that date came, however, Phi Sigma Delta had had no choice but to seek a merger partner, and in the fall of 1969 its forty-nine chapters, along with the energy and innovation of its national officers and staff, had been joined with Zeta Beta Tau.

The merger with Phi Epsilon Pi, a fraternity with a tradition and profile that were more similar to Zeta Beta Tau's than were those of Phi Sigma Delta, further appeared to strengthen the central organization of ZBT. Having merged with Kappa Nu in 1960, Phi Epsilon Pi in 1969 had chapters and colonies at approximately sixty campuses. Altogether, the merged brotherhoods of Kappa Nu, Phi Alpha, Phi Sigma Delta, Phi Epsilon Pi, and Zeta Beta Tau brought the fraternity's roll to a peak

The Phi Epsilon Pi chapter at the University of Buffalo football field in the relatively peaceful fall of 1967, holding aloft their fraternity's banner, two years before the merger with Zeta Beta Tau. Most face the prospect of being drafted into the Vietnam War. Both final exams and the planned May commencement ceremonies were canceled for the Class of 1970 members pictured here; Buffalo was too convulsed in violent student conflict following the Kent State shootings. To commemorate those tumultuous days, editors of their senior yearbook half-humorously printed photos of Buffalo police dressed in riot gear and shooting tear gas on the campus. Included here, hanging from goalpost, left to right: Robert Blackman '70, Alan Wolf '70, Shelly Ludwig '70, touching the shoulder of Mike Nusbaum '70; Steve Snyder '70 (sitting upright) and Judd Fink '70.

of 157 chapters and a living membership of over ninety-three thousand men. The leaders of Phi Sigma Delta and Phi Epsilon Pi, including Burton L. Litwin, Richard A. Wells, and Maurice Jacobs, the latter a distinguished Jewish communal leader and publisher, all participated in ZBT's Supreme Council, and the constitution and bylaws were changed to incorporate the antecedent fraternities' traditions, rituals, and insignia. From the perspective of later years, there was little doubt that the mergers did much to strengthen the core of Zeta Beta Tau, helped to bring in the energy of many new alumni, and helped to preserve elements of the antecedents' traditions and rituals, which would otherwise have been forgotten.

Trouble Times Three

In the short run, however, the mergers caused a bad situation to become even worse. Instead of having to deal with the collapse, unpaid debts, legal entanglements, real estate crises, and burgeoning undergraduate discipline problems of a single fraternity, Barry Siegel and the Supreme Council of ZBT suddenly found their difficulties tripled. Complications, problems, and lawsuits related to the mergers began immediately and continued for several years. The NIC, recognizing neither the merger nor the traditional rule that none of its constituent fraternities would be permitted to seize unfairly the chapters of another, allowed former Phi Sigma Delta and Phi Epsilon Pi chapters to be taken by other fraternities. In protest, ZBT withdrew from the organization temporarily, joining other fraternities that had become dissatisfied with the actions of their umbrella group.

At the chapter level, alumni and undergraduates out in the field, many of whom had been rivals for years, were appalled to discover that they were now supposed to be part of the same fraternity, and they refused to merge. In a series of "de-mergers," dozens of chapters either disbanded unilaterally or petitioned ZBT for release, while many alumni trustees of both the old ZBT and the antecedent fraternities refused to turn over their property to the new Zeta Beta Tau. Frequently, houses were sold off over the direct opposition of the local alumni, bringing about permanent termination of their years of support, and creating hatred for the national organization that never abated.

At the national level, the merger of three formerly independent organizations, each with its own facilities and operating procedures, presented a myriad of headaches, frequently about the most prosaic of details, such as what to do with the lease obligations of the antecedents' former national offices, how to secure and move the contents of their safe deposit boxes, and how and where to switch bank accounts. Which auditing firm should they choose? What would happen to old obligations and insurance policies? Who would sign checks now, and how would pensions and severance be paid to the retired officers of three different fraternities?

Barry Siegel, who in better times had been acknowledged as one of the most effective national fraternity leaders in the country, was shattered by Zeta Beta Tau's downfall and overwhelmed by the heroic efforts that were so obviously required to salvage it. No one knew better than he that he possessed neither the business nor the legal background to even begin to deal with this mountain of difficulties by himself. Yet as the months passed and harassed alumni volunteers gave up in exasperation, more and more responsibilities were piled on his shoulders. After weeks of agonizing over the decision and numerous conferences with Supreme Council officers, he finally tendered his resignation. The Supreme Council, announcing the decision at its meeting of March 6, 1971, passed a resolution commending Siegel for his eleven years of service to ZBT "beyond the call of duty" and designated Assistant Secretary James E. Greer Jr. (California State at Long Beach '64) as his successor.

Back from the Brink

Born in Bremerton, Washington, and raised in Orange County, California, James Greer had turned down bids from Sigma Alpha Epsilon and Phi Kappa Tau to join ZBT at California State at Long Beach in the spring of 1961 and became president of the chapter in his junior year. Upon graduation he intended to go into his family's business, but a phone call from Barry Siegel in 1965, inviting him to become a field secretary, changed his plans. Of his first year and a half working for the fraternity before being drafted into the armed forces, Greer, who had received a good Episcopalian Sunday school education and cherished the interfaith contacts that the fraternity offered him and his fellow members, recalled, "It was a great time to be associated with ZBT. To be associated with ZBT was to be associated with the best among all fraternities. It was known that it served a particular segment, the Jewish one; but without reservations you could walk with great pride in NIC circles. Our chapters had fine reputations; our alumni were fine upstanding men. It was a time that everyone would have preferred had stood still. It's gone forever."

Even while serving in Fort Riley, Kansas, Greer had been called upon to visit western ZBT chapters and to help with convention arrangements. Nine months before his discharge from the army in May 1968, Barry Siegel called once again to invite him to come to New York as assistant executive secretary and editor of ZBT's publications; and as Lee Dover had once done, the former Californian came and made the city his home. Not long afterward, the crisis began, and a bereft James Greer suddenly found himself cast into the maelstrom and searching for allies who could help pull the fraternity through its worst days. "I was too young and too dumb to know what we were doing," he recalled many years later. "If I knew then what I know now, I might not have done what I did."

Whatever was to be done would be done with less help than at any point in the fraternity's history. A number of stalwart alumni volunteers, among them past national president and now ZBT Foundation president Stanley I. Fishel, never missed a single meeting no matter how unpleasant or grueling they happened to be. Others, however, could hardly be blamed for avoiding what had once been an honor and a joy but had now been turned into a bitter and despairing job of full-time proportions. Only nine members of the Supreme Council showed up at the designated July 20, 1971, meeting, not enough even to achieve a quorum. Months went by without any meeting at all. As the normal alumni support structure of Zeta Beta Tau collapsed along with the undergraduate chapters, Greer gathered about him three men who, together with himself, literally held the fate of the fraternity in their hands. Supreme President Arthur J. Horwitz (Penn '48), an expert in mergers and acquisitions, provided financial knowledge and contacts along with an unshakable faith that ZBT must survive. General Counsel Saul D. Kassow (NYU Heights '46), retained by ZBT virtually full-time in June 1971, provided the necessary legal expertise. Finally, Douglas L. Maine (Temple University '70), who in later years would go on to become chief financial officer of the telecommunications corporate giant MCI, took upon himself the unenviable staff job of director of chapter affairs.

Not long after Greer had assumed his new position, however, it appeared that any efforts at reorganization would be fruitless and that ZBT was ready to join the the ranks of fraternities that were no more. It was in the late spring of 1971 that the twenty-eight-year-old executive secretary, realizing that he desperately needed help, called Arthur J. Horwitz—only recently installed as a member of the Supreme Council—and suggested a lunch meeting along with attorney Saul Kassow and ZBT treasurer Richard W. Cohen (NYU Heights '47) to discuss the future of the fraternity. At that fateful lunch at the Harmonie Club in New York City, he recalled, the group reviewed ZBT's financial situation and reached the conclusion that the fraternity was for all intents and purposes bankrupt. From a businessman's point of view, death through liquidation would have been the only sensible thing to do. "But this isn't a business," Horwitz declared angrily. "This is ZBT, damn it, and ZBT isn't going to go under. We can save it, we can turn it around—I know we can!"

Under Horwitz's direction, three more decisions rapidly followed. First, under no circumstances would Zeta Beta Tau declare bankruptcy in any form. Even if eventual reorganization was a possibility, the damage to its public standing and reputation would be irreparable. Instead, the officers would take upon themselves the responsibility of confronting every single one of the fraternity's creditors and negotiating a separate settlement. Second, there would be no recourse to recriminations or lawsuits against anyone connected with the antecedents who might have misrepresented or misstated the extent of their own indebtedness and thus compounded national ZBT's difficulties. Third, new corporate entities, beginning with the National ZBT Corporation, would have to be formed temporarily in order to provide some isolation and protection from the financial and legal problems of the undergraduate units.

Coping and Climbing Out

From the day of the 1971 lunch at the Harmonie Club until 1973 the triumvirate of James E. Greer Jr., Saul D. Kassow, and Douglas L. Maine effectively ran the fraternity from ZBT's national office, now relocated from the Statler Hilton Hotel to a small building in New York's suburbs. As in the years of the Great Depression, coping, muddling through, and an almost ruthless insistence that ZBT receive its due despite hard times became the order of the day. Chapter services and fraternity publications were cut to the bone. The officers negotiated to extend or forgive old bank loans and take out new ones. They dealt with chapter property on a case-by-case basis, sometimes selling, sometimes allowing foreclosure, sometimes taking out second and third mortgages.

Instances of drug abuse, criminal behavior, and antagonism at the local chapter level were similarly dealt with on a case-by-case basis. Kassow worked to find ways of indemnifying alumni so that they would not be liable for the debts and misdeeds of undergraduates. A determined fund-raising campaign by James Greer netted several thousand dollars and a renewal of support in some quarters. Gradually, a new core of volunteer officers formed. The constitution was rewritten to allow for a smaller Supreme Council, more undergraduate representation, fewer standing committees, and lower quorums for meetings and annual conventions. Most important of all, the National Permanent Endowment Fund, which had been started against a rainy day on the eve of the Great Depression, was finally called upon to serve its purpose, although it was evident that a long struggle would be necessary before the income could ever be replaced.

Additional problems and complications continued for several years. Attempts to merge ZBT and the antecedents were unsuccessful at many campuses, and alumni relations remained bitter. At the 1972 national convention the alumni officers and staff present resisted an effort by the undergraduates to allow coeducational chapters and a resolution that all future annual meetings be held in states with a drinking age of eighteen. Massive government spending for social programs and the Vietnam War, coupled with the aftereffects of the 1973 Arab-Israeli war in the Middle East, brought about both double-digit inflation and wide-scale unemployment, along with a severe gasoline shortage that forced the fraternity to hold its 1974 convention at a location as close to an airport as possible to minimize driving time. The general inflationary pressures of the postwar era in the United States had already made difficult the achievement of basic fraternity desiderata, such as a house for every chapter, at least one traveling field secretary, and a high-quality quarterly publication. As inflation continued through the late 1970s, these desires passed beyond the reach of many college fraternities, including Zeta Beta Tau.

Nevertheless, the signs of recovery slowly began to appear. In 1972, James Greer was able to write and distribute a new *Introduction to Membership* book—a small, mimeographed affair to be sure, unlike the grand publications of ZBT's past, but one that indicated a stable, functioning, and structured fraternity nonetheless, a reflection of returning campus stability overall. Campus antiwar protests were already quieting down in January 1973 as a cease-fire agreement was signed in Vietnam and the few remaining U.S. military personnel were withdrawn by March of that year. Two more years of fighting between North and South were to continue, and Saigon, the capital of South Vietnam, would fall to Communist forces on April 30, 1975—but American soldiers would no longer be there.

Also in the 1972–73 school year, undergraduates rediscovered the joys of parties and dating, even partaking in a national "nostalgia" craze that made marathon dances, modeled after those of the 1930s, a popular event for both entertainment and fund-raising purposes. By 1974, old chapters, including one at Trenton State College that the national had been assured was "dead," began to reorganize, and new colonies petitioned to join. To the category of "dead," in council parlance, was added the more hopeful "critical," "half-dead," "50–50 chance of survival," and finally "in revival." All in all, the Supreme Council noted with pleasure the positive news it was receiving from several campuses and the steadily rising rush figures, which had gone from 765 in 1972 to 940 in 1973 to a tolerable 1,112 the following year.

It was in January of 1974 that Arthur Horwitz, suffering from burn-out but widely acknowledged to have saved the fraternity, stepped down from the presidency before the end of his term and was replaced by ZBT veteran Rabbi Matthew Simon (Chicago '53), who promptly indicated that the period of "sackcloth and ashes" had passed and that the time had come for ZBT to assume a normal life again. James Greer began the year with a long memo on fraternity reorganization that aimed to remove responsibility for policy-making in ZBT from the "triumvirate" and restore it to the Supreme Council.

With a return to tradition and stability and a desire to incorporate the legacy of all five antecedent fraternities, the new Supreme Council designated a common Founder's Day, to be commemorated by all members. The annual convention reassumed its festive quality, and awards, such as the newly designated Barry Siegel Rushing Trophy for the chapter bringing in the most new members, were given once more. Supreme Council meetings no longer dealt with financial matters only and instead began to deal with issues such as house policy, accounts receivable policy, scholarship standards, prohibition of firearms, prohibition of hazing, fraternity legacies, and expansion.

In the last area the national fraternity was aided by the presence of Irving M. Chase (UCLA '74), a past president of his chapter who was appointed assistant director of chapter affairs shortly after his college graduation. After a month and a half of training at ZBT national headquarters, he spent long weeks in intensive chapter visits, lending his general expertise, providing visibility for the national organization, and aiding in programming and rushing. By the winter of 1974–75 it was evident that his efforts had borne fruit. The national officers were happy to report that each of the chapters he had visited, with the exception of one, all enjoyed significantly higher rush figures than they had had the previous year.

Conclusion

Through the latter part of the 1970s, despite numerous crises and setbacks, the outlook for ZBT markedly improved. Membership figures continued to grow. Many alumni who had been lost to the fraternity

At the University of Georgia in 1975. From left to right: Mike Topper '75, William Bezkor '76, and Rick Denman '76.

during its worst years were lost forever, but others remained, and at least a half dozen chapters were able to revive the happy custom of annual alumni homecoming reunions. Certainly, the danger that ZBT would go under completely was no longer present, and the campus atmosphere that automatically branded fraternities and related institutions as "frivolous" and "irrelevant" was a thing of the past.

The year 1976, the bicentennial of both the United States and the American college fraternity system, brought a renewed regard for tradition across the country, after the tumult of the Vietnam War years, and a collective rediscovery of America's heritage. Not coincidentally, within the Greek world it also brought a new historical awareness of their place within that heritage as a scholarly symposium on fraternity history was convened at the fraternity birthplace, Union College.

Rabbi Matthew Simon, a historian by avocation, urged in 1977 that the time had come to begin writing Zeta Beta Tau's own history. In this call he was joined by Stanley I. Fishel, who reminded the council that their 1978 convention would coincide with the eightieth anniversary of the fraternity's birth. Their seventy-fifth anniversary had come and gone during the nadir of 1972–73, when they could not even begin to celebrate it properly. Now, he insisted, the fraternity should do whatever it could to make its eightieth anniversary gathering the setting for an important alumni celebration. He did not say, although surely he must have thought it, that the fraternity's recent survival against tremendous odds deserved as much celebration as its birth eight decades earlier.

Nevertheless, despite its successful revival, there was widespread doubt that ZBT could ever duplicate the position it had enjoyed in earlier eras. Too much time had passed; the nation as a whole and the college campus in particular had undergone too many changes. The basic organizational structure might be secure, but the ZBT of the late 1970s, 1980s, and 1990s faced old problems revived in new and virulent forms. Exactly what stance, if any, it should take regarding its Jewish heritage remained a vexing problem. With the resurrection of "normal" fraternity life had come a revival of hazing, leading in 1974 to the first hazing death of an undergraduate within the ranks of ZBT. Drug abuse and alcohol abuse remained serious problems, complicated by new liability laws. Risk management soon became a primary preoccupation of fraternity officers on both the national and local levels, as public perceptions of the Greek system reached new lows.

The tumultuous days of the Vietnam War era were gone, but so too were the days of Lee Dover and Harold Riegelman. By the late 1970s, in the midst of its eightieth anniversary celebration, it had become evident that, much though ZBT might prize its legacy, it would never be able to go "home" again. A new reincarnation would be necessary if the fraternity were not only to survive but flourish in its second century of existence.

CHAPTER ELEVEN

FRATERNITY OR "ANIMAL HOUSE"?

ZBT *in the Age of Liability,* 1978–98

A noticeable return to college traditions and a resulting revival of interest in college fraternities were already well underway on American campuses in 1978, when the Universal Studios film *National Lampoon's Animal House,* set in a fictional small college town of the mid-1960s and portraying fraternity life as one nonstop bacchanal, was released to cheering audiences. Produced by Matty Simons and Ivan Reitman and written by fraternity veterans Douglas Kenney, Chris Miller, and Harold Ramis '66 (Ramis had been vice president of his ZBT chapter at Washington University in St. Louis), the devastating caricature of life at "Faber College" became one of the most popular films of the year and, indeed, one of the most popular comedies of all time. According to James Greer, in whose mind the memory of the near-demise of ZBT was still fresh, "It was one of the best rush films ever created—we couldn't get to the bank fast enough with the initiation checks."

College-bound young people took the cinematic caricature at full face value. From the start of that school year's fall semester, the music of the sound track boomed across countless college courtyards. Freshmen and sophomores from coast to coast bedecked themselves in bedsheets, swigged beer, and chanted, "Toga! Toga! Toga!" in imitation of the film's famous toga party scene, and food fights spread across the land. The nation's beer distributors, breweries, and related commercial interests saw *Animal House* too. Recognizing a good market when they saw one, especially in the opening week of the school year, they took to sponsoring promotions, contests, and other programs in conjunction with fraternity chapters, frequently promoting sales of their products by distribution of free samples.

Some viewers of the film were revolted by the scenes of wild parties, deception, road trips, vandalism, drunkenness, violence, pot smoking, hazing, statutory rape, drug use, academic cheating, students tossing the contents of their meals at one another, and a fraternity house so filthy it was on the verge of condemnation by the local board of health. However, to the average seventeen-year-old boy, as one ZBT who entered college in 1980 and who was significantly influenced by the film recalled, "You have to admit, it looked kind of fun."

There was nothing funny, however, in the way that thousands of impressionable teenagers were led by the film to believe that regular endangerment of life and limb was an inseparable part of fraternity life or that fraternity houses were proper havens for consuming alcohol illegally after states began to raise the drinking age from eighteen back up to twenty-one. There was nothing humorous in the influence that *Animal House* and its aftermath had on the nation's insurance companies, which soon began to rate Greek-letter groups among the top ten most risk-prone institutions in the country as a flood of lawsuits rained down upon them and the concept of liability broadened beyond anything previously known.

Teenagers might well laugh at the scenes of John "Bluto" Blutarsky (a role created by TV's *Saturday Night Live* comedian John Belushi) periodically crushing beer cans against his head and downing an entire bottle of whiskey in a single gulp. Freshmen did not understand that such behavior could land them in a hospital with alcohol poisoning or, worse, kill them. They did not understand that some of the more destructive aspects of pre-1968 "traditional" college fun and high jinks that the film glorified had once been tempered by the presence of chaperones, parietals, housemothers, and strict social codes, all of which had been jettisoned in the 1970s. They did not understand that society's attitudes in the 1950s had changed profoundly and that they could no longer depend on the indulgent societal attitude of "boys will be boys" to get them out of trouble.

In short, the new popularity of fraternity life garnered by *Animal House* came at a high price; the film ultimately caused "dreadful damage," as Greer noted, to the health and well-being of fraternity undergraduates and to the Greek system as a whole. For the ZBT leadership in particular, its appearance marked the beginning of an era when the values of brotherhood and fraternalism would almost be displaced in their minds by a relentless preoccupation with risk management and potential liability.

The General Fraternity Revival and ZBT

The extent of the damage to the fabric of the fraternity system was not yet clear at the turn of the decade, however, and at first ZBT and other national Greek-letter groups had cause to rejoice at their apparent good fortune. They had lived through predictions of the complete demise of college fraternities, yet now an unexpected upsurge in membership was cause for comment in the nation's media. The article "Columbia Fraternities Revive a Rite of Spring," appearing in the *New York Times* on April 10, 1981, noted that on the campus that had become almost synonymous in the public mind with student radicalism fully seventeen functioning fraternities, representing more than 10 percent of the student body, were reviving the tradition of an annual Spring Carnival. Similarly, the Bridgeport, Connecticut, *Post* noted on September 5, 1982, in its coverage of the opening of the academic year, that "the college fraternity system, an institution as old as the US . . . is no longer the sickly anachronism some said it was a few years ago," even if it was not as robust as it had once been.

Observers reflected that the change in lifestyle, a concurrent fashion of nostalgia within general American popular culture, and the new conservative tone of the country—heralded by the election in November 1980 of Republican President Ronald Reagan '32 (himself a loyal member of Tau Kappa Epsilon from his days at Eureka College in Illinois)—might have played a role in this upsurge, making it more possible for students who so wished to join fraternities without fear of embarrassment among their peers. Some members spoke of joining as a way to overcome feelings of "isolation" and "dehumanization" on campus; others reflected that fraternities were replacing the social bonds that had recently operated in social movements and student activist groups. Whatever the reasons, the growth in interest was undeniable. Even Princeton University, where fraternities had been technically forbidden for more than a hundred years, had sub-rosa chapters of two fraternities by 1982, with more to follow.

By 1979, Zeta Beta Tau in particular was clearly back on its feet again as a functioning national fraternity. Initiation figures were up, averaging twelve hundred to fifteen hundred men a year; new groups of chapter trustees were in formation; and expansion was aided by the reopening of the State University of New York to Greek-letter groups. Fund-raising was up, and ten colonies stood poised to become new chapters. The 1980 ZBT summer convention in San Diego, California, which was expected to draw an attendance of 150, drew 185 instead. Granted that the Lee Dover/Barry Siegel record of 100 percent chapter representation was never reached again in the 1980s, and the national officers were constantly contriving new techniques to force reluctant and impoverished chapters to send at least two delegates to the national convention. Nevertheless, enough came to make the conventions successful affairs, and a growing annual network of regional conclaves sprang up to link together far-flung ZBTs who would otherwise have been unable to travel across the country for a fraternity gathering.

ZBT's national office entered the personal computer age in 1983 with the purchase of a $10,000 system fitted with the WordStar program, an 8-megabyte hard drive, and their own "daisywheel" printer, which allowed the organization's paperwork to be processed with new efficiency. By January 1998, the fraternity's centennial year, ZBT would unveil its first page on the World Wide Web. The fraternity awards program was functioning once more, albeit sometimes on a sporadic basis, and in October 1982 national officers traveled to the University of Michigan both to dedicate the new chapter house and to give ZBT's Man of the Year prize to the university's president, Harold T. Shapiro (McGill, ZBT '56), who would go on five years later to become the eighteenth president of Princeton University. The ZBT Foundation's scholarship program was fully revived, and in 1980 it distributed over $32,000 in grants and loans; its assets grew to over a million dollars. In the area of social service, chapters were reported to be raising hundreds of thousands of dollars annually for local and national charities.

Most important of all, alumni interest and programming, which had been almost moribund during the lean years, appeared to be slowly returning. Some, like ZBT Foundation president Stanley I. Fishel, had never ceased their involvement. In 1980 he entered his fiftieth year as a member of Zeta Beta Tau, and the occasion was duly marked at the May 4, 1980, Supreme Council meeting by his election as honorary life member. Others, who for years had taken no notice of their fraternity, now contributed beyond expectations to the first Founder's Annual Appeal in 1980–81. An analysis and breakdown of funds received revealed that alumni from the oldest Zeta Beta Tau chapters—those with either a single Greek letter or an "alpha" designation—contributed the most.

The Antecedents: Phi Sigma Delta/Phi Alpha, and Phi Epsilon Pi/Kappa Nu

In addition to initiates from the pre-merger Zeta Beta Tau chapters of 1968, alumni originating from all five constituent historically Jewish fraternities were represented in the organization's revival. These might be counted as three, if one considered the Phi Sigma Delta/Phi Alpha merger of 1959 and the Phi Epsilon Pi/Kappa Nu merger of 1960. The official name of the fraternity was now "Zeta Beta Tau Fraternity: a Brotherhood of Kappa Nu, Phi Alpha, Phi Epsilon Pi, Phi Sigma Delta, Zeta Beta Tau." Without these mergers, the antecedents, along with their national directors, might well have vanished with hardly a trace and with no mechanism in place to transmit any of their history or traditions to succeeding generations. By absorbing the antecedents, assuming all their obligations, and incorporating aspects of their traditional terminology and insignia, national Zeta Beta Tau, in its own view, was rescuing its brother fraternities from total extinction.

On the local level, however, it was not always easy to erase years of loathing between groups that had once been bitter rivals. In one case, trustees of the University of Maryland chapter still insisted on retaining the name of Phi Sigma Delta thirteen years after the merger. They threatened to close the chapter down rather than remove the letters from their chapter house and allow Zeta Beta Tau to take over. At the University of Virginia chapter, alumni and undergraduates both found it unthinkable to hold any identity or name other than Phi Epsilon Pi, and they continued to identify themselves as such. Rather than allow themselves to be absorbed by Zeta Beta Tau, they withdrew to become a strictly local fraternity, still calling their chapter Phi Epsilon Pi years after the national, multichapter Phi Epsilon Pi fraternity had ceased to exist.

The psychic, legal, and financial shock of the upheavals and mergers of the late 1960s and early 1970s reverberated for years, and an unknown number of formerly active members remained permanently alienated from the fraternity. With chapters closed, open, merged, closed, and then open again, the traditional orderly progression of Greek-letter chapter designations within the fraternity's rolls became completely disrupted. But for the most part, the former leaders of the antecedents, particularly those of Phi Sigma Delta/Phi Alpha (whose officers comprised 40 percent of ZBT's governing board in the first year after the merger) became well integrated into the greater brother-hood of ZBT by the early 1980s.

Of the thirteen men who served as ZBT national presidents from 1970 through 1998, seven were originally initiated into one of the ante-cedents of Phi Sigma Delta, Phi Epsilon Pi, or Phi Alpha. Maurice Ja-cobs (University of Maine '17), the elder statesman of Phi Epsilon Pi, frequently attended Supreme Council meetings, in his last years, when able, and carried on an extensive correspondence with the ZBT na-tional office, working to bring Phi Epsilon and its alumni back into the fold. On April 10, 1980, he too was voted an honorary life member by the council. In the 1980–81 academic year, the Special Awards Commit-tee recommended that as many of ZBT's traditional prizes as possible be given to outstanding figures from the antecedents; the next Man of the Year trophy was awarded jointly to two members who had origi-nally been initiated into Phi Epsilon Pi and Phi Sigma Delta.

The initiated alumni of Kappa Nu, which had been a relatively small but intensely close-knit brotherhood, founded at the University of Rochester, also saw their origins acknowledged when the council per-mitted the Rochester chapter to take the Alpha designation—despite the strenuous objections of ZBT alumni of the defunct chapter at the City College of New York. (In common with ZBT, Kappa Nu's name originated from the Hebrew language; its insignia included the He-brew letters *kuf* and *nun*, which stood for *Kesher Ne'urim*, "the tie of youth.") In the Berkeley area, where Kappa Nu had ranked socially at the top of the ladder of historically Jewish fraternities, alumni peti-tioned to establish a scholarship at the University of California that would preserve their fraternity's name.

As the years passed, the most active Zeta Beta Tau alumni became ei-ther those who had joined post-merger and had never known any other identity or else leaders from previous years who were able to jettison the rivalries of another age in favor of the higher value of fraternalism. "We are perhaps unique among all fraternal organizations in America as a result of our mergers," declared ZBT treasurer Martin D. Braver (Boston '47), a past national president of Phi Alpha, speaking at a No-vember 1985 Supreme Council gathering at the University of Illinois to initiate honorary alumni. In his speech, recorded in the Council min-utes, he praised the state of the fraternity's union:

Here we stand, brothers in one fraternal bond, yet composed of men who while they were undergraduates, sometimes thought of each other as the enemy—cer-tainly that was probably true during the highlight of rush. Today, we are ZBTs and

Phi Eps and Phi Sigs and Phi Alphans and Kappa Nus—but we are all ZBTs. We are the stronger for that, and much envied for our ability to achieve the amalgamation that we have. . . . We have come to realize that there is a kind of motivation and loyalty that supersedes even regard for two or three particular Greek letters . . . a loyalty that is perhaps even higher than the loyalty to a specific identity. It's loyalty to fraternalism itself, a commitment to work with young people who without a doubt, are the future leaders of our cities and our nation.

In 1984, Braver, a senior partner in a Boston CPA firm, rose to the post of national president of ZBT. Other national alumni officers who led the fraternity through the 1980s and 1990s included Richard S. Simon (Michigan '43), a businessman and manufacturer in Pittsburgh and longtime trustee of ZBT's chapter at the university there; businessman Frederick E. Schatz, also a graduate of Michigan ('57); attorney Stephen P. Ehrlich (University of Denver '70); Philip M. Waxberg (City College '66), a New Jersey businessman; Ronald J. Taylor, M.D., a 1966 graduate of Washington and Jefferson College and a board-certified psychiatrist practicing in Baltimore; attorney Leonard Komen (Missouri '65); and Irving M. Chase (UCLA '74), a lawyer and businessman in Irvine, California, who had served on the ZBT national staff immediately after his college graduation and went on to become a director of the Supreme Council in 1982, national secretary in 1988, national treasurer in 1989, and national president from 1994 to 1998. In the National Office, James E. Greer Jr. continued as executive vice president, assisted by James S. Mamary (Rutgers '75) and later Raymond J. Woody (Rutgers '83); the latter had begun by serving immediately after his college graduation as expansion director of the fraternity.

Weaknesses

Despite the apparent resumption of "normal" fraternity life, however, Zeta Beta Tau in the 1980s faced a host of new problems, along with old problems now resurfacing in a more virulent form.

The general outlook for American colleges and universities, the hosts of individual chapters, was not bright. Changes in higher education continued to go in directions detrimental to the Greek system. Shifting enrollment patterns were one significant factor. For example, observers noted that greater numbers of students were now studying only part-time and taking five or six years to finish their courses instead of the traditional four. Such students were less likely to show an interest in fraternities. A contraction in the number of new campuses and potential fraternity members overall was a particular difficulty of the post-1970s years. By the early 1980s the bulk of the baby boomers had exited their college years, and the number of eighteen-year-olds in the United States had declined sharply. Residential colleges, competing for students among a more limited applicant pool, instead strove harder to make campus life desirable by supplying ever more luxurious and inclusive student living quarters, complete with everything from cable television to personal computers.

Government support for college students, once generous, was contracting as well. Legislatures and private donors who in the past had been among higher education's most loyal supporters could not forget the student excesses of the 1960s and early 1970s and had lost much of their earlier enthusiasm. In many such minds the dignified vision of "college men and women" had been replaced with the vision of "college kids" and "spoiled brats." The advent of a new, more conservative Republican administration also took an unexpected toll. After years of expanding government aid to all aspects of higher education and research, President Ronald Reagan and other government leaders sought to reduce federal college student aid and related programs. Accompanying tax cuts were insufficient to offset the disruption to student life caused by ubiquitous budget-slashing and the results of double-digit inflation in the late 1970s. As for the cold war, although serious tensions between the United States and the Soviet Union continued until 1987, the support of higher education was no longer automatically connected in the minds of the American public with the cause of security and national defense.

Within the bounds of the fraternity itself, the economic outlook was hardly any brighter. In real terms the national fraternity's operating budget was a fraction of what it had been two decades earlier, and the NPEF, the fraternity's endowment fund, had become too depleted in the course of the 1970s to be of further immediate assistance to the national organization. The cushion of both organizational and individual wealth that had sustained the fraternity in the past was gone. Finances at both the national and the local level became a constant worry, leading to tension about the equitable distribution of funds among chapters, national, and the three technically separate branches of Zeta Beta Tau—the fraternity, the foundation, and the NPEF. Officers at all levels were torn between wanting to offer members more services but not wanting to inflict more hardship by raising fees to pay for them. The

Deltan, now the name of the fraternity's magazine in deference to Phi Sigma Delta's former periodical, could be distributed only once a year, and the cost of maintaining a good field staff became prohibitive. A dispute on the benefits of saving money by moving the National Office out of the New York City area—perhaps to Indianapolis, where twenty-two national fraternities and sororities now had their headquarters—began in 1980 and raged on, with feelings running equally high on both sides, for almost fifteen years.

A number of methods to accrue additional income, including offering alumni discounts on hotels, car rentals, and insurance, met with limited success, as did attempts to share office space with other fraternities. More successful was the decision, in 1982, to revive the practice of mandatory undergraduate contributions to replenish the NPEF, as well as retaining a professional fund-raising firm to conduct ZBT's first capital fund-raising drive.

Alumni Activity

In the early 1980s the former characteristic high level of ZBT alumni involvement and support at the chapter and city levels also appeared to be a casualty of the years, not to be restored with the return to a more "traditional" American campus atmosphere. A large and dedicated group of volunteer alumni trustees and advisers was still the best indicator of chapter success, and chapters so blessed did well; but few of ZBT's units enjoyed the support of such a group anymore.

ZBT alumni had by tradition never been a great source of financial support at the national level. A survey conducted in 1980 revealed that while 17 percent of total operating costs derived from alumni contributions was the historical average within the National Interfraternity Conference (NIC) and in some fraternities the share of alumni financial support approached 50 percent, a relatively decentralized Zeta Beta Tau ranked almost at the bottom, with only 7 percent of its national budget through the years coming from alumni contributions. In terms of time and energy at the local level, however, ZBT alumni had given generously. In the past the national fraternity could count on a cadre of perhaps five hundred men across the country, the proverbial "backbone of ZBT," to lend their guidance and support to undergraduates in their area.

Now even those ranks had become seriously depleted. Bitterness from merger days; lack of outreach from the national; fear of liability; disgust with media reports of hazing, alcoholism, and drug abuse; a belief that college fraternities were a frivolity unworthy of serious attention; the gap in religious background and social class between older graduates and younger members; and sheer indifference all played a role. So did the advent of true nonsectarianism. Ironically, in the past, ZBT had benefited indirectly from the pervasive anti-Semitism in America's upper echelons. Adult Jewish men of accomplishment and ambition, as most ZBTs were in its early days, had almost been forced to rely on one another to overcome the obstacles that faced them at every turn, and this favored their uniting around their chapters of origin. Zeta Beta Tau, whose initials were popularly said to stand for "Zillions, Billions and Trillions" or "Zion Bank and Trust," had furthermore played a crucial role by allowing adult graduates to socialize and enjoy themselves in a manner commensurate with their relatively upper-class socioeconomic level at a time when equivalent Gentile fraternities and town and country clubs might be closed to them. In a freer and more democratic society, however, ZBT alumni activity was no longer necessary to serve that function.

The basic existence of ZBT at the undergraduate level had been secured by 1978, but it was evident that the once-active alumni clubs had faltered, and few graduates beyond the circle of national officers and remaining trustees cared to attend conventions. The chairman of ZBT's Audit and Finance Committee, when asked to report to the Supreme Council in 1980 on the prospects that new membership services would improve communications with ZBT alumni, had to conclude that the request itself was based on a questionable assumption: that some current relationship between the fraternity and its alumni constituency actually existed. "The Committee believes that such a relationship does not now exist between the fraternity and the overwhelming majority of its alumni," he wrote with frankness, "and that re-establishing such a relationship is of primary importance." He suggested that a new Committee on Alumni be formed "to see how this can best be accomplished." Indeed, by 1990 the national leadership concluded that it had long enough concentrated almost solely on building its undergraduate base and that reaching out to ZBT alumni should once more become a priority. By then they were able to depend on a base of fifteen years' worth of ZBT graduates who had never known anything other than the post-1970 merged fraternity.

Legacies

The legacy problem affected alumni participation as well. Occasionally, a yet-loyal alumnus from previous decades would retain enough of an interest in ZBT to wish that his son join ZBT also. If the son was accepted, well and good. If he was not, it was almost inevitable that the alumnus would be permanently alienated. "Drop dead" was a typical response from a ZBT graduate from Brooklyn to an October 1983 request for donations to the ZBT scholarship fund. "My son was blackballed as a legacy and you people have the colossal gall to ask me to make sure the people who blackballed him can finish school." Alpha Epsilon Pi had accepted his son, the man wrote, so he was choosing to donate $1,000 to their scholarship fund instead. James Greer's response on November 4, 1983, revealed that this was not an isolated incident and that, if anything, the legacy controversy was worse in the relatively progressive 1980s than it had ever been before:

While I am obviously not happy with your response, I want to let you know that I share your sense of hurt and betrayal. Unhappily there is not a year that goes by that we do not have two or three similar situations, Inevitably expressions of dismay are directed towards the National Office and they are among the most painful matters with which we deal. I wish I had the means to prevent such situations from happening. As you may know, universities removed the rights of nationals and alumni to control undergraduate membership selection a number of years ago. Our loss is AEPi's gain. (Supreme Council Minutes notebook)

Maintenance and Expansion

Overall, while the pledging of new members and the establishment of new chapters continued steadily, so too did chapter closings. Too many of the chapters that did remain suffered the inherent maladies of youth and weakness. A study conducted by James Greer in 1988 revealed that ZBT had essentially become a rebuilt organization. Of the 124 chapters on the roll immediately after the 1969–70 mergers, only 33, or less than 27 percent, had remained in continuous existence. True, the national fraternity had succeeded in reviving 32 of the 89 chapters that had "died" during the debacle of the early 1970s and had succeeded in adding approximately 18 completely new ones to the roll. But this still meant that the majority of ZBT's local chapters in 1988— 67 percent—had either been newly established or rechartered since

1973, and therefore their roots were not as deep nor their loyal alumni as numerous as the national leadership might have wished.

The changing character of the host ZBT campuses also caused friction between chapters, national officers, and alumni as they debated what the expansion policy of the new fraternity should be throughout the 1980s. The stress on absolute conformity to a single ZBT ideal that had ruled during the Lee Dover years—Jewish, handsome, well-mannered, rich, from a "good" family and attending a "good" college—was now a thing of the past. Younger ZBT members now came from varying religious and socioeconomic backgrounds and a bewildering variety of public, private, large residential, small residential, rural, urban, and commuter colleges. The change brought about a host of questions. How could a single set of standards be applied to such a variety of institutions? When the time came to expand, should priority be given to establishing revived ZBT chapters or those located on so-called prestigious campuses rather than establishing chapters at those schools with lesser social status? Were those eager to learn and move up the socioeconomic ladder, as many founders of Jewish fraternities themselves had been, not precisely the group that needed and wanted the values of fraternity more than any other? And were not their college administrations the most hospitable to Greek-letter groups otherwise despised and increasingly being eliminated from the older, more established campuses?

What was the value, furthermore, of nonsectarianism? Did not the maintenance of generational ties still dictate that preference be given to campuses where ZBT's "traditional group" was well represented? Why not take advantage of fraternity-minded parents who still believed that ZBT was a completely Jewish college social fraternity and for that reason would urge their sons to join it in preference to another group? Although the fraternity was no longer officially Jewish, most of the alumni and potential legacies were, and some council members argued that a strong correlation existed between the level of Jewish identity and the "strength" of particular chapters as measured by any criteria. Others argued for the universal value of fraternalism and brotherhood, stating that it was the students, not the campus, that made a fraternity chapter rise or fall and that the enormous expenditure in work and funds necessary to establish a single chapter at a "prestigious" school that also had a high Jewish student population might better be used to establish four or five chapters elsewhere.

Jewish Identity

Aside from its implications for deciding expansion policy, Zeta Beta Tau's Jewish heritage also presented a number of programming challenges. It was possible from time to time to affirm that heritage through positive activities that anyone of any faith or background could share in. The revival of ZBT's Roger Williams Day tradition in 1979 was one such instance, as was the leadership's decision, when planning a 1990s convention in Washington, D.C., to organize a trip both to the U.S. Holocaust Memorial Museum and a visiting exhibit of the Dead Sea Scrolls. The sensitivity to injustice and the universalistic spirit and ethos of American Reform Judaism, which was in many respects the religious cradle of Zeta Beta Tau, still informed the fraternity's actions and served as an anchor in a changing world.

All too frequently, however, reminders of ZBT's Jewish heritage surfaced in an unpleasant context. As in the case of all the other historically Jewish fraternities and sororities, ZBT chapters were still taken as "Jewish" by campus anti-Semites and suffered the consequences. Swastika paintings, dead pigs thrown on the lawn, vandalism, cases of other fraternities taunting them with "Hitler salutes" or playing "Third Reich music," as occurred at UCLA in the 1980s, did not occur often, but they occurred often enough for the fraternity to issue a standard procedure to all its chapters on how to deal with such incidents.

Rushing, the lifeblood of any fraternity, could be affected negatively as well. In the case of Alpha Epsilon Pi, where the issue of Jewish identity was hotly debated at their summer 1980 convention, Executive Director Sidney Dunn came down firmly on the side of stressing it if for nothing but the principle of self-interest. Unless they remained Jewish, he believed, AEPi would be unable to compete with the older and more prestigious historically Gentile fraternities. Indeed, ZBT's leadership was continually chagrined when, all too often, a good non-Jewish potential fraternity member, in complete ignorance of the fraternity's history, would rush ZBT, only to be warned away from "the Jewish house" by his peers and by his family. At the same time, the host of Jewish families, rabbis, and communal leaders who in the past would have gladly sent good rushees and financial contributions ZBT's way rather than to Sigma Chi or Sigma Alpha Epsilon no longer had any justification to do so. Ironically, by the 1980s it appeared that ZBT was suffering all the rushing disadvantages of being a historically "Jewish" house while enjoying very few of its benefits.

Sometimes anti-Jewish feelings, or at least discomfort with the Jewish aspects of ZBT's heritage, could surface within the fraternity's membership itself, as much from Jewish students as non-Jewish ones. In one example, during the fraternity's ninth decade of existence, the new chapter at Duquesne University expressed, through its trustee, strong discontent with the fees of the national organization. It was a common enough complaint within the fraternity world, but further investigation revealed the real reason: the members had decided that they did not wish to be associated any longer with a historically Jewish fraternity. Two chapters, Western Ontario and UCLA—the latter the very chapter that had graduated ZBT's president at the time, Irving Chase— were discovered to have set actual "rush quotas" for Jews so that by design they would not admit more than a certain percentage of Jewish men. During a general session at one of the fraternity's national conventions in the early 1990s, led by Dr. Ronald J. Taylor, a student rose to express his concern with the fraternity's historical association with Judaism, particularly as expressed through the presence of a traditional six-pointed Star of David on the membership badge. While he did not want to remove the star from the badge, the student suggested that it be rotated on its center horizontal axis by 90 degrees. That way, the meaning of the star would be less obvious, and only those within the bounds of the fraternity's own initiates would be aware of ZBT's Jewish origins.

News of these incidents alarmed alumni leaders. No one desired anymore that ZBT's chapters be 100 percent Jewish, but how could such things be allowed to happen in a fraternity founded by Dr. Richard J. H. Gottheil? And what good was their heritage if they could not guarantee that every one of their chapters was a place where a Jewish boy could at least feel at home?

Media Damage

The confluence of weakening chapter solidity, alienation of alumni, financial difficulty, and confusion over ZBT's historic mission came precisely at the point when solidarity and clear-headed leadership were most necessary. The excesses of the post–*Animal House* years brought an attack of negative media attention and front-page revelations of gross behavior among the nation's Greeks. Even the most loyal fraternity alumni leaders could not deny that with the increase in the legal drinking age from eighteen to twenty-one in the early 1980s, chapters were becoming havens for underage binge drinking accompanied by abuse of both property and people. Throughout the Greek system, behavioral problems became the rule rather than the exception. Chapter leaders who objected, bound by the ideal of brotherly loyalty, found it almost impossible to confront and remove such men from their midst. Furthermore, the sexism and racism that was being so thoroughly rooted out of most segments of society seemed to be finding a partial haven among campus Greeks, including ZBT. The general public did not differentiate between fraternities with better or worse records in this regard. Whenever an incident hit the newspapers and TV stations, all fraternities, ZBT included, were caught in the crossfire.

The rising toll of young men killed in the process of a fraternity hazing was of greatest concern. In the ten years between 1982 and 1992, as ZBT noted in its own introductory membership material, at least forty-five students were reported to have met their deaths through fraternity hazing rituals, and dozens more had been injured badly enough to require hospitalization. The real, unreported number could have been higher still. By 1985 several national fraternities had had their insurance policies canceled outright and their chapters permanently expelled from the campus in the wake of repeated incidents. ZBT's national leaders took no comfort that the Greek system's worst extremes of hazing and student misbehavior occurred outside their ranks; "There but for the grace of God go we" was the most common sentiment voiced at anxiety-filled Supreme Council meetings.

Mothers and other members of the victims' families now waged political campaigns to make hazing a criminal offense and a recognized threat to the public health. The campaign was aided by the American Medical Association, which in the mid-1980s published a study examining the medical consequences of typical hazing acts in gruesome detail and noting that there had been 168 cases of severe injury or death related to fraternity hazing in the United States between 1923 and 1983. In 1984 the New York state legislature introduced new antihazing legislation that toughened penalties and removed what had once been a major impediment to prosecution: the consent of the victim was no longer a defense against the crime, the victim could in no way be considered an accomplice, and proof of actual physical injury was no longer necessary. Other state legislatures passed similar laws.

Young college women as well as young men were victims of fraternity violence, assaulted on chapter house premises in the midst of drunken parties. Several well-publicized incidents included the gang-rape of a woman at the University of Pennsylvania in 1983, which led to a court case and the ultimate disbanding of the fraternity. A female sociologist on the faculty wrote a nationally distributed book describing the incident in detail and tracing its origins to the sexism inherent in male fraternity life. In the public mind "frat boys" became almost synonymous with sexual harassment and assault of women. The Greek system also became associated in the public mind with racism, which kept surfacing in public reports of general fraternity activities, particularly in the context of "theme" parties.

It was little wonder that, in the face of such publicity, increasing numbers of schools were deciding that fraternities, despite any revival of student interest in them, had no place on their campuses. In April 1983, for example, it was announced that the trustees of Princeton University had voted to continue their 108-year ban on official school recognition of fraternities and sororities—meaning that the three fraternities then on the campus, which had admitted eighty-four students, would continue to be denied use of university facilities or even use of the university's name. In November 1983 the faculty of Amherst College voted 90 to 29 to close all fraternities whose property was owned by the college.

Fraternity officials tried to defend themselves and their institutions against the charges leveled against them. In one case, the president of the NIC wrote a letter of protest to the president of ABC News after the airing on the evening of September 24, 1981, of a *20/20* television program entitled "The Rites of Passage," which concentrated on hazing, drinking, and drug abuse among fraternity members. After the January 1982 issue of *Playboy* magazine painted a similar picture in an article entitled "Fraternities: Are They for You?" Irving Chase of Zeta Beta Tau wrote to the president of Playboy, Inc., citing the article as perpetuating stereotypes and maligning an entire group of men unfairly:

[The author] would have one believe that every fraternity man is loud, bigoted, alcoholic, insensitive, selfish and a stupid boor who cares for nothing but his latest female conquest. A fraternity is a microcosm of society and like society, it would have individuals as just described; however, tᴏ generalize that *all* fraternity men are Neanderthals does a disservice to those of us who are proud of our fraternities. I have been associated with my fraternity for about 12 years, first as an undergraduate and presently as an undergraduate adviser, and have nothing but fond memories concerning my fraternity brothers. They were not loud, bigoted, alcoholic, insensitive, selfish and stupid boors, but rather fine men who have become the doctors, lawyers, dentists, accountants, teachers and businessmen of today. These men are the political and philanthropic leaders of tomorrow. (Supreme Council Minutes, Spring 1982)

Trouble within ZBT

ZBT and its extended family might have maintained for itself an image that overall its members hazed less, drank less, treated women better, studied more, and were more tolerant than those of other NIC Greek-letter groups. However, ZBT was not and had never been immune to the "Animal House" syndrome, and there were enough incidents of discreditable and sometimes outright criminal behavior within the ranks to convince the national leadership that they had a problem on their hands as well. All of ZBT was left open to charges of harboring racism when in October 1988 the University of Wisconsin ZBT chapter held a "slave auction" party and fund-raiser. The incident did "terrible damage" to the good name of ZBT, as the Supreme Council charged, as it was "insensitive and rightfully objectionable to any number of groups in the Wisconsin community." Of the 168 hazing deaths that the American Medical Association had enumerated from before 1983, one belonged to ZBT. The first and only such death in the one hundred years of the fraternity's existence occurred as early as 1974 when, during the nighttime digging of ritual graves on a New Jersey beach, the sandy walls collapsed on seventeen-year-old William Flowers and smothered him. His companions frantically tried to dig him out, but their efforts only caused the sand to collapse further. By the time the police arrived, the boy was already dead.

That summer, the 1975 ZBT national convention approved "An Act to Redefine and Prohibit Hazing," stating that chapters or individuals who hazed faced suspension and probable expulsion from the fraternity. Hazing in various forms, however, continued to take place, prompting complaints by parents and disciplinary action from school authorities. When an anonymous questionnaire on hazing was distributed to the delegates of the 1979 Montreal convention, including a detailed list of possible acts and a request to check off those that occurred in one's own chapter, 50 percent of the chapters reported none at all. However, the other 50 percent of the delegates responding reported such activities as pledge class line-ups; yelling at pledges or calling them names; road trips or kidnappings; personal servitude; forced calisthenics; deception; throwing whipped cream, water, paint, and the like on a pledge; and lengthy work sessions. More than 48 percent believed that hazing served a useful purpose by perpetuating tradition and creating pledge class unity and discipline; moreover, a large percentage of delegates considered fifteen of the twenty-eight acts enumerated in the questionnaire too mild to be considered hazing at all.

The results of the survey alarmed the national staff and Supreme Council and prompted to them to intensify their efforts. Over the next several years the national fraternity issued rules and requirements of increasing strictness in an attempt to put an end to hazing. First the chapter, then each individual was directed to sign an affidavit stating that they understood and agreed to abide by ZBT's antihazing policy, and James Greer insisted that each chapter invite a local law enforcement official to address them on their state's criminal and civil penalties for it. Year after year the undergraduate delegates at the annual convention dutifully endorsed the antihazing measures in principle. Yet year after year at least half of the chapters continued to haze in some form, believing, as visiting officers informed the council, that it was unthinkable not to perpetuate the tradition and that the ZBT national did not really "mean" what it was saying. Young men within ZBT continued to be injured by those purporting to be their fraternity brothers. Where bodily harm did not occur, the fraternity as a whole could still suffer unbearable embarrassment, as in February 1984, when the University of Pennsylvania reported to the council that pledges dressed only in jock straps and sneakers, led by fully clothed ZBT brothers, ran through the campus and onto Fortieth Street and had furthermore stolen property from a rival fraternity. The council and the ZBT national convention delegates could pass legislation in public to their hearts' content, but in reality there was no way to enforce complete, consistent compliance on the local level.

Situations involving intoxication, vandalism, and violence between fraternity chapters both within and without ZBT also occurred. The threat of litigation was ever present. At Carnegie Mellon University in 1983, in the course of a rush party, three freshmen rushees became ill and had to be hospitalized with alcohol poisoning; the dean of students charged the chapter with "gross irresponsibility" and withdrew recognition of them for a year. The local television and newspapers picked up the story. In this case the fraternity appealed; the chapter maintained that they had not been irresponsible, that they had been serving liquor in accordance with current university regulations, and that the charge of ZBT responsibility was circumstantial since the three students freely admitted to having drunk alcohol at other fraternity rush parties earlier the same evening. But the damage to ZBT's reputation and public standing was done.

In other "special chapter situations" discussed at a 1983 Supreme Council meeting, members considered what to do about a complaint by the Rutgers chapter that the visiting C. W. Post ZBT's had "wantonly damaged" their chapter house at a recent football weekend. At a party in South Carolina, they noted, an inebriated nonmember entered the house and got into a fistfight with a ZBT. The guest sued the brother for assault, and his attorney was threatening the entire chapter with litigation. At the University of Mississippi, members of both the Mississippi chapter and the visiting LSU chapter got into a fistfight with members of another fraternity. During the course of the fight, a member of the other fraternity pulled a gun on one of the ZBTs. No one was hurt, but the matter did not end there; as the officer reported, "Various legal charges are being brought."

Finally, drug use within the chapter continued to be a serious concern for ZBT national as it was for other fraternities. In 1980, for example, the field secretary had to report that their Syracuse University chapter was, as it had been for some time, "a center of drug traffic on the Syracuse campus" and that the situation could not be allowed to continue. Three years later, what was by then a relatively weak Washington and Jefferson chapter was further damaged by the arrest of its president for on-campus drug possession charges. He was expelled for three years and was serving time in prison. "The publicity," the official report noted, "has been extensive and damaging."

It was not necessary for a serious problem with drugs, alcohol, hazing, or general mayhem to exist for a ZBT chapter to be judged in serious trouble. Lack of sufficient adult supervision, neglect of insurance coverage, safety and health code violations, "atrocious" housekeeping, financial mismanagement, and general indifference could cause irreparable damage—and the national organization, away from the scene and with dwindling funds and personnel, was limited in what it could do. From the national point of view there was always the dilemma between the desire to be understanding and help the chapter on the one hand, and on the other the desire to cut the rotten branches off before they destroyed the entire tree.

The potential organizational problems that could "kill" a chapter, short of outright criminal activity, were legion. If a chapter did not rush sufficient new members to keep itself solvent, for example, a member of the national staff might be sent for an emergency visit and quick instruction in rushing techniques, or a nearby alumnus might be dispatched to render aid; if neither of those techniques worked, the chapter would close. In 1985, for example, under the heading "Special Chapter Situations," council members discussed a New York city chapter that had collapsed organizationally and whose members had already been evicted from their house. A midwestern chapter was dubbed an "Animal House" chapter by a visiting national staff member, who reported that the executive alumnus trustee had thrown his hands up in disgust and walked out early in the school year. The chapter continually bounced checks, presented behavioral problems at regional or national fraternity events, was in serious default on its NPEF and mortgage obligations, and had not yet fully repaired damaged caused by a fire in its kitchen the previous year. As a final straw, James Greer reported a recent phone call from a distraught father who called to complain that there were no windows in his son's room. As he reported to the council, he was forced to tell the father that at that point there was nothing the national could do: the group was "so deficient as a reasonable chapter of the fraternity" that its very recognition was in doubt and that it was the father's responsibility to do whatever he thought necessary to ensure the protection and well-being of his offspring.

Not all, or even most ZBT chapters ever reached such a deplorable state. However, the overwhelmingly negative messages about ZBT in particular and the fraternity system in general that the public was receiving took their toll and soon appeared to seriously compromise any Greek-letter "revival" of the sort that had followed in the wake of the system's most disastrous years. Why should young men agree to subject themselves to such indignities and jeopardize their academic standing, their personal safety, and their clean legal record? What parent in his right mind would allow his or her son to join such groups, which had apparently long since outlived their usefulness?

By 1982, ZBT's treasurer had to report a "dramatic turnaround" in rushing and initiation figures, with a sharp increase in "depledgings" and more than a half-dozen charter revocations contributing to a severe deficit. By 1984–85 no relief from this "rush recession" was in sight; between closings and revocations the number of chapters was down to sixty-nine, and expansion was everywhere being cut off by university administrations who wanted no part of ZBT on their campuses. That summer, the National Office was forced to lay off five members of its staff, and morale reached a new low.

Taking Steps: Dry Rush

The new crisis brought the first tentative steps toward a radical reordering of fraternity priorities in both ZBT and other national college fraternities. All realized that without policies regarding alcohol, hazing, general risk management, and their own legal protection, the fraternity system as a whole might not long endure. In March 1984, General Counsel Saul Kassow, warning that "we may not have seen the end of civil litigation or criminal litigation," endorsed and promoted the novel idea that all chapters be incorporated for their own protection and that all have a compulsory liability program. Above all, the national had to prove that it was not paying mere lip service in its rules against hazing; undergraduates had to be made to understand that by hazing they were jeopardizing not only the health and well-being of their own members but the welfare of ZBT and the entire Greek system.

In the fall of 1985, ZBT and other fraternities, acting in tandem for the first time, began to exchange specific ideas and regulations for risk management and for preventing alcohol abuse and underage drinking. The regulations grew increasingly elaborate as time went by. Undergraduate chapter leaders were warned: do not pay for alcoholic beverages with chapter funds (both to discourage their use and to avoid liability); use third-party vendors instead or hold legal guests responsible for bringing their own; have security guards stationed in the parking lot, at the door, and on the floor of the party itself; have someone collect car keys at the door and do not give them back if the person shows evidence of being drunk; have designated drivers and provide buses, vans, or taxis for those unable to drive home safely; card your members—don't permit minors to drink under any circumstances and don't allow nonmembers or uninvited guests to "crash" the party; provide nonalcoholic beverages in identical cups and sufficient food along with the liquor; start planning to have parties with no liquor at all; employ bartenders who will ensure that guests drink in moderation; stop serving alcohol at least an hour in advance of the closing of the party.

Also in the turning-point year of 1985, after witnessing the difficulty of maintaining legal drinking patterns at ZBT's annual summer convention, expansion director Ray Woody recommended a drastic policy: ZBT conclaves and conventions should no longer include alcohol at all. In the summer of 1987 the entire Zeta Beta Tau convention endorsed the "dry rush" policy advocated by the NIC. Not only was such a measure guaranteed to eliminate the risk of underage freshmen consuming liquor at an important official ZBT event; it also sent a strong message to prospective members that, contrary to popular perception, a fraternity was not a drinking society and anyone wishing to join one should go elsewhere. By 1990, ZBT joined several other fraternities in the NIC in permanently banning beer kegs, once almost an icon of college fraternity life, from any of its official functions. Still, illegal drinking continued to take place.

Antipledging and the Brotherhood Program

If the consumption of alcohol, which took place at public parties and gatherings, was difficult to regulate, the regulation of hazing, which had always been shrouded in secrecy, was even more difficult; yet there was no doubt anymore that any responsible fraternity had to make a do-or-die effort. Perhaps, as some national officers suggested, after years of wrestling with the problem of how to eliminate hazing, it was time to take a step back and find out why young men wanted and needed to haze. What were the psychological reasons for the persistence in hurting the very people one wanted as friends and fraternity brothers for life? If the roots and the basis of hazing could be more clearly understood, they suggested, and cases of successful antihazing initiatives studied in an organized way, then perhaps they could learn to eliminate it at its source.

In the fall of 1988 the ZBT leadership, distressed at continuing reports of hazing violations and behavioral problems from its undergraduates, assembled at a Chicago airport hotel for a special weekend-long meeting to discuss possible solutions. As officers and staff shared their evidence and experiences, one gradually presented itself. Hazing, they believed, was intimately and inextricably tied to the rhythm of fraternity life as it had existed for generations: rush, a trial period of "pledgeship" covering weeks or months, and finally, initiation into full membership. It was the period of pledgeship, emphasizing differentials in membership status between older and younger members, that was the "window of opportunity" that inevitably led to hazing. By tradition, pledges were considered second-class citizens, with no rights and no chance to refuse even the most outrageous demands of an older member unless he quit the fraternity. The very principle of pledgeship left the door open to injury and possible death, and any group that was subject to hazing in any form would inevitably want to do it to the next group, perpetuating a vicious cycle. Halfway measures would never solve the problem. Eliminate the entire institution of pledging, ZBTs national leaders concluded, and only then would you eliminate the danger of hazing.

Accordingly, in the aftermath of the Chicago meeting, ZBT's Supreme Council took the revolutionary step of abolishing pledging in ZBT altogether. In its stead they established a new set of rules, which came to be known as the Brotherhood Program, with minimum "Brotherhood Quality Standards" to be applied consistently and continuously to *all* members of Zeta Beta Tau during all their years in school. The Brotherhood Program was intimately tied to the new philosophy of risk management, in which prevention of possible liability was supposed to stand second after a brother's duty to keep his chapter, his fellow brothers, and all their friends and guests safe.

Under the new terms of membership, there was to be no differentiation or segregation whatsoever between one group of brothers and another. Secondary or subservient status was forbidden, and the very terms *pledge* and *pledgeship* were to be stricken from ZBT terminology. Candidates had to be initiated into Zeta Beta Tau within seventy-two hours of accepting a bid and thereafter were considered full brothers with all the rights, privileges, and responsibilities of everyone else in the chapter. In place of traditional pledging activities, all ZBT members were to participate in a prescribed series of "bonding activities" and could maintain their membership only through a "semiannual Brotherhood Review" conducted in the presence of the entire chapter. If undergraduates did not approve of the particular brotherhood programming supplied to them by the National Office, they were welcome to devise their own, but they would have to submit it to the Supreme Council for approval. Any chapter that did not adhere to these guidelines risked expulsion from the fraternity.

The Brotherhood Program and the nonpledging initiative was put into operation at the start of the 1989 fall semester, and "Join a Fraternity, Don't Pledge One" became ZBT's new recruitment motto. The change attracted extensive media attention, including features on the *Today Show, Larry King Live, Good Morning America,* and CNN News in addition to all three major networks' news programs. On the undergraduate level, however, the elimination of pledging was not received with unmitigated joy. It was so revolutionary, so contrary to accepted college fraternity norms, such a departure from what members saw leaders of other fraternities doing, and so complex that it was perhaps not surprising that many undergraduates responded to it with disbelief if not rage.

Ray J. Woody, who had authored much of the new program in consultation with the committee, reported on a nationwide tour of the chapters to inform them of the new rules in 1989. He described their reactions as corresponding to the five emotional stages that psychiatrist Elizabeth Kubler-Ross had established as the typical reactions of someone suffering from a life-threatening disease: denial and isolation, anger, bargaining for time, depression and grief, and finally, acceptance. Not more than half the chapters, in his view, were anywhere near the acceptance stage of the process. Frequently, there was a split within the chapter itself between one leader or faction that favored the program and another leader or faction that did not. The alumni trustees, he reported, were not always a help and required as much education as the undergraduates did. Filled with nostalgia for their own student days, many were unable to comprehend the need for the change and assured their student charges that things would go on much as they had before. The national staff itself, though gratified by the immediate reduction in hazing that the program brought about, worried about lack of compliance, spotty volunteer support, and the lack of human and financial resources to help carry out such a gargantuan task. Nevertheless, it was clear that there could be no going back: the future of the fraternity was at stake.

The change was far from easy. Between 1989 and 1996 the ZBT Supreme Council shut down fifteen chapters for violations of the nonpledging and risk management policy, while dozens of chapters and individual undergraduate members were disciplined by the Supreme Council. But no one had been killed or seriously hurt. In the fall 1991 issue of the *Deltan*, ZBT's executive director was proud to write that after two full years of the nonpledging experience, *"there have been no injuries in ZBT"* and that other national fraternities and sororities were investigating whether they too could incorporate aspects of ZBT's new program.

Minimum Chapter Standards

The trend toward uniformity and centralization within a fraternity, which was paradoxically becoming increasingly more diverse, also found its expression in the establishment of the Chapter Minimum Standards Program. As early as 1980 the Supreme Council had agreed on the need to establish some standards that could be applicable throughout all of ZBT's heterogeneous chapters. The difficulty lay only in deciding precisely what those standards should be. After years of debate, in fall 1985, the first criteria were crystallized by the appointed committee. Rush in a good chapter, they wrote, must equal at least 25 percent of chapter membership or meet the average rush total on the campus; grades must be equal to the university national average; rush and pledge retention had to fall within certain parameters. Most important of all, a good chapter had to have a good alumni trustee program, including at least one alumnus available to the chapter at any time. Ideally, there would be two trustee board meetings a year, meetings with the treasurer twice a year, contact with the president at least once every other week, visits to the house at least once a month, and publication of two alumni newsletters a year.

Between 1989 and 1992 the national fraternity further refined and attempted to enforce its criteria. In 1990 the council declared twenty men as the minimum size for any ZBT chapter regardless of location; any chapter that was not specifically excused from the requirement would be suspended until it complied. In 1992, on the theory that standards were best inculcated at the very beginning, the council set new, stringent rules for the recognition of new chapters. Any colony wishing to become a full-fledged chapter had to have a minimum of fifteen men. They were also required to have a building fund, at least one faculty adviser, an assembled trustee board, proper liability and fire insurance, willingness to incorporate themselves, a letter of support from both the local interfraternity council and the school administration, and a constitution and set of bylaws approved by the Supreme Council. If they had done all that and were also current in all their fees and dues, they could submit to the Supreme Council a petition for chartering signed by all their members. Only then could they be considered worthy to join the ranks of ZBT.

District Governors

In an attempt to duplicate the strong volunteer alumni supervision that had characterized the fraternity in the past, ZBT in the 1980s and 1990s also put effort into developing and intensifying its District Governor

Program—not quite the same as a good alumni trustee program but perhaps the next best thing. A district governor, as its name implied, was a strategically placed ZBT alumnus who would act as both liaison and supervisor of all the chapters in his area. Under the direction of Stephen P. Ehrlich (Denver '70), the ranks of good ZBT district governors grew, and the training they had to undergo increased in intensity and sophistication. There was also a concerted attempt to spot talent within the fraternity while members were undergraduates and groom them for future leadership positions as direct chapter advisers, district governors, or eventually as officers and directors in the national administration.

Interfraternal Cooperation

It was a benefit of the decline in sectarian divisions and the relative democratization of American Jewish life and fraternity life in general that ZBT did not have to face its challenges alone. Instead, it could depend on a high level of cooperation and mutual aid from all the other fraternities of the NIC, both those that were historically Jewish and those that were not. For example, in the 1980s it was now possible for Sidney Dunn of Alpha Epsilon Pi to visit the Zeta Beta Tau national office, have a cordial, courteous, and mutually beneficial discussion with James Greer, and then write a thank-you letter promising to return the courtesy at his own national office if he ever had the opportunity to do so. For Barry Siegel and his Alpha Epsilon Pi contemporary, George Toll, Dunn noted in his letter, the notion that they might ever have accomplished a mutual exchange of ideas was all but incomprehensible.

As for relations between ZBT leaders and the leaders of the historically Gentile fraternities, in ages past these groups would rarely have been able to conduct professional business comfortably in the same town and country clubs; indeed, they might hardly have spoken to one another. Now, facing common problems and needing common solutions, ZBT was integrated into the general college fraternity world to a degree not known before. Together with others in the NIC, for example, Zeta Beta Tau organized collectively to fight the universities that were blocking further fraternity expansion and helped to finance the establishment of the Center for the Study of the College Fraternity at Indiana University. Collective effort in turn brought collective honor. In 1989, Stanley I. Fishel was awarded the National Interfraternity

Conference Gold Medal, the highest award it could bestow; Richard S. Simon was similarly honored in 1997; and in 1992 both Dr. Ronald Taylor and James E. Greer, Jr. were awarded the NIC's Silver Medal in recognition of their contributions to the fraternity world. Also in 1992, for the first time since Harold Riegelman's selection sixty-five years earlier, a ZBT, Richard S. Simon, was elected president of the entire NIC organization.

Group Liability Insurance

Greater centralization coupled with the new spirit of interfraternal cooperation proved to be of special benefit when fixing policies regarding liability, risk management, and the purchase of insurance. Banding together in ever larger groups was the only way to fight against burgeoning risk, skyrocketing premiums, and the cancellation of individual insurance policies for several national fraternities. In 1985 the Supreme Council finally agreed to the umbrella purchase of group casualty and property insurance for all ZBT chapters. The next step was to join forces in common cause with chapters of as many other fraternities as possible. By 1992, thirty-four national college fraternities and sororities including ZBT were members of the Fraternity Insurance Purchasing Group (FIPG). All FIPG members were required to adhere to common standards designed to keep their members safe and the cost of insurance to a minimum.

Enforcement

If the staff and alumni volunteers could not be everywhere to enforce compliance with the rules, they could still attempt to educate the undergraduate members to internalize feelings of responsibility and shame. The fraternity's 1996 insurance and risk management manual was more than 130 pages long and filled with lists of regulations, forms, and legal details that might have taxed the brain of a third-year law student. Conspicuously, it was dedicated to the memory of a ZBT who had died in a chapter house fire in 1984. The national authorities thus freely acknowledged that they could not be everywhere all the time to uncover violations of their rules.

The national fraternity did, however, as the cautionary letter continued, frequently receive reports of violations from other fraternities, parents, angry neighbors, university administrators, opposing members within the chapter itself, interfraternity councils, and various members of the ZBT family of district governors, trustees, alumni, staff members, and Supreme Council members who happened to be in the vicinity for weekend visits. "When Brothers think they can violate the fraternity's risk management policy without actually being caught by the national fraternity, they may be correct," the manual warned. "The real question Brothers should ask themselves is whether or not they can violate the fraternity's policy without everyone else on the list above knowing. Ultimately, violations will be reported."

Hope and the Loss of Innocence

The need to emphasize risk management, however, came at a high price. It was perhaps a sign of the times that in the fifth edition (1996) of ZBT's *Successful Operations Procedures* (the 1990s equivalent of Lee Dover's classic *Manual for Chapter Administration*) more than half of the entries dealt with liability and legal issues. Gone were the long lists of chapter customs and traditions; gone were the rules regarding dress and etiquette, housemothers and chaperones; gone were the lengthy prescriptions for proper communal leadership and public service. Practically the only tie to ZBT's past days was the inclusion of Maurice Zellermayer's song, "Here's to Our Fraternity," which national officers urged the undergraduates to learn how to sing:

> Here's to our Fraternity,
> May it live forever,
> May we always faithful be,
> And its bonds ne'er sever.
> Though the troubles may be nigh, boys
> With our standard raised on high, boys
> We'll be loyal to our Z B T
> Ever loyal to our Zeta Beta Tau

Instead of learning long lists of traditions, new ZBT officers were instructed on such topics as how to deal with a serious injury or death, such as rendering first aid to someone dying from alcohol poisoning (care had to be taken not to permit him to suffocate in his own vomit); how to close down a chapter properly and safely (the National Office recommended hiring security guards because disgruntled evictees had been known to vandalize the house); how to survive a fire; how to handle a funeral; how to issue a press release in times of crisis; what to do in the event that they personally or a fellow member was arrested or accused of drug dealing, illegal weapons possession, rape, felony, embezzlement of fraternity funds, or theft; and how to respond if a fellow member was found to be suffering from AIDS.

Since 1898, Zeta Beta Tau had weathered virtually every imaginable obstacle. Its members had witnessed the golden age of Greek college life as well as college fraternities at their absolute worst. The joys of fellowship and friendship for which the fraternity had been intended were still there as ZBT approached its hundredth birthday. Muffled though they were by the ceaseless late-twentieth-century preoccupation with avoiding danger and social condemnation, the ideals and the old standards had not disappeared. Without the former, however, there was little hope that the joys of the latter would ever survive to nourish future generations of ZBTs.

The national fraternity stood ready to help and guard the membership in any way it could. "You have much going for you," declared Irving M. Chase, ZBT's president from 1994 to 1998, in his official address to new members. "The care and regard of a strong and honored National Fraternity, the love and support of your parents, the company of good friends, many of whom will last a lifetime, a college or university that wants you to succeed because when you succeed, they succeed . . . ZBT is where it is today at all levels . . . because in the face of 100 years filled with obstacles—obstacles that in a business context would have caused strong men to run from the field, ZBTs have stayed and fought. ZBTs have known that there is no such thing as failure, there is only giving up."

Ultimately, however, the fate and future of ZBT lay in the hands of the thousands of individual members who bore its name and wore its pin. "You have joined an old and honorable Fraternity and now it belongs to you," each new member in 1998 was told as the centennial year of Zeta Beta Tau was dawning. "For friendship's sake, take good care of it."

APPENDIX

Appendix I. Antecedents and Mergers

Zeta Beta Tau Fraternity in 1998 technically included members and chapters of four other fraternities of similar origin and traditions, known as the "antecedents"— Kappa Nu, Phi Alpha, Phi Epsilon Pi, and Phi Sigma Delta. The antecedents merged first with one another and then with Zeta Beta Tau when existence as separate, independent organizations was no longer feasible, in particular during the period of the Vietnam War and widespread campus unrest. These mergers were complete by 1970. The following chart depicts membership and merger patterns of the five constituent fraternities from 1959 to 1980:

MERGERS

	ZETA BETA TAU (founded 1898)	PHI EPSILON PI (founded 1904)	PHI SIGMA DELTA (founded 1909)	KAPPA NU (founded 1911)	PHI ALPHA (founded 1914)
1959	46 Chapters 18,600 Members	35 Chapters 13,504 Members	34 Chapters 10,083 Member	16 Chapters 5,500 Members	Merged with Phi Sigma Delta 17 Chapters 6,412 Members
1961	47 Chapters 19,000 Members	35 Chapters 14,025 Members	47 Chapters 16,583 Members	Merged with Phi Epsilon Pi 15 Chapters 5,700 Members	
1969	80 Chapters 30,000 Members	52 Chapters 25,900 Members	Merged with Zeta Beta Tau 49 Chapters 19,500 Members		
1970	115 Chapters 50,500 Members	Merged with Zeta Beta Tau 54 Chapters 26,800 Members			
1971	145 Chapters 78,300 Members				
1980	80 Chapters 89,000 Members				

In January of its centennial year Zeta Beta Tau consisted of 58 chapters, 12 "colonies," and an estimated 112,000 living initiates.

Appendix II. ZBT National Presidents 1898–1998

1898–99	*Rabbi David Levine	Founder
1900	*Louis A. Sable	Founder
1901–02	*Rabbi Aaron Eiseman	Founder

1903	*Maurice L. Zellermayer	Founder
1904	*Bernhard Bloch	Founder
1905	*Isidore Delson	Founder
1906	*Harold Kirschberg	Founder
1907–08	*Arthur S. Unger	Long Island Medical College ('05)
1909	*Arthur S. Leeds, Jr.	Columbia University ('07)
1910–11	*Samuel Stark	City College of New York ('03)
1912–20	*Richard J. H. Gottheil, Ph.D.	Honorary, Columbia University ('01)
1921–24	*Hon. Julius Kahn	Honorary, UC Berkeley ('23)
1925	*Harold Riegelman	Cornell ('14)
1926	*Harry Steiner	Columbia University ('18)
1927–28	*Judge Grover M. Moscowitz	New York University Heights ('06)
1929	*I. Emanuel Sauder	University of Pennsylvania ('09)
1930	*Judge William S. Evans	City College of New York ('06)
1931	*Herbert E. Steiner	University of Pennsylvania ('14)
1932–33	*Judge William S. Evans	City College of New York ('06)
1934–37	*Herbert E. Steiner	University of Pennsylvania ('14)
1938–41	*James R. Katzman	Syracuse University ('19)
1942–45	*Samuel R. Firestone	Ohio State University ('18)
1946–48	*James Frank, Jr.	Yale University ('28)
1949–52	Harold E. Grotta	University of Virginia ('33)
1953–55	*L. Reyner Samet	University of Virginia ('25)
1956–59	Stanley I. Fishel	Columbia University ('34)
1960–62	*Richard S. Graham	Cornell University ('37)
1963–65	*Jack London	City College of New York ('38)
1966–67	*Justin R. Wolf	Harvard University ('32)
1968–69	*Burton L. Litwin	Washington and Lee University ('51)
1970–71	Richard A. Wells	University of Texas–Austin ('54)
1972–73	Arthur J. Horwitz	University of Pennsylvania ('48)
1974–75	Rabbi Matthew H. Simon	University of Chicago ('53)
1976–77	Saul A. Fern	Boston University ('54)
1978–79	Seymour R. Brown	Case Western Reserve University ('48)
1980–81	Richard S. Simon	University of Michigan ('43)
1982–83	Bernard S. Kaplan	University of Chicago ('47)
1984–88	Martin D. Braver	Boston University ('47)
1988–90	Frederick E. Schatz	University of Michigan ('57)
1990–92	Stephen P. Ehrlich	University of Denver ('70)
1992–94	Leonard Komen	University of Missouri ('65)
1994–98	Irving M. Chase	University of California–LA ('74)
1998–	Ronald J. Taylor, M.D.	Washington and Jefferson College ('66)

*Deceased

Appendix III. Chapter Roll of ZBT before 1970

The following list indicates chapters of the fraternity before its mergers with the antecedents. Dates on the left indicate the year of the chapter's establishment. Dates in parentheses indicate the known year or years when a chapter became inactive. Note: By tradition, successive chapters in any national Greek-letter fraternity are themselves given individual Greek-letter designations, usually but not always in alphabetical order; i.e., the first established chapter is named "Alpha," the second is "Beta," the third "Gamma," etc. In internal fraternity communications, chapters are frequently referred to by their Greek-letter designation rather than by the name of the school.

1898 Home Fraternity (1903)
1903 Alpha, City College (1971)
1903 Beta, Long Island College Hospital (1914)
1904 Gamma, New York University (Heights) (1972–89)
1904 Delta, Columbia (1972–74)
1907 (Unamed) Jefferson Medical College (1908)
1907 Theta, Penn
1907 Kappa, Cornell (1982–88)
1908 Mu, Boston U. (1939–49) (1957)
1909 Lambda, Western Reserve U.
1909 Zeta, Case School of Applied Science (1928)
1909 Sigma, Tulane
1909 Eta, Union College (1933)
1910 Iota, Polytechnic Institute of Brooklyn (1920)
1911 Nu, Ohio State (1989)
1911 Xi, M.I.T. (1927)
1911 Omicron, Syracuse (1986–87)
1911 Pi, Louisiana State U. (1989)
1912 Rho, University of Illinois
1912 Tau, Harvard (1933)
1912 Phi, University of Michigan
1913 Upsilon, McGill (1969)
1915 Chi, University of Virginia (1985)
1916 Psi, University of Alabama
1917 Omega, University of Missouri
1918 Alpha Beta, University of Chicago (1975)
1918 Alpha Gamma, Vanderbilt
1918 Alpha Delta, University of Southern California (1972)
1920 Alpha Epsilon, Washington and Lee (1988)
1920 Alpha Eta, University of California (Berkeley)
1921 Alpha Lambda, Yale (1933)
1921 Alpha Zeta, University of Florida (1933–48) (1956)
1922 Alpha Theta, University of Nebraska (1962)

1922   Alpha Kappa, University of Wisconsin (1983–87)
1923   Alpha Xi, Washington University (St. Louis)
1924   Alpha Mu, University of Washington (Seattle) (1973–74)
1926   Alpha Omicron, University of Arizona (1969–83)
1927   Alpha Pi, University of North Carolina (1985)
1927   Alpha Rho, University of California at Los Angeles
1931   Alpha Sigma, University of Texas (1934)
1931   Alpha Tau, Franklin and Marshall (1988)
1935   Alpha Epsilon, Duke (1971)
1936   Alpha Phi, Miami U. (1974–89)
1942   Alpha Nu, University of Tennessee (1969)
1942   Alpha Chi, University of British Columbia (1970–79)
1942   Alpha Iota, University of Kentucky (1973)
1946   Alpha Psi, Penn State (1971–88)
1946   Alpha Omega, University of Miami
1947   Beta Alpha, University of Colorado
1947   Beta Gamma, Indiana University
1947   Beta Delta, Rutgers
1947   Beta Epsilon, Michigan State U. (1971)
1948   Beta Zeta, University of Maryland
1948   Beta Eta, Bowling Green State U.
1948   Beta Theta, University of Manitoba (1972)
1949   Beta Iota, University of Minnesota (1953)
1950   Beta Kappa, University of Arkansas (1955)
1951   Beta Lambda, San Diego State College (1968–88)
1956   Beta Tau, Johns Hopkins (1990)
1957   Beta Mu, Rider College
1960   Beta Xi, Brooklyn College (1973–90)
1960   Beta Pi, Long Beach (1975)
1961   Beta Rho, New York University (Square) (1972)
1962   Kappa Nu Kappa, Rennselaer Polytechnic Institute
1962   Beta Upsilon, Youngstown (1979)
1962   Beta Phi, Pittsburgh
1963   Beta Iota, Long Island (1968)
1963   Beta Psi, American U. (1971–84)
1963   Gamma Alpha, Washington and Jefferson
1964   Gamma Beta, California State at Northridge
1964   Gamma Delta, C.W. Post (1990)
1965   Gamma Epsilon, Marshall (1978)
1965   Gamma Zeta, Louisville (1972)
1966   Alpha Phi, Parson's School of Design (1972)
1966   Beta Xi, Baruch College (1968)
1966   Gamma Eta, Bradley (1973)
1966   Gamma Theta, Queens College (1973)
1967   Gamma Iota, Western Michigan (1971)

1967 Gamma Kappa, Adelphi (1972)
1967 Gamma Lambda, Hartford (1967–85)
1967 Gamma Mu, Memphis State (1972)
1967 Lambda, DePauw (1972)
1968 Beta Phi, West Chester (1973)
1968 Beta Tau, Widener (1988)
1968 Gamma Nu, California State at Los Angeles
1968 Gamma Omicron, Univ. of Wisconsin, Milwaukee (1972)
1968 Gamma Xi, California State Santa Barbara (1970–85)
1968 Zeta Tau, Seton Hall (1989)
1969 Beta Pi, Western New England (1980)
1969 Beta Psi, Drake (1976)
1969 Gamma Beta, New Haven
1969 Gamma Chi, South Florida (1970–86)
1969 Gamma Omega, Northern Illinois (1971)
1969 Gamma Phi, Hofstra
1969 Gamma Psi, Northeastern (1984)
1969 Gamma Rho, Eastern New Mexico (1972)
1969 Gamma Sigma, Lamar (1979)
1969 Gamma Tau, Arizona State (1972)
1969 Gamma Upsilon, Northeast Louisiana (1973)
1970 Delta Alpha, Kent State (1971)
1970 Delta Gamma, Oklahoma (1972)
1970 Delta Theta, Charleston (SC) (1989)
1970 Delta Zeta, Rutgers, Newark (1972)

Source: *Baird's Manual of American College Fraternities* (20th edition, 1991).

Appendix IV. Active Chapters of ZBT as of January 1998

SCHOOL	GREEK NAME	DATE OF INSTALLATION OR RECHARTERING
Alabama	Psi	1916
Alfred	Kappa Phi	1993
Arizona	Alpha Omicron	1983
Ball State	Zeta Phi	1997
Bentley	Delta Chi	1976
Berkeley	Alpha Eta	1921
Boston	Mu	1993
Bowling Green	Beta Eta	1946
Brandeis	Epsilon Phi	1988
Brooklyn	Beta Xi	1991

Cal. State Northridge	Gamma Beta	1964
UCLA	Alpha Rho	1927
Cal. San Diego	Epsilon Beta	1985
Case Western Reserve	Lambda	1909
Columbia	Delta	1904
Cornell	Kappa	1989
Delaware	Epsilon Theta	1982
East Stroudsburg	Zeta Pi	1993
Fairleigh Dickinson/Madison	Epsilon Tau	1984
Gannon	Zeta Xi	1992
Georgia Tech	Xi	1916
Hartford	Gamma Lambda	1997
Hofstra	Gamma Phi	1969
Illinois	Rho	1912
Indiana	Beta Gamma	1947
Kansas	Epsilon Mu	1984
Maryland–Baltimore	Zeta Kappa	1991
Maryland–College Park	Beta Zeta Epsilon	1996
Miami–Florida	Alpha Omega	1946
Michigan State	Beta Epsilon	1992
MIT	Xi	1993
Monmouth–Illinois	Delta Lambda	1971
Montclair	Epsilon Psi	1989
Northwestern	Gamma	1976
Penn State–Erie (Behrend)	Zeta Epsilon	1990
Pennsylvania	Theta	1907
Princeton	Zeta Sigma	1997
Ramapo	Zeta Delta	1990
Rider	Beta Mu	1957
San Diego State	Beta Lambda	1988
Stephen F. Austin	Zeta Lambda	1991
Stockton	Zeta Omicron	1992
SUNY–Albany	Epsilon Gamma	1986
SUNY–Stonybrook	Delta Psi	1977
Syracuse	Omicron	1989
Texas–Dallas	Zeta Upsilon	1997
Tufts	Omicron	1989
Tulane	Sigma	1909
USC	Alpha Delta	1995
Vanderbilt	Alpha Gamma	1918
Vermont	Zeta Rho	1995
Virginia	Phi Epsilon	1915
Virginia Tech	Delta Xi	1994
Washington & Jefferson	Iota Phi Alpha	1963
Washington–St. Louis	Alpha Xi	1923

Western Connecticut	Zeta Theta	1991
William Paterson	Epsilon Sigma	1995
York College–PA	Beta Alpha Chi	1989

Colonies: Clemson, Colorado, Edinboro, Emory, Fairleigh Dickinson/Teaneck, Florida, Kean, New Hamphire, North Carolina, Penn State, Rutgers, St. John's

Appendix V. ZBT Convention Sites

1898–06	No Conventions		1945	No Convention (WWII)
1907	New York		1946	Los Angeles
1908	New York		1947	Cleveland
1909	New York		1948	New York
1910	New York		1949	Miami Beach
1911	New York		1950	St. Louis
1912	Cleveland		1951	Chicago
1913	New York		1952	Seattle
1914	New York		1953	Atlantic City
1916	Boston		1954	Miami Beach
1917	New York		1955	Santa Monica
1918	No Convention (WWI)		1956	Chicago
1919	New York		1957	Washington, DC
1920	New York		1958	Montreal
1921	New York		1959	Miami Beach
1922	New York		1960	Denver
1923	Cleveland		1961	Chicago
1924	Norfolk		1962	New York
1925	Montreal		1963	San Francisco
1926	New York		1964	French Lick, IN
1927	None		1965	Grand Bahama Island
1928	Los Angeles		1966	Lake Placid, NY
1929	New Orleans		1967	Grand Bahama Island
1930	St. Louis		1968	Sun Valley, Idaho
1931	Boston		1969	Grand Bahama Island
1932	Cincinnati		1970	Grand Bahama Island
1933	Cleveland		1971	Columbus
1934	Kansas City		1972	McAfee, NJ
1935	Chicago		1973	Miami Beach
1936	New Orleans		1974	Washington, DC
1937	Washington, DC		1975	New Orleans
1938	New York		1976	New York
1939	San Francisco		1977	Lake of the Ozarks, MO
1940	Omaha		1978	Bal Harbour, FL
1941	Chicago		1979	Montreal
1942	No Convention (WWII)		1980	San Diego
1943	No Convention (WWII)		1981	New York
1944	No Convention (WWII)		1982	New Orleans

1983	Nassau, Bahamas		1991	Pittsburgh
1984	Chicago		1992	Kansas City, MO
1985	Anaheim, CA		1993	Washington, DC
1986	Boston		1994	Newport Beach, CA
1987	St. Louis		1995	Bloomington, IN
1988	Naples, FL		1996	Miami Beach
1989	Baltimore		1997	Oxford, OH
1990	Beaver Creek, CO		1998	Baltimore

Appendix VI. Chapter Rolls of ZBT Antecedents to 1970

PHI EPSILON PI

Founded November 23, 1904, at the City College of New York, by Max Shlivek, Alvin P. Bloch, Arthur Hamburger, Siegfried F. Hartman, Arthur Hirschberg, William A. Hannig, and Abraham E. Horn.

1904	Alpha, CCNY		1920	Delta, Washington and Lee
1905	Beta, Columbia (1928–58)		1920	Psi, Illinois
1911	Kappa Alpha, Rochester		1920	Omega, Cincinnati (1935)
1911	Epsilon, Cornell		1920	Alpha Alpha, Dartmouth (1922)
1913	Zeta, Pittsburgh		1920	Alpha Beta, Iowa
1914	Eta, Penn		1920	Alpha Epsilon, Johns Hopkins
1914	Theta, Penn State		1921	Alpha Gamma, Michigan
1914	Iota, Dickinson			(1942–57)
1914	Kappa, NYU (Square)		1921	Kappa Omicron, University of
	(1922–49)			Chicago (1934)
1915	Kappa Beta NYU (Heights)		1921	Kappa Pi, Alabama
1915	Lambda, Rutgers		1921	Kappa Nu, California
1915	Mu, University of Georgia		1922	Kappa Sigma, Tulane (1956)
1915	Nu, University of Virginia		1923	Alpha Delta, Minnesota
1915	Kappa Delta, Union College		1925	Alpha Eta, Wisconsin (1937–66)
	(1925)		1926	Alpha Zeta, Harvard (1935)
1916	Xi, Georgia Tech		1928	Alpha Theta, South Carolina
1916	Omicron, Tufts		1929	Alpha Iota, Miami (FL)
1916	Pi, University of Maine (1925)		1930	Alpha Mu, George Washington
1916	Rho, Rhode Island State (1922)			(1952)
1916	Sigma, Brown (1918)		1932	Kappa Upsilon, Arkansas (1941)
1916	Tau, Auburn (1920)		1932	Alpha Nu, Muhlenberg
1916	Upsilon, Connecticut (1964)		1932	Alpha Omicron, Ohio State
1916	Phi, Carnegie Tech (1922)			(1964)
1917	Kappa Zeta, Buffalo		1932	Alpha Xi, Boston U.
1917	Kappa Iota, Union		1933	Alpha Kappa, Western Reserve
1917	Chi, Syracuse			(1955–66)
1920	Gamma, Northwestern		1933	Kappa Phi, Alfred

1933 Alpha Pi, Louisiana State (1958)
1933 Alpha Rho, Ohio U.
1935 Alpha Sigma, Mississippi
1948 Alpha Tau, Queens College (NY)
1949 Alpha Upsilon, Memphis State (1959)
1949 Alpha Phi, North Carolina State (1962)
1950 Alpha Chi, Omaha (1955)
1951 Alpha Psi, McGill
1952 Kappa Alpha Delta, UCLA
1952 Kappa Alpha Gamma, Wayne State (1963)
1956 Beta Alpha, Houston

1957 Beta Beta, American U.
1958 Beta Gamma, Brooklyn College
1959 Beta Delta, Rensselaer Polytechnic Institute
1960 Beta Epsilon, Florida
1961 Beta Zeta, Philadelphia Textiles
1961 Beta Eta, Indiana
1962 Beta Theta, Maryland
1963 Beta Iota, Long Island U.
1965 Beta Lambda, Northern Illinois
1966 Beta Mu, C.W. Post
1966 Beta Xi, Baruch College
1967 Beta Omicron, DePaul
1967 Beta Sigma, Southampton

PHI SIGMA DELTA

Founded at Columbia University in New York, November 10, 1909, by William L. Berk, Herbert L. Eisenberg, Maxwell Hyman, Alfred Iason, Joseph Levy, Herbert K. Minsky, Joseph Shalleck, and Robert Shapiro.

1909 Alpha, Columbia (1933–55)
1912 Beta, Cornell
1913 Gamma, Rensselaer Polytechnic
1913 Delta, NYU (Heights)
1914 Epsilon, Union College
1916 Zeta, University of Pennsylvania
1916 Eta, University of Michigan
1919 Theta, University of Colorado
1920 Iota, University of Denver
1920 Kappa, Western Reserve
1920 Lambda, University of Texas
1921 Mu, University of Chicago
1921 Nu, M.I.T. (1927)
1921 Xi, Boston U. (1933)
1921 Omicron, Ohio State
1922 Pi, University of Wisconsin
1923 Rho, Johns Hopkins
1925 Tau, Lehigh (1933)
1927 Sigma, Penn State
1927 Upsilon, University of West Virginia
1928 University of Vermont
1929 Chi, Duke (1936)
1929 Psi, University of Alabama (1939)

1931 Omega, University of Missouri (1964)
1943 Alpha Alpha, University of Connecticut
1947 Alpha Beta, UCLA
1947 Alpha Gamma, University of Illinois
1948 Alpha Delta, Ohio U.
1949 Alpha Epsilon, Syracuse
1949 Alpha Zeta, University of Miami (1966)
1952 Alpha Eta, Colorado State
1952 Alpha Theta, Rutgers
1952 Alpha Iota, NYU (Square) (1966)
1955 Alpha Kappa, University of Utah (1961)
1957 Phi Alpha Kappa, Hunter College
1957 Alpha Lambda, Detroit
1957 Alpha Mu, University of Massachusetts
1957 Alpha Nu, University of Wisconsin, Milwaukee
1958 Alpha Xi, C.W. Post

1959	Alpha Omicron, Pratt Institute	1963	Alpha Sigma, Michigan State
1959	Phi Alpha Mu, CCNY	1964	Alpha Tau, Long Island U.
1961	Kappa Nu, Brooklyn College	1965	Alpha Upsilon, Adelphi
1963	Alpha Pi, University of Rhode Island	1965	Alpha Phi, Parson's Institute of Design
1963	Alpha Rho, Washington (MO)		

KAPPA NU

Founded at the University of Rochester on November 12, 1911 by Joshua Bernhardt, Louis Gottlieb, Joseph A. Lazarus, Morris Lazerson, Harold Leve, and Abraham Levey.

1911	Alpha, University of Rochester	1921	Omicron, University of Chicago (1934)
1915	Beta, NYU (Heights)		
1915	Gamma, Columbia (1926)	1921	Pi, University of Alabama
1915	Delta, Union University, Albany NY (1925)	1921	Rho, University of Cincinnati (1923)
1916	Theta, Albany (1919)	1922	Sigma, Tulane
1917	Epsilon, Boston U. (1934)	1922	Tau, University of California, Berkeley
1917	Zeta, University of Buffalo		
1917	Iota, Union College	1932	Upsilon, University of Arkansas (1941)
1918	Eta, Harvard (1934)		
1918	Kappa, Rennsaeler	1933	Phi, Alfred
1919	Lambda, Western Reserve (1932)	1939	Chi, Louisiana State U. (1942)
1919	Mu, University of Michigan (1953)	1951	Omega, NYU (Square)
		1951	Alpha Beta, Cornell
1919	Nu, University of Pennsylvania	1952	Alpha Omega, Wayne State
1921	Xi, University of Pittsburgh	1952	Alpha Delta, UCLA

PHI ALPHA

Founded October 14, 1914, at George Washington University in Washington, D.C. by David Davis, Maurice H. Herzmark, Edward Lewis, Reuben Schmidt, Hyman Shapiro.

1914	Alpha, George Washington U.	1921	Kappa, University of Pennsylvania (1939–52)
1915	Beta, University of Maryland (Baltimore)		
		1921	Lambda, DePaul U. (1927)
1916	Gamma, Georgetown	1922	Mu, University of Virginia
1919	Delta, Northwestern (1924)	1924	Nu, Clark University
1919	Epsilon, University of Maryland (College Park)	1924	Omicron, University of New Hampshire
1920	Zeta, Yale (1925)	1924	Pi, Boston U.
1920	Eta, Johns Hopkins (1938)	1925	Rho, University of Richmond (VA)
1920	Theta, NYU		
1920	Iota, Columbia (1923)	1925	Sigma, Brooklyn Polytechnic

1927 Tau, William and Mary

1927 Upsilon, University of Chicago

1927 Phi, Duquesne U.

1927 Chi, Trinity College (1929)

1928 Psi, University of Tennessee (1930)

1928 Omega, University of North Carolina

1928 Alpha Alpha, University of West Virginia (1935)

1929 Alpha Beta, Temple

1930 Alpha Gamma, Wayne State U.

1930 Alpha Delta, University of Detroit

1937 Alpha Epsilon, St. John's College (MD)

1938 Alpha Zeta, St. John's University (NY)

1940 Alpha Eta, CCNY

1941 Alpha Theta, Washington U. (1942)

1953 Alpha Iota, Cornell

INDEX